FACING
TED WILLIAMS

FACING TED WILLIAMS

PLAYERS FROM THE GOLDEN AGE OF BASEBALL RECALL THE GREATEST HITTER WHO EVER LIVED

EDITED BY DAVE HELLER

FOREWORD BY WADE BOGGS

AFTERWORD BY BOB WOLFF

SPORTS PUBLISHING

Sports Publishing books may be purchased in bulk at special discounts for sales promotion, corporate gifts, fund-raising, or educational purposes. Special editions can also be created to specifications. For details, contact the Special Sales Department, Sports Publishing, 307 West 36th Street, 11th Floor, New York, NY 10018 or sportspubbooks@skyhorsepublishing.com.

Sports Publishing® is a registered trademark of Skyhorse Publishing, Inc.®, a Delaware corporation.

Visit our website at www.sportspubbooks.com

10 9 8 7 6 5 4 3 2 1

Library of Congress Cataloging-in-Publication Data

Facing Ted Williams : players from the golden age of baseball recall the greatest hitter who ever lived / edited by Dave Heller ; foreword by Wade Boggs ; afterword by Bob Wolff.
    pages cm
(hardcover : alk. paper) 1. Williams, Ted, 1918-2002—Anecdotes. 2. Williams, Ted, 1918-2002—Friends and associates. 3. Baseball players—United States—Biography. I. Heller, David Alan.
GV865.W5F33 2013
796.357092—dc23
    2012048683

Print ISBN: 978-1-61321-769-6

Cover design by Brian Peterson
Cover photograph courtesy of the Boston Public Library

Printed in the United States of America

For my wife, Shelly. When she walks down the street,
they should say, "There goes the best damn wife there ever was."

CONTENTS

Contents

Contents

FOREWORD

TED WILLIAMS IS who John Wayne wanted to be when he grew up.

Growing up, I was a huge Ted Williams fan, and I mean *huge*. Coincidentally, I was drafted by the Red Sox in 1976. I wore No. 9 in high school and read *The Science of Hitting* my junior year. I never thought in my wildest dreams that I'd actually have the opportunity of meeting him.

Well, it did happen. The first time I met Ted was when I was starting out in the minors. It was my first spring training. I'm eighteen years old and standing in line at the movie theater two days into spring training, and standing two people behind me is bigger than life Ted Williams. I went up to Ted and introduced myself, said I was drafted the year before and played in Elmira,[1] and grew up admiring him as a hitter.

And he just went into this conversation about "how do you hold your hands, how do you do all of this"—right in line. Just firing off this and that, what kind of hitter was I in high school, and I thought I had just died and went to heaven. It was truly one of those monumental experiences that you are afforded in life, and for me, having had the opportunity to meet Ted, it was truly overwhelming.

So, I can imagine how these young pitchers felt when they got the opportunity to face Ted Williams. It had to be mind-blowing. And

---

[1] The Emira Pioneers (or Elmira Red Sox, as they were known) were a Red Sox affiliate in the New York–Penn League.

now I can see why Ted Williams walked so much—because guys were scared to pitch to him!

He was a John Wayne-esque figure; very intimidating, very brash. It was pretty much an R-rated conversation every time Ted would get going; definitely wasn't for Little Leaguers. But this is the way Ted carried himself. He had that aura about himself that very few people carry.

You knew right when he walked in the room, like in that old commercial: If E. F. Hutton is talking, you listen. Every time Ted would say something, the whole room would get quiet. That was the intimidating part about him. When you are young and impressionable, he really stands out. That was the great part about Ted.

During my minor league days, Ted would just sort of be roving around in a golf cart. He'd stop by maybe once during the day while I was in Double-A or Triple-A, and he'd stand behind the batting cage while guys were swinging and talk to various players. It was more of casual conversation than sit down and instruct.

"What did you do in the game yesterday, kid?"
"Two-for-three, Ted, with a walk."
"Where were your hits?"
"Line drive left-center base hit, ground ball in the hole for a base hit, grounder to short."
"You didn't pull the ball?"

Just certain conversations like that, rather than sitting down in the cage and doing it that way.

When I was in Triple-A, he said you have to get that 2–0, 2–1 pitch, and you just have to get those hips going and get those hands out in front. And that really wasn't my style. I stayed inside the ball and hit it the other way. I felt like when I did that, I rolled over a lot to second base and hit weak ground balls. I didn't have a good concept on how to pull the ball.

I sort of stuck to my guns, but it's tough when you're listening to the greatest hitter that ever lived, and he's telling you to do one thing, and then you're doing your own thing. It wasn't a thing of going against Ted Williams. Everyone has their own mechanical philosophy, and for me to try to change, I think that would have destroyed my whole swing.

I thought I was better utilized in Fenway Park if I could reach the wall rather than hit deep fly balls to right field for outs. It just didn't compute in my brain to where that made sense, and leaving the wall to didn't make sense.

But later on, Ted did say, you get that 2–0, 2–1 pitch, look for that pitch to drive. And I really did that. I hit the ball to left-center and it would be high off the wall. In Wrigley Field, that's a home run. In Houston,[2] that's a home run. And parks that didn't have the big 37-foot monster, you had the chance to hit the ball out of the park. It probably took some homers away, but it also gave you some hits. You could hit high fly balls to left field and then scrape the wall, which were outs in other parks.

Probably about 98 percent of the time I took the first pitch. There were instances when I'd jump on the first pitch and felt comfortable doing so, but I felt—another chapter out of Ted—that the longer you faced a guy, the more chances he was going to make a mistake. The more pitches I saw, I felt I had the upper hand, that the guy was going to make a mistake. He wasn't going to make that good pitch early in the count to get me out. If I had five, six, seven, or eight pitches, I had the upper hand. It's demoralizing for a pitcher to foul off a ball, foul off a ball, foul off a good pitch, and foul it off and not put it in play. He gets somewhat upset, makes a mistake, and that's when you capitalize on it.

---

[2] Boggs is speaking of the Houston Astrodome, which was home to the Astros from 1965–1999.

He would show up about once a year when I was with Boston. The Red Sox never had an old-timer's day, but Ted would make it a point to come up for a weekend series unannounced. He would just walk in. He'd be there for Friday, Saturday, and maybe a Sunday game, and then you wouldn't see him the rest of the year.

He always made sure to come over and find me, and then we'd sit down in front of my locker and chat. I have great pictures of us sitting in front of my locker, looking bright-eyed and very astute, with Ted doing his hand gestures. Those are very fond memories.

The funny part about it was, when he would come over, he'd never ever let any reporters eavesdrop on our conversation. He'd basically shoo them away and we'd talk for fifteen to twenty minutes. All the reporters would come up after, and their first question was, "Did you guys talk about hitting?" In actuality, Ted and I would talk fifteen to twenty minutes on nothing but fishing. During those chats, we would never, ever, talk about hitting. It was kind of funny. Every time we'd sit down, he'd want to know what kind of fish I caught in the offseason, what kind of line I used, where I was fishing, and various things like that. Hitting never really came up. He would like to talk about hitting with other players and young guys, but the majority of the time when Ted and I got together, it was non-stop fishing.

This is one of my worst regrets in life—that I had the opportunity to ask him to go fishing down in the Florida Keys and never did. But I never make the same mistake twice, because I had the opportunity to ask Curt Gowdy[3] to go fishing with me down in the Keys, and he graciously accepted. Although it wasn't Ted, I sort of got the same

---

[3] Curt Gowdy was the voice of the Boston Red Sox from 1951–1965, the host of *The American Sportsman*, and was elected into the National Baseball Hall of Fame in 1984. He was also a fishing partner of Williams.

thing, because Curt had a lot of stories about Ted. I didn't have Ted, but I had the next best thing. Listening to Curt recall fishing stories about time spent with Ted in the Keys, while sitting out back after a day of fishing, was just incredible.

But that is the one regret in life I do have; that I never pulled the trigger on asking Ted to go fishing. And I'm sure Ted would have accepted, and it would have been the greatest day ever, to bonefish with Ted down in the Keys.

Once I got to know him later in life, his voice started to calm down, but his presence was still there, and that was the great thing about him. All the way up until Ted passed away—I had seen him a couple months before he passed away—so from about the age of eighteen to Ted's passing, I had seen him periodically throughout the years.

Although Ted was basically a pull hitter throughout the majority of his career, he did hit the ball to left-center on some occasions. But I was more an inside-out hitter, and Ted was more hips ahead of hands, which enabled him to pull more balls than myself. So, our mechanical philosophies were different, but I think our cerebral philosophies were basically the same.

Work the pitch, get a good strike zone, work the counts, and if you don't get a good pitch to hit, then you accept the walk. All those points are the keys to being a disciplined hitter, and that's what Ted preached more than anything: Knowing the strike zone. And when you see the big strike zone in Ted's book, *The Science of Hitting*, you can see that the areas that gave him difficulty were basically bad pitches to swing at. But when you put the ball in the sweet spot, his average naturally went up.

And that was more or less my philosophy. If you put it in an area to where I can make solid contact, then I have an opportunity to hit the ball to the wall. And that's why I utilized Fenway Park for eleven years to my advantage, unlike Ted.

I mean, they had the very first shift on Ted, and he would beat the shift and still hit .400. I think that's what made it so amazing. They'd throw everyone on one side of the field, and he still hit .400. By the way, I've been an advocate that hitting .400 will never be done again . . . and Ted did back in 1941. Personally, to hit .400, I think those days are long gone.

There's very little that Ted hasn't done—serving our country during war and losing five years of a valuable career, just to come back, never missing a beat, and win another batting title. He's the greatest in my mind.

In 1986, Ted, Don Mattingly, and I were able to sit down over dinner one night with Peter Gammons to talk about hitting for an article he was writing for *Sports Illustrated*, and it ended up lasting for about five hours. We got to the restaurant at about 5:00 and I think we left between 10 and 10:30, and it was nonstop talking the whole time.

When I got inducted into Ted's Hitters Museum, Ted was still alive, and we had a couple of nights to sit down and talk about baseball and fishing. We actually talked more about baseball than we did during my playing days. Once I had retired, Ted and I would talk about various games, young players, and things of that nature. But I still told Ted about fishing trips in the offseason and catching sailfish. And now I'm into marlin, and Ted once caught a 1,000-pound marlin, and he said, "You have a ways to go if you want to catch me, kid."

But I have been over several times to his hitter's museum, and I have a cubicle of Red Sox stuff there. It's an extreme honor to even be in that museum. If anyone can get over to Tropicana Field and check it out, it's a wonderful museum and a tremendous place to go.

Speaking of Tropicana Field, when they had a ceremony for my 3,000th hit, Ted was there. That was very moving. We had sent out the invitation, and it came back that Ted wasn't feeling too well and wouldn't be able to make it. But lo and behold, I turn around in the clubhouse, and Ted walks in. It was very moving that he would come down and be a part of that. It was *extremely* special, it really was. And he tipped his cap to me. The greatest compliment a player could ever get is if Ted Williams tips his cap to you. That was '99 when he did that, the same year he had that moment at the All-Star Game at Fenway, which some of the former players in this book also talk about. I would have loved to have been there and wheeled him out. It was a monumental moment in baseball.

I have a lot of books in my library and pictures around the house of Ted's stuff. I have pictures of Ted in just about every room, so my house is somewhat of a shrine to him. He left me a shotgun, a fly-rod reel, and a spinning reel in his will when he passed away. I was completely shocked at that. Dave McCarthy, the curator of the Ted Williams Museum, called and said that Mr. Williams has left me some items in his will, and I was just overwhelmed that he would think of me and make such a gesture. That's goosebumpville.

And it would have been special, really special, if Ted could have been at my Hall of Fame induction, but he had passed away a few years earlier.

I was looking forward to reading this book; to see the psyche pitchers when a terrific hitter came to the plate. I know how they think now: They walk him and pitch to the next guy. That's why guys walk so much nowadays. It's not because they have a good eye, it's that guys just don't throw strikes to where they can swing the bat. They'd rather pitch to the guy behind him, who is either in a slump, isn't doing well, or isn't the same caliber of player.

In my opinion, *Facing Ted Williams* is a must-read because it's great to hear about the approach that pitchers, catchers, and fielders of that era dealt with a hitter like Ted Williams. I think facing Ted Williams as a young player would have been *so* intimidating. But when you look back at that era, there were a lot of intimidating players—just so many great players of that era—that pitchers were facing greats all the time. But it's always nice to read something about Ted.

It is extremely special, the journey I had with Ted. My dad's favorite player growing up was Ted Williams . . . well, Ted Williams and Mickey Mantle. Just having my dad sit down with Ted Williams during minor league and big league days, me sitting down and talking with him, making it to the Hall of Fame and being mentioned in the same breath as him, and wearing a Red Sox cap into the Hall of Fame—which Ted and I share—is extremely special.

I don't think Hollywood could have scripted anything better than a little, snotty-nosed kid from Tampa, Florida, who gets to be alongside his idol in the Hall of Fame and grow up to even be mentioned in the same breath as him.

It is an incredible journey. Growing up, I dreamed about being Ted Williams . . . that dream sort of manifested itself into myself. But there will never be another Ted Williams. His persona—not only on the field, but off—and to also be an American hero? I mean, wow. The legacy he left behind is what people aspire to, and it's a pleasure to have been able to know somebody like that.

—Wade Boggs, November 2012

INTRODUCTION

IS TED WILLIAMS the greatest hitter of all time? I believe that it's a question that will always be up for debate. I'm not sure there will ever be—or can be—a definitive answer. And who would know best, anyway? That is the purpose of this book; to find out from those whose opinions matter most: The people who went up against him.

But maybe I'm getting ahead of myself just a bit.

When I was in the sixth grade, I decided to replay a baseball season with my dice simulation of choice (APBA), and chose the 1941 American League. Certainly, it wasn't for the great pennant race, because there wasn't more than one team who was in it that year. (The Yankees won by 17 games, and there were only three teams at .500 or better in the AL.) Quite simply, it was the prospect of being able to replay the last time someone hit .400 in a season.[1] Later, when I was eighteen, I was fortunate enough to get a kind of backstage pass to the Hall of Fame induction ceremonies in Cooperstown. I got to see a lot of hall of famers make their entrance (and also got to taste rum for the first time, but that's another story), including Ted Williams. In fact, a friend I was with said he heard someone ask Williams what he'd hit if he were right-handed. Now, this guy could tell a joke with a straight face better than anyone, so I have no idea if this is true, but I did take a picture of Williams, and if I can recall correctly, he had a quizzical

---

[1] With two games left in the 1941 season (a doubleheader against the Philadelphia Athletics), Ted Williams had the choice of sitting out, as he had a .39955 batting average, which would have been rounded up to .400. That wasn't acceptable for Ted. Instead, he played in both games of the doubleheader, going 6–8 on the day, and finishing with a .406 batting average for the season.

9

look on his face. We've always heard theories from ballplayers about what it takes to be a great hitter. Rogers Hornsby used to say not to watch movies because it would hurt your eyes, and there are entire books written by the likes of Ted Williams and Tony Gwynn on the art of hitting.[2]

But what about the strategies of those who had to face him? How did they pitch to Williams? Did they play the Williams shift and, if so, did it really do any good? And how good was Williams, really?

Obviously, one of the issues in finding out these things is time. It has been over seventy years since Williams made his major-league debut (1939), and over fifty years since he had his last at-bat (a pretty famous home run, which is recounted within these pages). This means that many players from that era are no longer with us, including Williams, who died on July 5, 2002.

But there were over 236 former pitchers and ballplayers out there who I was able to get in touch with to chat about "The Splendid Splinter."

Those whom I spoke to had some great stories and memories. It really is kind of funny how certain themes would come across in the responses I got—like umpires not calling a strike on Williams if he didn't swing. And that's just one of many examples.

One of the first ballplayers I spoke with was Virgil Trucks, who recounted a home run Williams hit off him in 1940. After we were done talking, I went to verify what he had said, and discovered that, after seventy years, his details were spot-on. I mention this because, when I called one ex-pitcher and asked if he could share his memories against Williams, he told me, "That was over fifty goddamn years ago!" It wasn't said with malice or disgust, but rather just laying out the facts.

---

[2] Ted Williams' book, *The Science of Hitting*, came out in 1986 and is not only still in print, but continues to sell successfully.

While every former ballplayer in this book didn't have his details down pat like Trucks, I didn't feel it was my job to argue or confront these men with the "true" details. Because after all . . . this book is about their memories.

I do represent the true facts of game events that were incorrectly related. I don't do this to show up the ballplayers or to make them look bad, but rather to present an accurate, historical account.

And really, the details were usually correct. But minor things—like perhaps the situation (runners on base, inning, score)—weren't exactly the way it was. So he struck out Williams in the fourth inning, not the ninth, or there was no one on base, instead of two. The fact is, Williams did indeed strike out, so the memory of the pitches and the strikeout were, in my opinion, likely correct—just not the situation. And that's what's important.

And speaking of statistics, while the availability of stats has increased tremendously over the years, there are still some years in which box scores are not available (pre-1946 for the most part, plus some scattered games here and there post-1946). Thus, not all the statistics for Ted Williams vs. certain pitchers are complete. We've noted them within these pages, but have given the best representation possible.

While many of those who faced Ted in his prime are long gone, the ballplayers I spoke to were able to share their memories with me, and, in the end, gave wonderful stories that most of us would have never heard.

I hope you enjoy them as much as I did.

Section One: Pitchers

Dave Baldwin

Right-handed pitcher

1966–69: ....Washington Senators
1970: .... Milwaukee Brewers
1973: .... Chicago White Sox
Career statistics: .... 6–11, 22 saves, 3.08 ERA

Note: Baldwin did not play against Ted Williams, but was managed by him in 1969 with the Senators.

WHEN THE WASHINGTON Senators went to spring training in Pompano Beach, Florida, in 1969, we had high hopes despite a dismal last place finish in '68. We had good reason to be optimistic. Our new manager was a legend, a baseball icon, a combination of Teddy Roosevelt, John Wayne, and Hercules. Our new manager was Ted Williams.

Ted was the perfect manager for the '69 Senators. Our roster was made up mostly of the '68 Senators team—not an encouraging situation—but Ted was bursting with confidence and that was infectious. We needed a leader who was authoritative and self-assured. Ted was that in spades. The players felt that just his presence in the dugout would be enough to lift a last place team into the first division.

Having those characteristics, Ted might be assumed to be egotistical, but his players didn't see him that way. He was focused on his team, trying to help each player become the best he could be. He demanded that his players have a can-do attitude. He was a larger-than-life, fifty-one-year-old cheerleader who convinced his team that they could be playing for the pennant. That was crucial to the Senators' success, but a manager must do much more for his team.

Ted realized he needed a coaching staff that would complement his abilities. First, he chose to retain Sid Hudson, a Red Sox teammate of

Ted's, for his pitching coach. He relied heavily on Sid's advice on all pitching matters. Then, Ted hired Joe Camacho to be his advisor on strategic and tactical decisions during games. Joe had been a senior instructor at Ted's baseball camp in Massachusetts. Ted's bullpen coaches were Doug Camilli and George Susce, two veteran catchers who were well acquainted with the Senators' pitchers.

Ted added veteran infielders Wayne Terwilliger (the manager of Buffalo in '68) and Nellie Fox to make our on-field operations run smoothly. Nellie also served another important function: at times he was a court jester, needling Ted to the amusement of the players. He goaded Ted more than anyone else dared. When Nellie looked at Ted, all he saw was a target. And there was Nellie, holding a handful of darts. "You know I had more hits than you did, don't you?" he would ask with a gleam in his eye. "And only about a third the strikeouts you had," he added, just to be sure he made his point.

Another thrust that always worked was "You would have been a hell'uva hitter if you could have gone to the opposite field." And his favorite jibe, "You were too predictable. I always knew right where to play you." This earned the perfect rustic yet colorful response from Ted.

This teasing by Nellie allowed Ted to look human and, therefore, approachable by his players. I don't know whether Nellie and Ted arranged for these little interactions for our benefit or whether they were acting on intuition, but it worked well, contrived or otherwise.

Whenever Ted expounded on any topic, he was an impressive show. Imagine a player asking him a question about hitting a baseball—his favorite subject. First, if Ted was sitting, he stood up—he had to be on his feet for this. Then, to make sure the player paid full attention, he would grow taller and lean back, the way he used to swing at a nickel curve. His audience would be awestruck. It was like driving past Mount Rainier. To emphasize his parameters, Ted would throw potent expletives and rapid-fire gestural metaphors at the player from all angles. *POW, BAM, ZAP,* and other cartoon interjections rattled windows as he punctuated his punctuations. Before long the player would be exhausted.

It *was* overwhelming, but this animated lecture could be an invaluable education for a pitcher. Ted was providing insight into how one of history's hardest-thinking batters thought about his business. The pitcher-batter battle was partly a mind-reading exercise and partly a guessing game. With Ted's enlightenment, it became more the former, less the latter.

Besides educating his pitchers, Ted was a great mentor for his hitters, of course. Eddie Brinkman was his prize pupil. Eddie batted only .208 over several seasons prior to '69, but under Ted's tutelage Eddie stopped uppercutting the ball so much and began to hit line drives instead of lazy fly balls. He hit .266, the highest batting average of his career.[1] In fact, the whole team hit much better under Ted. We had finished next to last in the American League in hitting in 1968 with a team average of .224. (Only the pathetic Yankees were worse. They had a season-long slump of .214, one of the poorest team batting averages in baseball history.) Under Ted, we improved to .251—tied with the Red Sox for third best in the 12-team league.

I wonder how often manager Williams thought, *Maybe I'll just take a few cuts.* Once, near the end of batting practice, he couldn't stand it any longer. He grabbed an unattended bat, shouted, "Let's see what you've got" to the pitcher (one of the coaches, probably Terwilliger or Fox) and stepped into the cage. Everyone in the park was transfixed as Ted hit nine or ten line drives against the right-field wall on as many pitches. He made perfect contact on every pitch. Although he was fifty-one, considerably hefty, and hadn't swung a bat in a game in nine years, he was still the best hitter on the team. He batted 1.000 that day, and that was the last time I ever saw him hit.

---

[1] Brinkman would hit .262 under Williams in 1970. He was traded to Detroit before the 1971 season and never hit higher than .237 again.

In that one incident, we saw conviction win out against the risk of pride. Ted was so sure he could pick up a bat and hit line drives cold it probably didn't occur to him he might look foolish in front of his whole team. No other manager was better at leading by example.

Charlie Beamon

Right-handed pitcher

1956–58: ....**Baltimore Orioles**
Career Statistics: ....**3–3, 0 saves, 3.91 ERA**

Ted Williams vs. Charlie Beamon

4-for-9, 1 double, 4 RBI, 0 walks, 0 strikeouts, 1 double play, .444 batting average, .444 on-base percentage, .556 slugging percentage

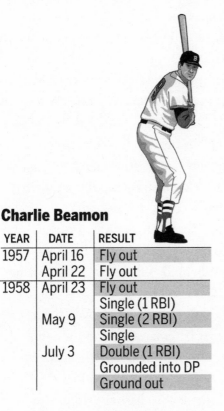

Charlie Beamon

YEAR	DATE	RESULT
1957	April 16	Fly out
	April 22	Fly out
1958	April 23	Fly out
		Single (1 RBI)
	May 9	Single (2 RBI)
		Single
	July 3	Double (1 RBI)
		Grounded into DP
		Ground out

IT WAS A serious situation [the first time I faced Williams]. I believe that I came in relief with a couple of men on. He just looked so relaxed. And I mean, I was really impressed; I had read so much about him, and this was the first time I had a chance to pitch against him.

I was pretty relaxed, though. I had a good sinker—a real good sinker—and Ted, to me, seemed to be a high-ball hitter from the few times I had seen him hit. So I just kept the ball down low on him. He hit it *very* hard, but it was right at some-body; you know, a ground ball.

But that was about it. I was very impressed with him, because he didn't waste any motion. When he moved, he swung the bat. I admired him more than anything from what I had read and seen.

If he wasn't going to swing, he wasn't going to [use] a lot of [motion]. But he picked that ball up real quick, and when he committed himself . . . boom! That was that. He was all about hitting. He wasn't about looking pretty and all that stuff, even though he did have a beautiful swing.

You had to watch him [when pitching], because he would move a little farther out of that on-deck circle to where he could really see the spin of the ball. When I came in and warmed up, he had moved over a little bit, but the umpire told him to get back in there—back in the on-deck circle.

But he was a keen observer of the game and had a real sharp mind; any advantage that he could get, he took. He was just tremendous.

When I got to the big leagues, I knew I was ready. I had been in the minors for three or four years and had pitched against some real good hitters in the Coast League—nothing like Williams—but I had faced some good hitters.

They didn't say too much [on how to pitch Williams], but the starting pitchers would talk about how they were going to pitch to hitters. So they didn't say too much to me; I just kind of observed and took it all in, picking up what I could. I knew what got me to the big leagues, and I was not going to change my way. I'd match my strength against any of them, including Ted Williams. I had an excellent changeup, too; so when I got behind, I'd throw changeups and different stuff.

[Our team used the Williams shift as well.] Waaaay over; the second baseman was almost next to the first baseman, and the shortstop was on the other side of second base (the right field side). But he was so quick; I mean [you knew] he was going to pull the ball. Half the time—even with the shift—he hit the ball so hard, he'd hit it right to them. It didn't matter.

I never got a chance to talk with him, but as far as talking with fans and kids—he really talked a lot with kids when I'd seen him. Sometimes coming into the ballpark, there he'd be, talking to three or four kids on the way into the park. He was quiet but very friendly to players and kids. I don't think he liked the media too much, but they were kind of weird anyway. Everybody wanted a story, which is okay; everybody has their purpose.

Ted was really something special. He was an outstanding hitter. He wouldn't swing at bad pitches and the umpires would not call a strike on him if he didn't swing. He was very patient, and he had a real good attitude about things, as far as the umpires and stuff like that. If they happened to call something he didn't think was a strike, he never said anything. All he needed was one pitch anyway, you know [laughs]. Yeah, he was a tremendous hitter.

He was alright. Ted was the man.

Ted Bowsfield

Left-handed pitcher

1958–60:	**Boston Red Sox**
1960:	**Cleveland Indians**
1961–62:	**Los Angeles Angels**
1963–64:	**Kansas City Athletics**
Career Statistics:	**37–39, 6 saves, 4.35 ERA**

Ted Williams vs. Ted Bowsfield

0-for-2, 0 RBI, 0 walks, 1 strikeout, .000 batting average, .000 on-base percentage, .000 slugging percentage

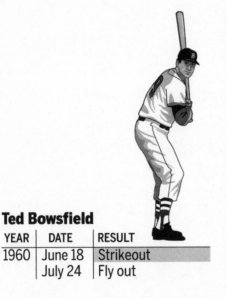

Ted Bowsfield

YEAR	DATE	RESULT
1960	June 18	Strikeout
	July 24	Fly out

I ONLY FACED TED Williams twice in my career. In regards to my strategy against him, I don't think many teams had a strategy as far as how they were going to pitch to him. I think the general consensus was that you tried to get him out with your best stuff, whether it be a fastball or breaking ball. There was no point in trying to nibble around the plate, because if Ted took the pitch, the umpires generally called it a ball.

Generally, pitching to Williams was based on game situations. For example, when we played the Yankees in Yankee Stadium and in Boston, Jackie Jensen—a fine right fielder for the Sox—always hit in the No. 4 slot behind Williams. [Yankees manager Casey] Stengel, if the game were on the line, would always walk Williams and pitch to Jensen. I think the results were more favorable to the Yankees than they were to the Red Sox in those situations. Teams like Cleveland did use the Williams shift, but a lot of teams didn't, because he was such a great hitter that he'd usually hit the location of the pitch to any part of the field. This happened more as he got older.

Was he the toughest out I ever faced? Of course! I'm glad I didn't have to face him too often, but Al Kaline was the toughest batter for me.[2]

I faced a lot of great hitters [in my career]. Not all of them during regular season—some in spring training. But the likes of Willie Mays, Stan Musial, Mickey Mantle, Harmon Killebrew, Harvey Kuenn, Yogi Berra, Elston Howard—all of those players were great hitters. Mays was probably the best all-around player; Mantle would be a close second.

It was an honor to just watch Williams hit in 1958, '59, and '60, even as the years were getting on for him. In spring training, if we were left behind, we would pitch batting practice to Williams. For it to be a challenge, he would make the conditions always be Game 7 of the World Series, winning run on base, 3–2 on the hitter, and he would tell us to throw any pitch we wanted. I can remember Bill Monbouquette, and I did this several times with him. It was great fun and, of course, a great learning experience.

Ted was a good friend for a long time. Our paths continued to cross in Anaheim [while I was their traveling secretary] when he managed the Washington Senators, and in Seattle, when I managed the Kingdome [as the stadium director], he would stop by on his way to Alaska on fishing trips. The end of his life saddened me a great deal, because he was a wonderful man, not always understood. He didn't care for the press very much, but he was a wonderful teammate and treated everybody who played with him just great.

---

[2] In 34 plate appearances, Al Kaline went 8–25, with 1 home run, 5 RBI, 2 walks, 0 strikeouts, a .320 batting average, .370 on-base percentage, and .680 slugging percentage.

Williams always said that it was easier to hit when you faced the same pitcher four times, like he did a lot in his early career. He maintained it was getting tougher to hit when he had to face three or four pitchers [in one game] later in his career.

The one thing he mentioned to me was that the pitchers who gave him the most trouble was the ones that had good control and changed speeds. The toughest pitcher he said he ever faced was Herb Score.[3] It's too bad that Herb has passed away, because I'm sure he would have had some great stories regarding their match-ups.

---

[3] In 34 plate appearances against Score, Williams went 6–25, with 4 home runs, 7 RBI, 9 walks, 2 strikeouts, a .240 batting average, .441 on-base percentage, and .760 slugging percentage.

Dick Brodowski

Right-handed pitcher

1952, 1955: ....Boston Red Sox
1956–57: ....Washington Senators
1958–59: ....Cleveland Indians
Career Statistics: .... 9–11, 5 saves, 4.76 ERA

Ted Williams vs. Dick Brodowski

1-for-1, 0 extra-base hits, 0 RBI, 2 walks, 0 strikeouts, 1.000 batting average, 1.000 on-base percentage, 1.000 slugging percentage

MY MEETINGS WITH Ted were only a few, but they were very exciting, because I was nineteen years old and Ted was already a legend. He had a great personality and was a great guy.

I met him in the spring of 1952, which was my first opportunity to go to a major league spring training camp. In June of 1952, I came up to the Red Sox and he wasn't there—I believe he went to Korea in 1952.[4]

In spring training of 1955—I went into the military in 1952 and 1954 (drafted)—I always remembered that he would check every pitch the pitcher threw and what his

Dick Brodowski

YEAR	DATE	RESULT
1957	April 25	Walk
		Walk
		Single

---

[4] Williams only played in six games in 1952 before being recalled to active duty to serve in the Korean War.

best pitch was, so if a pitcher was to get beat, he was to get beat on his best pitch. That made hitting much easier for him.

I remember facing him in spring training—I [think] in San Diego—but what we were doing there I don't know. I decided that I would throw pitches I didn't normally throw. I threw a nothing fastball, knuckleball slider, and fastball, and he hit a topspin ground ball through the right side. Also, the hit during the season was the same—which ain't bad for a "Triple-A" pitcher. I think we all used the Williams shift—he usually hit that way [right side]. The middle of every lineup was my toughest out.

I enjoyed the year of 1955; to watch Ted play ball for a full season . . . and it was an all-star season!

Bob Bruce

Right-handed pitcher

1959–61: ....Detroit Tigers
1962–66: ....Houston Colt .45s/Astros
1967: .... Atlanta Braves
Career Statistics: ....49–71, 1 save, 3.85 ERA

Ted Williams vs. Bob Bruce

2-for-5, 1 home run, 1 RBI, 1 walk, 1 strikeout, .400 batting average, .500 on-base percentage, 1.000 slugging percentage

Home Runs Allowed:

No. 505, June 30, 1960, at Boston

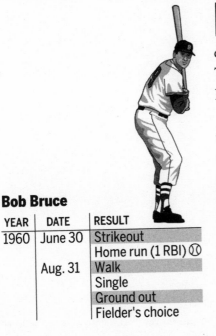

Bob Bruce

YEAR	DATE	RESULT
1960	June 30	Strikeout
		Home run (1 RBI) ⓧⓍ
	Aug. 31	Walk
		Single
		Ground out
		Fielder's choice

I REMEMBER TED WILLIAMS well. He was the best hitter I ever saw. I was a rookie with the Tigers when I first started against Boston.

Clem Labine and I were new teammates—I being a rookie and Clem a proven veteran. Clem was a locker mate of mine, and before the game, he leaned over and whispered, "Do you realize you and I are the only pitchers on the Detroit staff that Williams does not have in his book [referring to home runs]?" To make a long story short, I struck him out the first time up. The second at-bat, he hit the ball 400 feet for a homer.

Clem relieved me in the eighth, and Ted put him in his book quickly after that. When the game was over, we couldn't help but laugh. I said, "It didn't take him long, did it?"[5]

---

[5] Bob Bruce pitched 3⅔ innings against Boston on June 30, 1960, and was relieved in the fourth inning by Paul Foytack. Clem Labine did pitch the eighth inning, but he intentionally walked Williams. Williams would homer off Labine just over a month later, on July 31, in the first game of a doubleheader.

Art Ceccarelli

Left-handed pitcher

1955–56: ....Kansas City Athletics
1957: .... Baltimore Orioles
1959–60: .... Chicago Cubs
Career Statistics: ....9-18, 0 saves, 5.05 ERA

Ted Williams vs. Art Ceccarelli

4-for-6, 0 extra-base hits, 3 RBI, 1 walk, .667 batting average, .714 on-base percentage, .667 slugging percentage

ACTUALLY, I'M A little crazy, because I walked a man purposely my first time to face him. I walked Billy Goodman in front of him, and [Ted] got up and hit a ground ball, thank God. It was my first time pitching against Boston,[6] and there were two outs, and I wanted to pitch to him.[7]

I very seldom had sports heroes, but he was one of mine, so I wanted to face him. I was not really nervous, more hyped-up than anything else.

Art Ceccarelli

YEAR	DATE	RESULT
1955	July 21	Ground out
	Aug. 6	Single
	Aug. 7	Single (2 RBI)
1957	May 30	Single
		Ground out
		Single (1 RBI)
	July 6	Walk

---

[6] Ceccarelli faced Boston once previously, on May 13, 1955—his rookie season—but Williams did not play in that game.

[7] According to retrosheet.org, on July 21, 1955, in Kansas City, Ceccarelli entered a 4–3 game in the top of the ninth. He retired Frank Sullivan on a liner and Billy Goodman on a fly out before Billy Klaus singled to bring up Williams, who grounded out to first base.

It was a fastball. It was about the third one [he swung at]. Believe me, in those days, if a hitter had a reputation, you didn't get him called out on strikes; they had to be right down the middle. It wasn't a career highlight, but it definitely was a good feeling.

Luckily, I just faced him two or three more times. Thank God he didn't get many hits off of me. He hit the ball well a couple of times. He hit two pretty good shots to second base, but I got away with them.

It would have been good if he did hit a home run off me. I taught school after I left baseball, and one of my students was at the Hall of Fame and said to me, "Hey, Mr. Check, I didn't know you were in the Hall of Fame." And I knew exactly what he was going to say. He probably went to Williams, [Mickey] Mantle, and [Willie] Mays to see if they hit any home runs off of me. He was right on a few of them! Mantle got one, Mays got one, [Yogi] Berra got two . . . but not Williams.

They used the shift. The only thing the shift did was make Williams more determined to hit the ball through the right side. I used to watch him in batting practice, and he could hit the ball to the left field fence any time he wanted to, but he would not do it in a game for some reason. He was going to beat that shift. With his average, I guess he proved he could.

It was very easy to talk to him on the ball field, I'll tell you. I guess after the game he was somewhat of a loner, but I never had a problem with him. . . . And I haven't talked to any [ballplayer] who did.

I just happened to talk to him about something different [than baseball]. There was a Cuban ballplayer, Mike Fornieles, on the Boston team at that time. We had played together in the minor leagues [and Ted and I] were kidding him about [Fidel] Castro.

Unlike most people who think he was nonsociable, he was fine, just so long as he was talking to one of the guys. He didn't care for the reporters too much. Basically, he was very polite to the guys on the field. So generally, other ballplayers had no problem with him.

Well, I know he didn't like reporters, but they weren't the easiest people in the world [to get along with], to be honest with you.

Gene Conley

Right-handed pitcher

1952:	Brooklyn Dodgers
1953–58:	Milwaukee Braves
1959–60:	Philadelphia Phillies
1961–63:	Boston Red Sox
Career Statistics:	91–96, 9 saves, 3.82 ERA
National League All-Star:	1954, 1955, 1959

Ted Williams vs. Gene Conley in All-Star Games

0-for-1

1959: With the American League leading 3–1 in the fifth inning with one out and a runner on first, Williams struck out vs. Conley

Q. What was your strategy against Williams, and how do you think you fared?

A. Real good. Ha.

Gene Conley

YEAR	DATE	RESULT
1959	All-Star Game	Strikeout

I SPENT SEVEN YEARS in the National League. The year I was traded to the American League (1961), Williams had just retired. I was given his locker, however, right next to Frank Malzone.

He had left his bat and a few t-shirts in his locker. The bat was the [one he hit his] last home run on at the end of 1960. I gave the bat away to a kid in Rhode Island, and my wife didn't speak to me for a long time. (She read it was worth several thousand dollars later on. Ha. Oh well.)

It's hard for me to compare, as in the fifties there was some great hitters, which I'm sure you must know. From what I hear from [ballplayers] that I've talked to, he was probably the best of all the greats in the fifties. I feel like I didn't need the challenge.

Frank Malzone told me he played pepper[8] with him a lot. When Williams was finished with the pepper game, there would be just one spot on his bat where the ball always hit. I would say that must have been great hand-and-eye [coordination], especially playing pepper, when the throws weren't always strikes.

---

[8] Pepper is a game where one player hits ground balls to a group of fielders who are standing close by.

Glenn Cox

Right-handed pitcher

1955–58: ....**Kansas City Athletics**
Career Statistics: .... **1–4, 0 saves, 6.39 ERA**

Ted Williams vs. Glenn Cox

0-for-2, 1 walk (intentional), 1 strikeout, .000 batting average, .333 on-base percentage, .000 slugging percentage

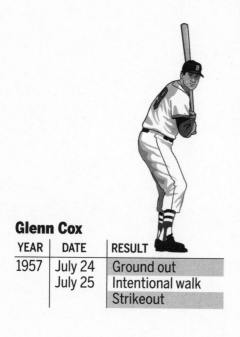

Glenn Cox

YEAR	DATE	RESULT
1957	July 24	Ground out
	July 25	Intentional walk
		Strikeout

WHEN I PITCHED against Ted Williams, it wasn't the way that you have it here.[9]

I came in with no outs. The first batter who I pitched against was Ted Williams.[10] I'd heard that, from other pitchers, if the ball was not perfect—on the corner or something—that the umpire gave him a break.

So my first pitch was a fastball—a good fastball—right on the outside corner. The umpire called it ball one.

Well, I was young and cocky. So I wound up, and the next

---

[9] At the time of my letter to Cox, Retrosheet.org only had Williams' appearance against Cox on July 24, 1957. The other game—July 25, 1957—was missing from their data and was only recently added.

[10] In the game on July 24, Williams was the first batter Cox faced when entering the game. Williams grounded out to first base in that appearance. In the game on July 25, the at-bat Cox describes came with two out in the seventh inning.

pitch was beautiful, right on the outside corner, and Ted just looked at it. Ball two.

So I walked in, which you're not supposed to do, but I kept my mouth shut. I just walked in, and I think the umpire, I remember the name—well I did remember the name—but I walked in and got about five feet from home plate, and the umpire said, "You open your mouth punk and you're gone."[11]

I never said a word. And I walked a couple more feet and turned around and started back towards the mound. I turned around and Ted Williams was there, and I said, "Ted, I'm going to tell you what's coming, and you still can't hit me." This is all true. I said, "I'm going to throw you nothing but fastballs."

And I walked [back] to the mound. The next pitch was a little bit above the waist and he swung and fouled it off. And then he fouled off another pitch.

He didn't realize that I had a good screwball. And the next pitch, well, I made a perfect pitch and he swung and missed it. He just stood there and looked at me. I know he thought I threw him a spitter[12] or something, because that sucker just went *pshoo*. It's just like yesterday that it happened.

He was probably one of the great hitters that ever played the game. I just believed in myself, I guess.

---

[11] As per baseball-reference.com, the home plate umpire for the game was Larry Napp.
[12] Spitball

Bud Daley

Left-handed pitcher

1955–57:...Cleveland Indians
1958–61:..Kansas City Athletics
1961–64:...New York Yankees
Career Statistics: .... 60–64, 10 saves, 4.03 ERA
American League All-Star: 1959, 1960

Ted Williams vs. Bud Daley

9-for-24, 2 doubles, 2 home runs, 7 RBI, 3 walks, 4 strikeouts, 4 hit by pitches, .375 batting average, .516 on-base percentage, 1.224 slugging percentage

Home Runs Allowed:

No. 502, June 21, 1960, at Kansas City
No. 503, June 21, 1960, at Kansas City

I DON'T KNOW IF you remember the old Kansas City ballpark, but it had two fences. It had one down below then a hill up, and a fence up on top, so people couldn't look in.

Anyway, I'm pitching one night and we score six runs in the first inning, and Williams is the first hitter in the second inning.[13] I called the catcher[14] out and said, "Hey, I've never thrown a slider and I've been working on it. Let's throw him a slider." So I threw him a slider and he hit it over the fence for a home run.

---

[13] On June 21, 1960, the A's scored five runs in the bottom of the first. Williams, who batted third, had hit in the first inning and grounded out. Daley retired the first eleven batters, with Williams coming up with two out in the fourth.
[14] Harry Chiti

Bud Daley

YEAR	DATE	RESULT
1957	May 22	Walk
		Single
		Hit by pitch
	June 20	Reached on error
	Aug. 22	Single (1 RBI)
1958	July 16	Strikeout
		Hit by pitch
	Sept. 18	Double
		Ground out
		Hit by pitch
		Ground out
1959	July 25	Single
	Aug. 19	Strikeout
		Fly out
		Strikeout
		Line out

YEAR	DATE	RESULT
1960	June 21	Ground out
		Home run (1 RBI)
		Home run (2 RBI)
		Single
	July 2	Foul out
		Foul out
		Walk
		Walk
		Double (2 RBI)
	July 15	Hit by pitch
		Ground out
		Ground out
		Single
		Strikeout
	Sept. 9	Ground out

So in the ninth inning he comes up, and the score is 10–1.[15] I told the catcher, I said I'm going to try that slider again. This time he hit it over the second fence. There've only been two homers hit over that fence.

The catcher comes out and says, "I think you better work on that pitch some more." I think that was the last slider I ever threw.

---

[15] It was actually the sixth inning with the score 8–1.

The first time I ever faced Ted Williams was in Boston, and I had two strikes on him. I threw a fastball right down the middle. He took it, and the umpire said ball.

So the next inning, I come out to bat. The catcher is out talking to the pitcher. I said to the umpire, "Hey, what was the matter with the pitch to Williams? It was right down the middle."

He says, "Son, let me tell you. People don't come here to see him strike out, they come here to see him hit."

I didn't realize he hit that much off of me, because I don't really remember him really hurting me in a ball game. [Actually,] I don't *ever* remember hitting him. That was the thing that really shocked me. I don't remember hitting him, and I'm sure I never hit him with a fastball.

I know he told me one time, "Your curveball is the hardest curveball to hit I've ever seen." He says, "Most curveballs come in and they kind of stop. Yours just keeps going and going and going." But I guess, apparently, he didn't have too much trouble.

One day we were warming up. You know how the pitchers catch the ball in for the outfielder during infield practice? Well, Williams is standing right behind me warming up, and I'm catching the balls from the outfield. He says, "Hey, Bud." I turn around and he says, "Watch this."

And he threw this little-bitty curveball that broke about three or four inches, and says, "You know what? I should have been a pitcher. I think I wasted a good career."[16]

---

[16] In his career, Ted Williams had one pitching performance. He pitched two innings, gave up three hits, one earned run, and one strikeout, finishing with a 4.50 ERA.

He was a heck of a nice guy. I really liked him. I think he's the best hitter I ever saw, [although] I wasn't as worried with him as I was with a couple [of] other guys.

I don't remember pitching to him too much, but when he came up, evidently I wasn't in a jam. But I would probably say that if I found myself in a jam, then I would have been really concerned . . . but hell, when you're up 10–1, you're not worried about it.

I always say that the best hitter I ever saw was Ted Williams; the most power was always Mickey Mantle; and the best all-around player I ever saw was Willie Mays.

Jim Derrington

Left-handed pitcher

1956–57:	**Chicago White Sox**
Career Statistics:	**0–2, 0 saves, 5.23 ERA**

Ted Williams vs. Jim Derrington

0-for-1, 0 RBI, 1 walk, 0 strikeouts, .000 batting average, .500 on-base percentage, .000 slugging percentage

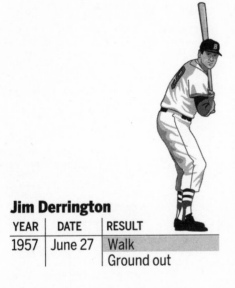

Jim Derrington

YEAR	DATE	RESULT
1957	June 27	Walk
		Ground out

THAT WAS A very long time ago. I do remember the time Williams grounded out to our first baseman, Walt Dropo. Williams hit it so hard that Dropo came by the mound and reminded me that he had a wife and family back in Chicago and to try and pitch Williams outside.

Our pitchers seemed to agree that the best way to pitch to him was to keep the ball low and hope he got a single. As you know, I only faced Williams twice [in my career]. For me, the toughest of the great hitters that I faced was Al Kaline.

Chuck Estrada

Right-handed pitcher

1960–64:	Baltimore Orioles
1966:	Chicago Cubs
1967:	New York Mets
American League All-Star:	1960
Career Statistics:	50–44, 2 saves, 4.07 ERA

Ted Williams vs. Chuck Estrada

4-for-7, 1 double, 2 home runs, 6 RBI, 2 walks, 1 strikeout, .571 batting average, .667 on-base percentage, 1.571 slugging percentage

Home Runs Allowed:

No. 514, August 20, 1960 (Game 1) at Baltimore
No. 515, August 20, 1960 (Game 1) at Baltimore

WELL, THERE'S A great story that I tell when I talk to different organizations about Ted.

What happened was, when I first got to the big leagues before my first start, I pitched in relief two or three times. So, I pitched in relief in Boston my third time out before I got my first start.[17] And we were in Fenway and had a six-run lead—a six- or five-run lead in the sixth inning and the phone rang and the manager of the team said just get some work in.[18] So I was just down there throwing.

Anyway, Boston ended up getting the bases loaded with nobody out. So as the story goes, they eventually called me in. Anyway, I struck out

---

[17] Estrada actually pitched in relief three times to start his career in 1960, then got two starts in early May before being used in relief in Boston on May 15, in the second game of a doubleheader.
[18] Baltimore led, 7–2.

the first hitter and popped up the second hitter behind home plate.[19] And lo and behold I called time out and I was walking back to the mound and Brooks Robinson, our third baseman, came over and says, "Hey, Chuck, how are you going to pitch *this* guy?" I say, "what are you talking about?" He said, "Turn around." Well, it was Ted.[20] So I said, "Hell if I know, but I'm going to find out [laughs]."

So anyway, as the story goes, I got fortunate and struck him out with the bases loaded to end the inning. And the fans gave me a standing ovation for striking out the greatest hitter ever, right?

Chuck Estrada

YEAR	DATE	RESULT
1960	May 15	Strikeout
	July 5	Double
		Walk
		Fly out
	Aug. 12	Fly out
	Aug. 20	Walk
		Single
		Home run (3 RBI)
		Home run (3 RBI)

Well, that's not the funny part of the story.

The next day—they don't do this anymore—but during the infield, like they did in the old days, I was on the Boston side of the infield. And we were doing our infield drills warming up and I was shagging balls for the fungo hitter to left field. And all of a sudden I hear this voice.

"Hey, kid."

And I'm saying to myself, *I ain't no damn kid*. But anyway, that voice says, "Hey, kid!"

So now I get a little upset and I turn around and it's Ted. And he said, "I want to tell you one thing." And I said, "What?" And he said, "You're going to be one hell of a pitcher." And that's what I remember about Ted [laughs].

---

[19] Estrada relieved Hal Brown after Boston loaded the bases on two singles and an error. Estrada then struck out Lou Clinton and got Gary Geiger to pop to the second baseman.
[20] Williams was pinch-hitting for pitcher Dave Hillman.

But I was fortunate enough to see his last at-bat, hit the home run off of Jack Fischer. They say he tore his uniform off, went down the runway, and said that's it. But even at that age, whatever it was, I couldn't believe how quick a bat he still had. Even though I struck him out—of course I was blessed with a very good arm—but at that time I had no clue what was going on. I was just amazed at how fast his bat still was, because I was a fastball pitcher.

So anyway, that's the story I tell everybody. As I look back now as I'm an old man, and I say, that was quite a story. As far as I knew, I was just trying to get an out.

No, I didn't have a scouting report. I can still see the four pitches I threw. I went strike one away. I went strike two away. I threw him a high fastball that he swung at. And I swear to God I could just hear that bat, and he fouled it off. Then the next pitch I threw a fastball down and away and he took it for strike three.

I was just a raw kid. I'm a country boy. And I thought, *wow, this is something special.*

I was in the dugout [for Williams' last game]. He was amazing. It was just a beautiful swing. Well, most left-handers have that, but not like *him*. But he was a real treat to try to get out.

That was later in the year [he hit home runs off him]. Hey, he's the best ever. He's going to get you. To be perfectly honest with you, the wind was blowing out to right field and I thought they were just fly ball outs. And it got up into that wind and they ended up two home runs in the right-field bleachers in Fenway. So he got back at me.

I don't remember if we won the game or not, but the bottom line is I was fortunate enough to play against some really great players.[21]

---

[21] Estrada and Baltimore lost, 8–6, as Williams had a pair of three-run homers.

His numbers proved that. Amazing. I've just never seen anybody with that quick a bat. Even at *his* age, then. So I hate to guess what he was like when he was young. I faced some great players in my career before I got hurt, but Ted was the one I always remember.

I never talked to him. The one thing that Ted always did, though, especially at the end of his career, they used to have . . . he would send people over and say if you want an autographed picture of me I'll sign it. But I was totally against hitters then and I didn't. All the other players did. I said to hell with him. But it was a treat.

From all the stories, the shift didn't matter. They did shift, but they didn't play deep enough [laughs]. Because he defied you. He'd hit the ball so damn hard it would sink over your head. Most guys the ball would rise. But he would get topspin and it's amazing how he'd get a ball on the ground and it would pick up speed, because he had a great top hand. That always amazed me. Balls would just shoot through the infield. And I'd see balls go head high over the infield and just hook down into the ground because he had so much topspin. Those are the things I remember about Ted.

I'd hate to even guess what he was like even in the prime of his career.

When Ted hit the ball there was that sound, that sound that very few players had in the time I was there. You *knew* who was hitting. Just by the sound you'd say, oh, Ted is hitting [laughs] and you'd turn around and sure as heck.

I can tell you a funny story about Ted, though. We were playing a game in Baltimore and Piersall was playing center field. And Baltimore had a little quirky left field. Ted came in and the ball was hit down the left-field line. And if it got past the outfielder it would curve around the fence, you know. Well, Piersall never left center field. There was a ball hit down the line and Ted couldn't get to it. So he ran over and just stopped and the ball went around and Piersall still sat in center field. And they had a little discussion about not backing him up. I don't know if they got along very well.[22]

Yeah, I wish I could have played against him when he was in his prime. That would have been fun. I would have done what I did with everybody. First thing I found out was can they hit my fastball. That's the first thing I always did. I never listened to, this guy does this. I learned at a very young age find out for yourself. They say, well, you can't throw this guy a fastball. I found out early in my career that I'm going to find out if he can hit *my* fastball before I decide to throw other pitches. Because I got burnt.

I think that's what he did when he came up to pitch it. Because I was a rookie and they didn't know who the hell I was. When I came in with the bases loaded, he wanted to see what this guy has got, his history. And he found out [laughs]. The story that he told me the next day at the time I didn't think much of it, but now that I'm old I think it's pretty cool.

---

[22] Piersall was not on Boston in 1960, which was Estrada's rookie year, so this could well be a story told to him by someone else, or it was a different center fielder.

Bob Feller

Right-handed pitcher

1936–1941, 1945–1956: .... Cleveland Indians
Career Statistics: .... 266–162, 21 saves, 3.25 ERA
American League All-Star: 1938–1941, 1946–1948, 1950
Elected to the National Baseball Hall of Fame in 1962

Ted Williams vs. Bob Feller (incomplete data)

43-for-129, 10 doubles, 2 triples, 9 home runs,[23] 23 RBI,[24] 34 walks (5 intentional), 10 strikeouts, .333 batting average, .472 on-base percentage, .651 slugging percentage

Home Runs Allowed:

No. 131, May 4, 1946, at Boston
No. 141, June 12, 1946, at Boston
No. 203, May 9, 1948 (game one),[25] at Boston
No. 210, June 16, 1948, at Cleveland
No. 227, May 5, 1949, at Cleveland
No. 330, August 30, 1953, at Cleveland
No. 351, July 22, 1954 (game one), at Boston
No. 353, July 29, 1954, at Cleveland
No. 374, June 19, 1955, at Boston
No. 416, September 15, 1956, at Cleveland

---

[23] Of the known available box scores, Williams hit nine home runs off Feller. But the data is available for all of Williams' 521 career home runs, and he ended up with 10 off Feller.

[24] Retrosheet.org has more data of Williams vs. Feller, but does not include RBI. Baseball-reference.com lists Williams with 23 RBI in 72 at-bats (90 plate appearances) vs. Feller.

[25] This states that the home run in question was part of a doubleheader.

Bob Feller (data incomplete; missing 1939-'41, 1946-'47)

YEAR	DATE	RESULT
1948	May 9	Line out
		Home run (1 RBI) ☉
		Walk
		Strikeout
	June 10	Walk
		Single
	June 16	Single
		Double
		Double
		Home run (2 RBI) ☉
	July 31	Single (1 RBI)
		Walk
		Fly out
	Sept. 22	Fly out
		Fly out
		Line out
		Ground out
1949	May 5	Walk
		Grounded into DP
		Fly out
		Home run (1 RBI) ☉
	June 1	Fly out
		Ground out
		Single
		Single (1 RBI)
	June 14	Walk
		Double (1 RBI)
		Strikeout
		Ground out
		Single (2 RBI)
	July 29	Walk
		Fly out
		Fly out
	Aug. 29	Single
		Ground out
		Double (RBI)
		Fly out
	Sept. 21	Sacrifice fly (1 RBI)

YEAR	DATE	RESULT
1950	May 3	Ground out
		Fly out
		Single
	June 2	Walk
		Fly out
	June 13	Intentional walk
		Single (1 RBI)
		Fielder's choice
1951	May 1	Strikeout
		Ground out
		Walk
		Ground out
	May 19	Grounded into DP
		Walk
		Single
		Single
	June 8	Ground out
		Fly out
		Walk
		Strikeout
	June 18	Fly out
		Fly out
		Single
		Fly out
		Walk
	July 17	Fly out
		Foul out
		Ground out
		Ground out
	July 28	Double (1 RBI)
	Aug. 26	Double
		Double
		Fielder's choice
1953	Aug. 30	Home run (1 RBI) ☉
		Walk
		Fly out
1954	July 22	Fielder's choice
		Walk
		Home run (2 RBI) ☉
		Walk
		Fly out
	July 29	Home run (2 RBI) ☉
		Walk

YEAR	DATE	RESULT
1955	June 19	Home run (2 RBI) ☉
	July 27	Strikeout
	Aug. 23	Intentional walk
1956	June 11	Double
		Walk
	Sept. 15	Strikeout
		Fly out
		Home run (3 RBI) ☉
		Grounded into DP

WHEN HE FIRST came up, he was a dead low-ball hitter, and you had to pitch him high and tight. . . . And after he was up there about a year, why he got to be fouling off the high fastball. He always was a better low ball hitter throughout his career. You had to throw strikes to him. He would not swing at a ball unless it was over the plate—or he thought it was. He *seldom* ever took a called third strike that I know of.

If he got back too far [in the count], you'd try to throw a slider and catch the outside corner. . . . And you'd only throw the fastball inside to him so he couldn't get the barrel of the bat on the ball. He was a very good fastball hitter. Trying to throw a fastball by him was like trying to sneak a sunbeam past a rooster in the morning . . . very difficult. He might not hit it square, but he would certainly foul it back. He'd seldom miss. Most of your home run hitters are fastball hitters. He hit 10 home runs off me during his career, and his batting average against me was around .241 or .242, as far as I know.

Did our team use the Williams shift? Yes we did. [Actually,] we invented it, [though] it didn't effect him too much.[26] He'd hit those sinkers over the infield—those line drive sinkers—or hit one out of the ballpark.

The Boudreau shift didn't really hurt him any, as far as his average went. I only once saw him hit the ball to left field, which was a home run in Cleveland in our old ballpark—Old League Park. We had the shift on, the Williams shift, and he hit one purposely down the left field line about 10 feet fair for an inside-the-park home run.[27]

Was he the toughest out [I ever faced]? No, I had a dozen fellows that were tougher than Ted. A lot of left-hand hitters like Tommy Henrich and Taft Wright, Stan Spence and Roy Cullenbine, who was a switch-hitter, Johnny Pesky, Nellie Fox, Rip Radcliff—they were all tougher than Ted. DiMaggio hit me pretty good [as well]. He liked the ball away and he had a stance where you couldn't pitch to him inside, because he would have got hit if the ball got away from you. He would not move. He was anchored right there at the plate and he wouldn't get out of the way of the ball, so you had to be careful if you tried to

---

[26] The shift used against Ted was created by Indians manager Lou Boudreau after game one of a doubleheader between Cleveland and Boston in July of 1946. It was known as the "Boudreau" or "Williams" shift.

[27] On September 13, 1946, Williams hit an inside-the-park home run at Cleveland against Red Embree in the top of the first inning in a 1–0 Boston victory. It was the only inside-the-park home run of Williams' career.

pitch him inside, as you were very apt to hit him. He was very close to the plate.

Ted hit as well as any hitter in any [era]. He was very good in the clutch, like he was in the 1941 All-Star Game.[28] Williams went 4–4, including a three-run home run off a blooper pitch thrown by Pittsburgh's Rip Sewell in the bottom of the eighth inning during the 1946 All-Star Game in Fenway.

[Ted] was a good friend of mine. We were very friendly socially away from the ballpark and even at the ballpark before the game. He spent quite a bit of time at my museum out in Iowa and helped me raise money to finish the museum—he and his son, John Henry.

Ted was three months older than me. He came up in 1939, and I came up in 1936,[29] though I didn't start pitching regularly until 1937. I got in a month and a week in 1936, and I became a regular pitcher in 1937, even though I missed a month because I slipped during a wet opening day game in Cleveland and tore up some ligaments in my elbow. I was out about a month in 1937, so I didn't pitch all that much. My first complete year of pitching, taking my turn every day, was 1938.

I have no idea why he didn't hit a home run off me before the war, but he just didn't do it; though he hit 10 home runs off me in my last ten years.

I only struck him out two or three times that I can remember. The first time was in Cleveland. It was just after the war or just before the war. He was very difficult to strike out. I'd throw him a changeup around his ankles and he'd pull it foul, and then I'd throw a slider around his fists—right around his belly button, around the belt buckle—and that was a good pitch for him. I don't know how many times he struck out

---

[28] Williams hit a game-winning three-run home run off the NL's Clause Passeau in the bottom of the ninth inning to give the AL a 7–5 win.

[29] At the age of seventeen.

in his career, but it couldn't have been many.[30] DiMaggio was tough to strike out, too, but Ted was a much better hitter and had more power, but he was not much of an outfielder when you got him out of Boston. He was a good outfielder in Fenway Park.

He had good, quick wrists and was a big, strong guy, and he had a big, heavy bat that he could handle very well, like a toothpick. He could hit to left field if he wanted to, but he rarely wanted to.

He was seldom called out on strikes. The umpires respected him. I never thought that the umpires gave him the benefit of the doubt. I never had any problem with that, not at all. I always thought the umpires were calling it right when Ted was up to bat while I was pitching. As far as I'm concerned, he didn't get any favorable calls. He had a good eye and very good hand-eye coordination, which is what made him so great.

---

[30] Williams struck out 709 times in 9,791 plate appearances. He struck out over 50 times in a season just three times, and all of those occasions occurred prior to World War II, in three of his first four seasons in the majors.

Don Ferrarese

Left-handed pitcher

1955–57:	Baltimore Orioles
1958–59:	Cleveland Indians
1960:	Chicago White Sox
1961–62:	Philadelphia Phillies
1962:	St. Louis Cardinals
Career Statistics:	19–36, 5 saves, 4.00 ERA

Ted Williams vs. Don Ferrarese

1-for-7, 0 extra-base hits, 0 RBI, 2 walks, 1 strikeout, .143 batting average, .333 on-base percentage, .143 slugging percentage

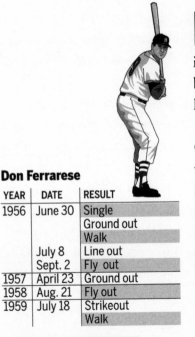

Don Ferrarese

YEAR	DATE	RESULT
1956	June 30	Single
		Ground out
		Walk
	July 8	Line out
	Sept. 2	Fly out
1957	April 23	Ground out
1958	Aug. 21	Fly out
1959	July 18	Strikeout
		Walk

HE [TED] GAVE me a big picture that he signed, I'm looking at in my office right now, and on the bottom, it says, "Tell him he can stick his curveball up his ass."

In 1956, my first start was against Cleveland, and I struck out 13 and was a big hero. My second start, I had a no-hitter against the Yankees, beating them 1–0[31] and was on the Ed Sullivan show. My third start was against Detroit, and I again did well.[32] In my fourth start, I faced Ted in Fenway. Of course, he had just

---

[31] Ferrarese actually had a no-hitter through eight innings, but Andy Carey led off the ninth with a single. He finished with a two-hitter.

[32] Ferrarese had a shutout through eight innings, but he'd be pulled after allowing two runs in the ninth in an eventual 3–2 loss.

come back from the Marine Corps. As he was going out to left field, he passed me and said, "Hey, you're the kid I hear who has the good curveball."

So anyhow, we did the shift and Billy Gardner was our second baseman, playing way out in short right field. Ted comes up to bat, and I throw him a curveball, and he stood up there and didn't make a move. Just took it, strike one. And the second one, strike two. Never moved at all.

I'm sure other people have told you that when he was ready to swing, he swung; and if he didn't, he wouldn't lunge. No lunging. The third time, he hit the son of a bitch so hard that he knocked Gardner over, and he snow-coned it. The force of it knocked him over. He knocked the crap out of it. Gardner said, "Jesus, you sure didn't fool him, did you?"

And as he rounded first, he spit in the air and looked at me and said something. Mickey Vernon was our first baseman. I asked him, "What'd he say?" Vernon said, "Tell that little shit to stick his curveball up his ass."[33]

That was my story with Ted. I did know his dad, Sam, by the way. He passed away in Walnut Creek, California. My dad had a liquor store in Walnut Creek, and Sam used to get letters from Ted, and he used to share them with me. I was playing in the minors at the time and whenever Sam had a letter, he'd let me read it. I don't think they were very close, but they did communicate.

I didn't really know Ted because I only pitched against him a couple times. It's interesting that I pitched against him seven times. I didn't know that; I don't remember all that stuff. I didn't even know that I struck him out.

---

[33] The game Ferrarse is likely referring to was on July 8, 1956, when, in a 4–4 tie in the fourth inning with two out and runners on the corners, Williams is credited by retrosheet.org with a line out to second base. Mickey Vernon was the Red Sox first baseman that day (he never played for the Orioles); Gus Triandos was at first for Baltimore.

He sure was a hitter. His hitting was unbelievable. I'm sure they'll tell you, too, that the umpires had a hard time . . . you had a hard time striking him out. I mean, they wouldn't call him out. Ed Runge got his butt chewed out as a rookie umpire when he called him out on a called third strike. The commissioner[34] gave him hell because they came to see Ted hit. They didn't publicize that, but that was the story amongst the ballplayers.

Even the great pitchers—like I played with Robin Roberts—and Williams said that Roberts was known for his control, and he used to get pitches. You earn that, I guess, and he certainly earned it. But he was a hell of a hitter. He loved to talk hitting with the guys.

As far as pitching him, I remember Gary Bell of Cleveland when we were in Cleveland together. Gary had struck him out four times in a game that went extra innings, and Ted was on deck waiting to hit, and he was taking that bat and twisting it around like he was making powder out of the damn thing. He couldn't wait to hit against Gary Bell . . . and he ended up hitting a home run off of him.[35]

He was definitely a special guy.

---

[34] Ed Runge was a rookie umpire in 1954, and the commissioner at the time was Ford Frick.

[35] The game Ferrarese refers to is likely from August 3, 1958, when Williams hit a home run in the top of the ninth off Bell. (Bell only allowed one other home run to Williams, and it was in the third inning of a game on June 28, 1959.) However, Bell did not strike out Williams on August 3, 1958. He did strike Williams out twice on two occasions: June 24, 1958—Williams' last at-bat that day was a single in the seventh, and September 12, 1958—Williams' last at-bat that day was a single in the eighth. Retrosheet.org does not show Bell ever facing Williams in extra innings, and the only time he faced Williams in the ninth inning was then he hit the home run on August 3, 1958.

Bill Fischer

Right-handed pitcher

1956–58: .... Chicago White Sox
1958: .... Detroit Tigers
1958–60: .... Washington Senators
1960–61: .... Detroit Tigers
1961–63: .... Kansas City Athletics
1964: .... Minnesota Twins
Career Statistics: .... 45–58, 13 saves, 4.34 ERA

Ted Williams vs. Bill Fischer

9-for-24, 2 doubles, 2 home runs, 7 RBI, 7 walks (2 intentional), 3 strikeouts, 1 double play, 1 sacrifice fly, .375 batting average, .516 on-base percentage, .708 slugging percentage

Home Runs Allowed:

No. 467, June 29, 1958, at Detroit
No. 473, July 29, 1958, at Detroit

Bill Fischer

YEAR	DATE	RESULT		YEAR	DATE	RESULT
1957	May 19	Single			Sept. 21	Grounded into DP
		Intentional walk				Strikeout
		Single				Double (1 RBI)
	June 27	Strikeout		1959	May 24	Walk
		Ground out				Ground out
	Aug. 3	Fielder's choice			May 29	Walk
1958	May 6	Intentional walk				Single
	May 25	Walk				Ground out
	June 7	Single				Fly out
		Single			July 2	Fly out
	June 27	Ground out				Ground out
	June 29	Home run (3 RBI)				Ground out
	July 18	Double		1960	Aug. 5	Pop out
		Walk			Aug. 30	Fly out
	July 28	Walk				
	July 29	Home run (3 RBI)				

HE WAS ONE of the greatest hitters of all-time they say, and I guess he was. He was the last guy to hit .400 and was a big and strong guy.

I pitched against him . . . oh, 1958, when I was traded to Washington from Detroit. I started a game in Fenway, and he came up to bat with the bases loaded and struck out. . . . And he was mad he struck out; he took the pitch and it was strike three. He made an imaginary swing after he was called out and then took his bat and threw it and it went over the Red Sox dugout and hit somebody in the stands. Well, they didn't know who it hit, but the umpires and both managers got together and said, "If we throw him out of the game, then he did it on purpose. Then whoever the bat hit could sue him." So they didn't throw him out of the game.

He then came up in the eighth inning and hit a two-run home run off me, and we lost 2–0.[36] When a guy strikes out, they throw the ball around and you wait to get the ball back. I didn't even really know what happened. That was an incident which was pretty big at that point in time.

I think he hit a couple of home runs off me . . . two, I believe. I know in Detroit, when I was with [the Tigers], he hit the ball above the second deck in old Tiger Stadium, where there was a wooden grandstand that people used to stand on.

He was always interesting to watch. One time when I was with the White Sox, he had three home runs in the game and came up the fourth time with nobody on base and two outs, and they walked him on purpose. [White Sox manager] Al Lopez said, "no one guy is ever going to hit four home runs against my team." So he walked him. I think the Red Sox won the game, 4–3.[37]

---

[36] The game took place September 21, 1958, in Boston. Williams struck out looking in the third inning and would later hit an RBI double in the sixth inning in a game Boston won, 2–0.

[37] The game was May 8, 1957, in Chicago. Williams hit three home runs, then was walked in the ninth inning with two out and a man on second. Boston would win 4–1.

When I coached with the Red Sox for seven years,[38] Ted was still [around the ballclub]. He used to come by spring training a lot and you'd see him during the season. When you'd see him coming, you didn't want to be around, because he'd ask these questions that you couldn't answer. Like, when do you start your curveball? Behind your head, in front, or wherever. It was never a question you could answer, because one guy would say this and another guy would say that. When he was around, he would talk loudly so that everybody knew he was there. . . . And he was always giving pointers on how to hit and how he would hit this guy. He was just fun to listen to. He was outspoken . . . very outspoken.

I know that the last time I saw him was with the All-Century Players [introduced at the 1999 All-Star Game at Fenway Park]. Then after that he got sick, but he was still around a lot. I got to know him very well. He never was a flashy dresser; sometimes you thought he didn't have any money at all. But he was a baseball man. When he talked, it was always about baseball.

The first time I faced him, I didn't strike him out; I know that.[39] In one game I saw in Detroit, Jim Bunning had a no-hitter with two outs [in the ninth], and Ted was at bat and Al Kaline was in right field. [Ted] hit a ball and Kaline had his back against the fence in right field. If he wouldn't have put his glove up, it would have gone into the bullpen. He just missed a home run.[40]

When facing Ted, I tried to keep the ball down so he'd [hit] the ball on the ground. If you pitched him up, he could hit the ball up in the air and get that backspin on the ball and it would just carry. The ball

---

[38] Fischer was Boston's pitching coach from 1985–91.

[39] Fischer first faced Williams on May 19, 1957, as a member of the White Sox. Williams singled to left field his first time up against Fischer.

[40] That no-hitter was July 20, 1958, in Boston.

would go up and you'd think, "well, it was a fly ball." Then you'd say, "oh my God, it's not going to come down right away."

But he was fun; the people enjoyed the way he played. The last year he didn't play a lot, because if he didn't feel right, he didn't play. But if [fans] knew he was playing, the stadium always had a few thousand more fans; so he was good for the game.

He was good at everything he did: fisherman, flyer, hunter, big-game hunter. He did everything 100 percent, full bore.

He was forty years old, thirty-five to forty when I faced him. He still had good reflexes and good eyesight. His strike zone was as big as a postage stamp. He got a lot of pitches that were strikes that the umpires gave him because he didn't swing. . . . And they didn't like to call him out. The fans wanted to see him swing. There ain't many of those guys around today, and it will be a while yet before there's another.

Paul Foytack

Right-handed pitcher

1953, 1955–63: ....Detroit Tigers
1963–64: .... Los Angeles Angels
Career Statistics: .... 86–87, 7 saves, 4.14 ERA

Ted Williams vs. Paul Foytack

12-for-45, 2 doubles, 4 home runs, 11 RBI, 11 walks, 3 strikeouts, .267 batting average, .404 on-base percentage, .578 slugging percentage

Home Runs Allowed:

No. 404, August 1, 1956, at Detroit
No. 438, June 30, 1957, at Boston
No. 450, August 27, 1957, at Detroit
No. 462, May 27, 1958, at Detroit

IT WASN'T FUN.

He was the greatest hitter that I ever faced, that's for sure. I talked to him about hitting, asked him why he stood with his right foot even with the front of home plate. He said, "Well, Paul, first of all, there's no one that can throw the ball by me." And I said, "Well, I can vouch for that." And he caught the curveballs and sliders before they got in too far on his hands. They didn't get a chance to get way in deep if you stand way in the box, and I guess they have a chance to get in on you, and he said, "I don't let that happen." And I said, "Oh boy, no wonder you're making more money than me, Ted." He was a great guy, but a tough, tough out.

My first concern when facing him was that I didn't want to get hit by a line drive. He hit me in the ankle one day and I'm hopping around, hopping around looking, and our first baseman said, "The ball

Paul Foytack

YEAR	DATE	RESULT
1955	June 22	Ground out
	July 29	Fly out
	July 31	Fly out
	Aug. 25	Ground out
	Sept. 7	Ground out
1956	May 15	Fly out
	June 6	Lined into DP
		Pop out
		Ground out
		Walk
	Aug. 1	Home run (3 RBI)
		Fly out
		Walk
		Fly out
1957	May 15	Fielder's choice
	June 30	Single
		Double
		Foul out
		Home run (3 RBI)
	July 13	Fly out
		Walk
		Walk
	Aug. 27	Single
		Ground out
		Home run (2 RBI)

YEAR	DATE	RESULT
1958	May 27	Fly out
		Home run (1 RBI)
		Ground out
		Ground out
	June 9	Single
		Walk
	June 12	Double
		Ground out
	June 29	Walk
		Fly out
		Single
	July 18	Fly out
		Walk
	Sept. 14	Ground out
		Flied into DP
		Ground out
		Foul out
1959	May 17	Strikeout
		Sacrifice fly (1 RBI)
	June 10	Pop out
		Foul out
		Single
	June 23	Walk
	Aug. 2	Line out
		Pop out
		Walk
		Walk
		Strikeout
1960	June 16	Walk
		Single (1 RBI)
	June 30	Strikeout
		Pop out

is right over there! The ball is right over there!" And I said, "I'm not looking for the ball, I'm looking for my foot!"

But as for trying to get him out, we just hoped that he would hit the ball at someone. He was a tough strikeout. That's all you could do. We weren't going to let him beat us in a ball game. We would intentionally walk him if we had to. We weren't going to let a hitter like that beat us in a ball game.

And I was good friends with Ted. Every time he'd take batting practice, it would be a 3–2 count, Tiger Stadium, ninth inning, two out—that's how he'd take his batting practice at Detroit. He was a great hitter, a great hitter.

He wouldn't [swing at a bad pitch], but the umpires had a tendency to sometimes give him a ball call when it was a strike only because he didn't swing at it. I said that's okay with me, don't ever swing at it! Like I said, the only thing you could talk about was don't let him beat you in a ball game if the score is tied or you're one run ahead or something. He was really something else.

We did not use the Williams shift that I could remember. He was certainly the toughest out. I never really thought about it. He wasn't going to hit the ball to left field anyhow. I don't know if that made him feel bad that he was going to give in and do that, but we really didn't have the shift that I can remember. And I didn't care, because all I thought about was, gee, I hope he doesn't hit me with a line drive.

One time—the only time I did this in my life—I don't know what the count was, but I got a little sweat from the back of my head and I threw him a spitter. It was wet, and halfway in he started to swing at it. I heard him say, "Oh, shit," and the ball hit the bat and bounced back to me. It was the only time I ever threw one. But he knew what it was right away when he saw it going down like it did.

He could see if you had the ball with the seams or across the seams and different things. He told me once, "Paul, if you had better control, you would win a lot of games." I was kind of a wild pitcher. Did I say kind of wild? I was very wild. I asked him about hitting one time. I said, "Did you hit a lot when you were in school?" He said there was a custodian at his school who would throw batting practice to him about an hour every morning before he went to class. I said, "Well, you big donkey, no wonder you can hit."

He was a good guy. He and I became real good friends, believe it or not. Talked about fishing one time and during the conversation, I mentioned that my uncle was the fly-tying champ of Pennsylvania; he used to make little flies for bait . . . make bugs and that. After that conversation, [Williams] invited me over to his hotel room. To cut a long story short, we called my uncle, and my uncle could not believe it and sent him about a dozen flies he had tied. And I swear, I thought Ted got the winning lottery number every month. That's how much he appreciated it. And he would *not* let me leave town without having dinner with him at least one night every trip.

We became good friends . . . but just during batting practice or right after a game. But no, he was not about to let up during a game. He was not that kind of person. He was going to hit and he didn't care who was on the mound.

He was something, boy. So good . . . and he did have a great eye. He would not swing at a bad pitch. He just didn't do it. If I had to throw one, and I threw it down the middle, oh boy. Almost wave bye-bye to it.

He hit .267 off of me. Actually, that's not too bad.

Bob Friend

Right-handed pitcher

1951–65: ....Pittsburgh Pirates
1966: ....New York Yankees
1966: ....New York Mets
Career Statistics: .... 197–230, 11 saves, 3.58 ERA
National League All-Star: 1956, 1958, 1960

Ted Williams vs. Bob Friend in All-Star Games

0-for-4

1956: First inning, 2 out, none on, tied 0–0, struck out; third inning, 2 out, runners on first and second, NL up 1–0, grounded out to first baseman Dale Long.

1958: Sixth inning, 1 out, runner on first, tied 3–3, reached on error by Frank Thomas.

1960: Second inning, 2 out, runner on third (after a balk and wild pitch), NL up 4–0, grounded out, Bill Mazeroski to Joe Adcock.

Bob Friend

YEAR	DATE	RESULT
1956	All-Star	Strikeout
	Game	Ground out
1958	All-Star	Reached on error
1960	All-Star	Ground out

I **NEVER FACED HIM** a hell of a lot, you know. Maybe spring training. Then you'd hear about how [he had] quick hands, a quick bat, and how he studied pitchers. After facing him, I agree with all of that.

But my strategy was not to get behind. Throw strikes and throw my best pitch, which was a hard sinkerball.

Okay, here's what happened in the all-star games: In 1956, I pitched three innings and got the win. But in the third inning, the bases were loaded and Williams was up. I went 3–2 and struck him out swinging. He swung at a curveball on the last pitch. So that's a mistake there. He had runners on first and second with two outs in the third inning, and the NL leading 1–0, and he grounded out to first. No, sorry, he struck out. Bases loaded, I got 3–2 on him.[41]

I again faced him in 1958. He came up in the sixth inning with one out and the score tied 3–3, and Frank Thomas made an error on the play. It was a bouncing ball to Thomas that he just fumbled. We had a fantasy camp in Bradenton that year, and they had the All-Star Game on. The groundouts weren't hit that big. Like I said, it was a key spot in the '56 All-Star Game. Went down to 3–2 with the bases loaded, and that would have been the ball game. So I felt pretty good about getting him out in a key position. He probably hadn't seen me enough. I had pretty good stuff in those all-star games.

They always talked about Williams. You may get him out one or two times, but he was such a great study of pitchers that he'd have you figured out. Well, I didn't face him much; I didn't give him a chance.

As I didn't pitch in the American League, we never had to use the Williams shift. I think they probably fared pretty well with it, because it kept being used. He was probably one of the greatest hitters of all time, no question about it. I can't remember that [being used in the all-star game].[42]

It [the all-star game] was pretty important when we played in it. We'd pitch three innings unless we got knocked out. I had pretty good

[41] Listening to the broadcast from the 1956 All-Star Game, Williams struck out in the first inning with two out and no one on base, and in the third, he grounded out with two out and two on.

[42] Listening to the broadcast from the 1956 All-Star Game, the National League put shortstop Roy McMillan to the right side of second base and second baseman Johnny Temple halfway between first and second. First baseman Dale Long played four steps off the line. All three played deep on the outfield grass, while the outfielders were also shifted to the right.

luck in those games, as I won two and lost one with an ERA of probably one.[43]

He didn't get a hit off me—he got an error—and that wasn't bad. So I'll take it and won't comment on it anymore!

Was he the toughest hitter I ever faced? By reputation, yes. I had to go with my best stuff. You couldn't be scared of him; you had to stay ahead. And I had some pretty good luck with some pretty good hitters, and that's the way it was.

It's pretty tough to compare him [to other ballplayers] because he studied how to hit. He was really something. I think if you were going to look at the way to hit, you'd watch him up there. He's the one you wanted to [emulate]. Now someone else I faced a lot was Stan Musial. He had a different stance. He also put the wood on the ball and had a lot of infield hits and home runs.

Yes, [people in the National League talked about Williams] all the time. He studied hitting better than everybody. He knew the hitting, he knew all the pitchers, and he had a *great* memory. In fact, after I struck him out in the '56 All-Star Game, I ran into him at the Pompano racetrack down in Florida. I went over and introduced myself. "Bob Friend, Ted Williams, nice to see you."

He says, "Oh, I remember you. You struck me out with that curveball. I didn't think you were going to do it."

So that's the kind of mind he had with hitting and everything else . . . and that was twenty years later! That's the way he operated. He had a photographic memory and knew the pitchers.

Ed Bailey, my catcher, knew he was sitting on a fastball. You know, 3–2 in the All-Star Game; but I broke off a real good curveball, and he

---

[43] In 8.1 innings pitched over three all-star games, Friend had a 1.08 ERA.

swung and missed. I felt real good about it, but there was no reaction from him. I'm sure he was disappointed that he didn't get what he was looking for.

I didn't talk to him too much. I'd run into him a little bit and he was always nice. He was a ballplayer's guy; all the players liked him. Everything he did was first class. His service in the military flying jets, I mean, the guy did everything. He came back and was still playing well. The players definitely respected that.

Ned Garver

Right-handed pitcher

1948–52: .... St. Louis Browns
1952–56: .... Detroit Tigers
1957–60: .... Kansas City Athletics
1961: .... Los Angeles Angels
Career Statistics: .... 129–157, 12 saves, 3.73 ERA
American League All-Star: 1951

Ted Williams vs. Ned Garver (data incomplete)

40-for-97, 10 doubles, 9 home runs,[44] 26 RBI,[45] 27 walks (1 intentional), 6 strikeouts, 2 double plays, .412 batting average, .540 on-base percentage, .794 slugging percentage

Home Runs Allowed:

No. 213, June 27, 1948 (game two), at St. Louis

No. 245, July 22, 1949, at St. Louis

No. 272, May 7, 1950 (game one), at Boston

No. 282, June 9, 1950, at Boston

No. 337, September 17, 1953, at Boston

No. 375, June 21, 1955, at Boston

No. 385, July 31, 1955 (game one), at Boston

No. 422, April 30, 1957, at Kansas City

No. 436, June 23, 1957 (game one), at Boston

No. 459, April 30, 1958, at Boston

---

[44] Of the known available box scores, Williams hit 9 home runs off Garver. But the data is available for all of Williams' 521 career home runs, and he ended up with 10 off Garver.

[45] Retrosheet.org has more data of Williams vs. Garver, but does not include RBI. Baseball-reference.com lists Williams with 26 RBI in 84 at-bats (111 plate appearances) vs. Garver.

Ned Garver

YEAR	DATE	RESULT
1948	May 26	Strikeout
		Fly out
		Ground out
		Single
	June 3	Walk
		Walk
		Walk
		Double
	Aug. 4	Fly out
		Single (1 RBI)
		Out (unknown)
1949	May 8	Walk
		Strikeout
		Fly out
		Walk
	May 26	Walk
		Grounded into DP
		Fly out
		Walk
		Single (2 RBI)
	June 8	Walk
		Double
		Single
		Fly out
	June 23	Double
		Fly out
		Walk
		Double (RBI)
		Double
	Aug. 2	Single
		Ground out
		Double
		Walk
		Walk
1950	May 7	Walk
		Home run (1 RBI)
	May 25	Walk
		Sac fly (1 RBI)
	June 9	Home run (2 RBI)
		Ground out
		Double
		Fly out
	June 25	Ground out
		Single
		Single
		Fly out
1951	May 7	Walk
		Single (1 RBI)
		Line out
		Walk
	June 1	Single
		Ground out
		Fielder's choice
		Fly out
	June 16	Single
		Fly out
		Walk
	July 15	Walk
		Ground out
		Fly out
		Ground out
	July 31	Single
		Single
		Ground out
	Sept. 13	Walk
		Fly out
		Strikeout
		Strikeout
1953	Sept. 17	Fly out
		Foul out
		Foul out
		Home run (2 RBI)
1954	May 17	Walk
		Line out
		Ground out
		Intentional walk
	July 16	Foul out
		Double
		Walk
	July 30	Fly out
		Pop out
		Strikeout
		Line out
	Aug. 24	Fly out
		Single
1955	June 21	Fly out
		Foul out
		Walk
		Home run (3 RBI)
	July 31	Walk
		Ground out
		Home run (4 RBI)
	Aug. 25	Walk
		Double
		Single (1 RBI)
		Grounded into DP
1957	April 30	Single
		Ground out
		Double
		Home run (1 RBI)
1958	April 30	Fly out
		Walk
		Fly out
		Home run (2 RBI)
	June 13	Single (1 RBI)
		Ground out
		Single (1 RBI)
	Aug. 24	Single (1 RBI)
1959	May 21	Single
		Fly out
		Pop out
	Aug. 5	Single
1960	July 3	Walk

LET'S FACE IT, Ted Williams was the greatest hitter during my fourteen years in the big leagues. . . . The greatest hitter that I ever knew. So let's start out with that.

But the first time that you faced him as a pitcher—the first time you faced him—he had never seen you. That was the best chance you had of striking him out. So the first time I pitched against him, it so happens, he did strike out and went back to the dugout and hit his bat on something and cracked the bat.[46]

Our clubhouses in Boston [sic] were side-by-side. You had to go through their dugout to get to our clubhouse. So if you got knocked out of the game, you had to go through their dugout to get to the clubhouse! And there were two Orlando brothers who were the clubhouse men. So my trainer, who was Bob Bauman at the time with the St. Louis Browns, asked for that guy to give him that cracked bat and he did. He fixed it and put a couple of nails in it. He kept it from 1948 till about, maybe it was 2001 or something like that, when I made a trip to St. Louis to speak at the SABR[47] organization meeting. Bob knew I was going to be there and called me and said he was going to move into a smaller place and he needed to get rid of some stuff, and if I wanted, I could have the bat. I said yes and to bring it down to the ballpark—I was going to the Cardinals game—so he brought it down to the ballpark.

I ended up telling Ted about it. He was down in this town of Avon Park one time because he owned a part-interest in a fruit-shipping warehouse. He came to sign autographs and I went down to see him, and we had lunch. I told him that I had that bat. He said to bring it down next spring when I'd come and he'd sign it for me. So I did.

I brought it down and called him, and he invited me over to see his museum and to dinner. I got to spend several hours with him in the afternoon and have supper with him, and then he signed the bat.

I have three children, and I knew that the bat was pretty valuable, so I sold it after his death. But then last year, when I was down here in Florida, a guy from Miami, I think he's a lawyer, sent me some photos of that bat and the story that I wrote about the bat. He asked me if I'd notarize the letter and send it back to him. So I did. But then I asked him how much he paid for that bat, and he said $28,000. So that

---

[46] Garver first faced Boston on May 26, 1948, pitching eight innings in a 5–3, ten-inning loss at St. Louis. Williams went 1–4 against Garver with that strikeout.
[47] Society for American Baseball Research

was pretty interesting. That bat, the first time I ever pitched to Ted Williams, has now been sold for $28,000. That is something. And it was a cracked bat. A game-used bat is worth more than one that was not used.

For some reason or other, Ted was always nice to me. One time during a game, he got on third base and made a break like he was going to steal home. Well he wasn't, but he charged up the line. I didn't balk or anything like that, but then when he got back to third base, he looked back at me and gave a little smile. That made me feel at home, you know. For a big guy like that to horse around with you a little bit, that made you feel good. Made you feel like you belonged.

I have interviews where he was with [Fay] Vincent—that used to be commissioner—where he and [Joe] DiMaggio were being interviewed and Ted told them all that I could throw my glove out there and get him out and all that crap.

Well, I pitched against Ted an *enormous* amount of times. You played in each town four times a year. I pitched against Ted all four times in Boston, and if he came to bat three times, that would be twelve times a year, and I pitched against him for I'm sure ten years. That adds up to being a heck of a lot of at-bats—just pitching to him in Boston! And I pitched against him in St. Louis, too.

I think somebody up there in New England once sent me—and he paid me pretty well to sign them, too—but he was getting an autograph of every living pitcher that had thrown a home run ball to Ted Williams. He would send you the number of balls that he hit home runs off of you, with the date on there that he did it, and then wanted you to sign that, and I did. I think it was 10.

So he hit 10 home runs and still went on like he couldn't hit me. I will say this: He always hit the ball to left field on me. There were very few people that he tried to go to left field on. He used to say that he didn't want to start swinging at balls out of the strike zone just because he could hit them—like Yogi [Berra] did—because he said a guy like [Eddie] Lopat or Garver will keep leading you out, leading you out, and the next thing you'll forget what your strike zone is. But he'd go to left field on me and even hit a home run to left field in Fenway Park.

He had trouble hitting what I threw, see. He said I had a slider that he couldn't pick the spin up on. I had two sliders: one that I threw to right-handers that broke out and down, and another I threw to left-handers, which was pretty flat. But I held it like a football, and I would try to throw it just about waist high, so that when the ball would break, it would break in on their fists. I have a picture at home on my wall of Ted Williams breaking his bat on me. That means I had hit him on the fists. He hit a little pop-up to second base in that at-bat.

Well, now that's the reason I threw it that way. When I threw that flat slider to left-handed hitters, they couldn't adjust their hands back very far. They could only bring it back about so far, and that's why you could hit them on the fists and keep it in the ballpark. It wasn't a strikeout pitch, but it would do the job and kept them from hitting the long ball.

So he said he had trouble picking the spin up on that ball. In other words, most of the time, as soon as the ball left the pitcher's hand, he knew what it was going to do. He could pick the spin up on that ball. I threw him a dang-blum knuckleball one time after about eight or ten years, maybe twelve, I don't know. But anyway, I threw him a knuckleball, and I'll tell you, he just exploded out of that batter's box. He had never seen it; he didn't know what was going to happen, I guess. I don't know.

But as soon as that ball left your hands . . . I want to tell you; I watched him very closely when I was on the bench not pitching. And he could pick up the spin on the ball even [from] a left-handed pitcher. We had a little left-handed pitcher down there at St. Louis, and he kind of short-armed the ball, and I figured it was tough to pick up, as it would be coming out of the guy's uniform—old Sam Zoldak. But anyway, I'd see him relax before that ball got to home plate because he could see it was out of the strike zone, see it didn't have the spin on it to bring it back into the strike zone . . . and I want to tell you now that this all happened in a very short time; but I'm telling you, he did it. That's how good he was.[48]

But I loved pitching to guys like that. I loved to pitch against guys like [Mickey] Mantle and DiMaggio and people who were recognized as the great ones. If they got a hit off you, well, what the heck, he's supposed to get a hit; he's a great one. But if you got him out, then that was an accomplishment.

And I always figured that the fans came to see guys like Williams, DiMaggio, and Mantle. They were the ones that put the fans in the ballpark and they surely didn't come there to see them run bases or to field their positions. They came there to see them hit. That's why I never agreed with the fact that the manager would tell you before the series started, "Now be sure to get the ball over to Dominic DiMaggio or [Johnny] Pesky, don't walk those guys . . . but if you walk Williams, well, that will be all right."

What the heck? Walk Williams? People came from Arizona and Wyoming and places like that to see him hit when we were in Kansas City. They didn't come to see him walk to first. So I figured, what the heck, I ought to pitch to him.

That's just the way I wanted to do it, but I have to go by what the manager says. If he says to go out there and hit somebody, you hit them. If he says to walk Williams or pitch him nothing but screwballs off the plate, you throw it off the plate and outside. If he wants to let them hit, you let him hit. But that wasn't my way of doing things.

I tell that you one time I had played all year with a bad knee. It would pop out sometimes, and even my first baseman, Walt Dropo, would have to put it back. But we had a special brace to put on it, and the trainer would wrap it before the game. Because of this, players bunted a lot on me to try to have my knee go out. So after it came out about the second time, I'd have to come out of the game. But I played

---

[48] It depends on the speed, but a batter usually has 0.4 seconds to make the decision to swing.

all year with my knee like that. Then I was planning to go hunting in Wyoming in November, but I had to have my knee operated on. So we were in Boston, and Fred Hutchinson was our manager. He said to me, if you pitch here in Boston with two days' rest, I'll let you go [have surgery] when we're going back to Detroit. We're not going to be in the pennant race, and we have some minor-league people up here. So if you pitch here on two days' rest, when we go back home to Detroit, then I'll let you go and get your operation, so that you'll be able to go hunting in November.

So [laughs] I had them shut out 1–0 through seven innings. In the eighth, there was a man on second base and two out, and Williams was the batter. George Kell was their third baseman and their cleanup hitter at the time. The count was 2–1 on Williams, and I threw a pitch on the inside corner of the plate that I thought was a strike, but the umpire called it a ball, making it a 3–1 count. The umpires were not inclined to call a strike on Ted unless he swung at it. He knew his strike zone very well. But at the same token, that doesn't mean that there isn't sometimes that he ought to be called out.

But anyway, he took that pitch, and the catcher knows more than the pitcher, because the catcher is real quiet and the pitcher is out there moving around. Well anyway, I thought it was a strike and they called it ball three. I knew that Kell was a better hitter leading off an inning than he was with men on base. I always could lead him away—he might get a hit—but I could lead him off the plate with men on base because he was too eager to drive in runs.

So I decided that's it, I'm not pitching to Ted anymore with the count 3–1. I'm going to put him on base and pitch to George Kell.

Well, I didn't even take a sign. Frank House was my catcher. I just got the ball back and went into my stretch. You need to understand that Ted hardly ever swung at a ball that wasn't a strike. So I just come up and throw the ball at a pretty good speed up about shoulder high on the inside part of the plate. As I didn't have a sign with my catcher, he didn't know I was going to make a pitch out, but I didn't want to throw the ball to the backstop. I just threw it in there plenty bad and Williams stepped back and hit that sucker for a home run.

Now that's really the only home run I can remember beating me at the time. You know that Ted Williams can beat you, so you don't want to pitch to him if the game is at stake and you can pitch around him. But at the same token, I thought I had him at a 2–2 count, but the umpire said ball three, so now I'm trying to walk him and he hits a home run to make it 2–1 and win the ball game. He might have gotten suspicious when I didn't take enough time to get a sign. I never talked to him about that, but I wish I would have.[49] That was a big deal, the one he hit off of me, because I had them beat 1–0. I mean, it looked like I wasn't going to let him beat me, and then I let him beat me. That one sticks in my mind. I've given up a lot of grand slams, but I don't remember cussing one of them. I don't think they beat me in a ball game. I'm just grateful that I had the opportunity to pitch against him, I'll tell you that.

When he had a stroke, he was in a Gainesville hospital, and I was in Ohio. The paper where I read the story only said that he was in Gainesville, but didn't mention what hospital. So I wrote a letter and I addressed it to Ted Williams, baseball's greatest hitter, and sent it to Gainesville. That's all the address I put on it, and he got it.

So the next spring, the Major League Alumni were having a reunion over in St. Petersburg, Florida. In the hotel they had a whole bunch of us in a big room. Mickey Vernon was there, Bob Feller was there, the old third baseman from Minnesota who hit all the home runs— [Harmon] Killebrew—was there, Roy Sievers was there; there were a whole bunch of good old players. We were all in a circle and fans could buy a ticket and could come get everybody's signature that they wanted.

Well after a while, some big guy tapped me on the shoulder and said, "I'm John Henry Williams. My dad is back in another room making a television interview, but he'd like to see you." I supposed it might be

---

[49] That game was September 17, 1953. Garver retired the first two hitters in the eighth inning, then allowed a single to Jimmy Piersall before Williams homered.

because I sent him that letter saying he was the greatest hitter ever, but I didn't know for sure. But for him to single me out of that bunch, to ask me over there, to have me come over there and say hello, that made me feel pretty good.

I only pitched against DiMaggio for three years, and I'm sure he hit me well.[50] Of course I pitched to Williams a lot more years, but I consider [DiMaggio] a great hitter because he didn't have a weakness, though I still consider Williams to be the best. God gave him more ability than anybody else. He could see better than [most] people. But on top of that, he was so dedicated and worked exceptionally hard.

Mantle had a weakness. I had good luck against Mantle. I told him, "I wished I could [always] pitch against guys like you, as I'd be in the Hall of Fame."[51]

If [Ted] was going to be the second hitter of an inning, let's say the guy ahead of him was Pesky. Pesky wouldn't be up there at the plate measuring me on every pitch I threw, you know. But Williams would be. Williams would charge into that dugout, get a bat, and get up there. If he was going to be the second hitter, he was up there, watching my pitches, measuring me. He really was conscientious about getting prepared, getting the most out of what he had. And he, believe you me, worked at it.

He also knew the important things, too. Today, they put a left-hand pitcher in no matter who they got up there that's a left-hand hitter, but for Ted, he could hit anybody. He could hit Whitey Ford, he could hit Herb Score, he could hit 'em all. In fact, he probably bore down on them more than anybody. But at the same token, he could hit them because he knew his strike zone. He of course could pick up the pitches, but he knew his strike zone. He didn't swing at bad pitches. He knew what it took to be a hitter and he didn't deviate from it. I never saw Williams start a swing and foul it off or something

---

[50] Of the known data, Joe DiMaggio was 12–23 (.511) with 1 home run off Ned Garver.

[51] Mickey Mantle was 15–53 (.283) with 1 home run against Ned Garver.

like that and take a half-cut. No, no, when he swung at the ball, he swung at the ball. Baseball was so lucky to have a person like that.

When Boudreau managed us at Kansas City, he was a guy that he wanted to, you know, do unusual stuff. He'd have the pitcher hit eighth, crazy stuff like that. I don't know, I thought he couldn't play anymore, but he wanted his name in the paper once in a while. He'd also do stuff like [the Williams shift]. I'm not saying that's bad because Williams was a guy [laughs] where, if he wanted to, he'd get a hit every cussed time up with the shift on. I'm telling you the God's honest truth. But he wouldn't do it. You don't even see Jim Thome doing that. I don't understand why they don't learn to hit the ball to left field. They'd cut that crap out. Why, good Lord, Williams hit me to left field, so I know he could hit anyone to left field. If he hit to left field, then you're in trouble when you got that shift on. But then good Lord, if he hit a line-drive single to right field, your second baseman caught it. He hit that ball like a bullet time after time after time. What the heck, they could throw him out from right field. He hit that ball hard, and if the shortstop—who was playing by second base—didn't get it, the second baseman would be out there stationed toward the middle of right field, and he could field that ball and throw it to first and get him out. I'd get tired of getting thrown out on base hits.

Sure, the shift was a good idea, because he was bull-headed enough to try to hit into it all the time. So you'd take some base hits away. He didn't get any base hits as a result of that, by him hitting into the shift. The only way he got base hits is if he hit a little grounder toward third. But he wouldn't do it. He was just bull-headed enough that he was going to hit .400 no matter what he did.

He did some unusual stuff while he was in the service. He got a wounded plane back to base. And he never mouthed off, he never complained, he never did anything. He just went in there and was one of the best pilots that ever was, I'm sure. And that was probably another challenge for him, and that's why he did it so dang-blanged good.

But I can tell you one year, the first time he came back, it was against us in Detroit. We played a doubleheader, and I think he hit three home runs, one off Al Aber, a left-hand pitcher we brought in there.[52] He just hit that ball like . . . I mean, you thought, well, he's been gone all this time, he might not be so sharp. Holy crap, I mean, he took that out of your head in a hurry.

Briggs Stadium was a good hitting ballpark, especially for a left-hander, as it was kind of a short right field. He'd hit that ball into the upper deck like a bullet. He was just capable of doing great things. When you figure he was in that great big ballpark in Boston. Heck, how many balls did he hit in Boston that would have been out of the park in Briggs Stadium? Just an untold amount of balls. And I don't know what you would have had done. The managers would have probably had to say that you would walk him every time up, like Sparky Anderson did to George Brett.

One time against the Yankees, he had a couple of home runs off the Yankee pitcher, and Yogi complained because he called ball four on him, and the umpire said, "Well, at least I held him to one base." If you walked him, he only got to first. If you pitched to him, you didn't [know] what the hell was going to happen.

I have nothing negative to say about Ted Williams. There was a lot of controversy up there in Boston because the writers would write

---

[52] Wiliams's first game back from the Korean War was on August 6, 1953, in Boston, against the Browns. Williams played in three games against the Tigers in '53: September 2 (game one of a doubleheader); September 3 in Detroit; and September 17 (game one of a doubleheader), in Boston. The latter was the game Garver described previously, allowing a two-run homer to Williams in the bottom of the eighth inning of a then 1–0 game. Williams did homer twice in his career off Al Aber, both of those coming in 1955.

stuff—like when they had that first baby, how he wasn't home—and he got permanently aggravated at them. So he just wouldn't cooperate. I figure that I respect his decision there. If he decided he didn't want to talk to them because of the unfair abuse, well, I think that's his option.

Ted was, as far as I'm concerned, an inspiration. He showed it in his work ethic and *love* of the game of baseball; his complete dedication to the game. I mean, I loved the game of baseball. It meant a lot to me. I don't like to see people go out there like that dag-blammed [Johnny Damon], when he was playing for Boston, or that [Manny] Ramirez; they look like bums. I don't like to see the way they dress going to the ballparks now. You're a professional; you should act and dress like a professional. You ought to show a little respect for the game, that's the way I feel about it. . . . And Ted Williams did all of that. He never deviated from it. Now, [he] had the greatest ability of anybody, but he didn't take advantage of that and act like an idiot. These guys now, they get really good, they think they can do anything. They think they can mistreat anybody and act any way they want because they're not going to fire you. What the heck, they're not going to do anything to you because you're too good a player. Back in my day, those guys didn't act like that. DiMaggio, Williams, they didn't act like that. They were leaders, they led by example. And I take my hat off to 'em.

I'm pretty good friends with Bob Feller. I've had him come to where I live up north to speak and stuff like that. When I was over Ted's, I asked him who he considered the greatest pitcher he ever saw, and he immediately said Bob Feller. Now, he had hit against Lefty Grove; he hit against Lefty Gomez; he hit against Whitey Ford; he hit against that guy over there in Cleveland, that left-hander—Herb Score—he hit against all guys who were considered tough left-handers, and he said Bob Feller.

So I asked Bob Feller—the Major League Alumni had an event in Cleveland, and we had a get-together up there at the ballpark the night before, so Bob I and were at that and our wives were at the same table—so I asked him who he thought was the toughest hitter, and Bob said Ted Williams, just like that. So he'll tell you that Williams was the greatest.[53]

---

[53] While Bob Feller passed away in 2010, the interview with Ned Garver took place while Feller was still alive.

Jim "Mudcat" Grant

Right-handed pitcher

1958–64:	Cleveland Indians
1964–67:	Minnesota Twins
1968:	Los Angeles Dodgers
1969:	Montreal Expos
1969:	St. Louis Cardinals
1970:	Oakland A's
1970–71:	Pittsburgh Pirates
1971:	Oakland A's
Career Statistics:	145–119, 53 saves, 3.63 ERA
American League All-Star:	1963, 1965

Ted Williams vs. Mudcat Grant

9-for-26, 1 double, 2 home runs, 3 RBI, 4 walks (1 intentional), 1 strikeout, .346 batting average, .433 on-base percentage, .615 slugging percentage

Home Runs Allowed:

No. 486, June 27, 1959, at Cleveland
No. 507, July 22, 1960, at Boston

WHAT STOOD OUT when I faced Ted Williams? *Everything* stands out when I faced Ted Williams! The name Ted Williams [laughs]. I faced him a couple years. But his batting stance, his knowledge of the strike zone, all of that became evident as you worked against him.

I don't think he every really changed in terms of attacking the ball and stuff like that. In terms of what I saw when I was in the minor leagues years before then and stuff I had read about him, I didn't see any particular change in his approach to hitting.

Most of us guys back in those days, we were taught to throw strikes. We were taught to make the hitter hit the ball with something on it.

Jim "Mudcat" Grant

YEAR	DATE	RESULT
1958	June 3	Double
		Ground out
	July 14	Reached on error
	Aug. 2	Single
		Single
		Ground out
		Fly out
	Aug. 21	Fly out
1959	May 15	Fly out into DP
		Ground out
		Fly out
		Line out into DP
	June 27	Fly out
		Pop out
		Home run (2 RBI)⊗⊗
	July 30	Fly out
		Strikeout
		Single
		Ground out
	Sept. 15	Single
1960	June 7	Walk
		Ground out
		Pop out
	July 22	Home run (1 RBI)⊗
		Walk
		Walk
	Aug. 23	Ground out
		Single
	Aug. 25	Intentional walk
		Single

So the strategy was not to throw it in the zone where left-handers particularly like to hit the ball. And even though a lot of pitchers didn't do it, my thought was to pitch him up and in, no matter what he thought.

He was not only going to get the call, he was going to hit it if it was a strike. But you know, I look at pitchers from the time I retired to the time that I started, and part of the game was to try not to throw it in the area where they extended themselves to hit the ball. So I pitched him in most of the time, but he was devastating up and away. You knew he could see that ball real well. He was going to get a good part of the bat on the ball, so you sort of keep it away in that area. But nonetheless, you didn't try to be macho about it because it was Ted Williams. You tried to keep it in the areas where he didn't like it the most.

I remember walking him with the bases loaded. I was leading 3–1 and back in them days, if you had pretty good stuff, the manager didn't take you out. So I remember I had the bases loaded with two out, and I was leading 3–1, and walked him with the bases loaded. And I remember him gesturing [lowering voice], "Throw the ball over the plate." I said, "Go ahead, go ahead." And I struck out Jackie Jensen to end the game.[54]

We did use the shift, because I saw him bunt the ball. He bunted it down the third-base line. It was a rare occasion, but I remember once with the Cleveland Indians, he bunted against us and laughed all the way to first base.[55]

Well, he had to be up there among the great hitters. He has to be in the top three among the guys I played against.

You say that Ted hit two home runs off me? Man that was great. But I remember he was kind enough to sign a photo for me, "To Mudcat, thanks for helping me [get] in the Hall of Fame."

By the way, Mickey Mantle said the same thing in the photo he signed for me.

---

[54] It is unknown what game Grant could be referring to. Grant walked Williams four times in his career, and they all came in 1960. Jackie Jensen was not with the Red Sox in 1960.
[55] Williams bunted for a hit against Cleveland's Gary Bell in the first game of a doubleheader on July 24, 1960, in the bottom of the first inning.

John Gray

Right-handed pitcher

1954:	**Philadelphia Athletics**
1955:	**Kansas City Athletics**
1957:	**Cleveland Indians**
1958:	**Philadelphia Phillies**
Career Statistics:	**4–18, 0 saves, 6.18 ERA**

Ted Williams vs. John Gray

1-for-7, 1 home run, 1 RBI, 2 walks, 1 strikeout, 1 double play, .143 batting average, .333 on-base percentage, .571 slugging percentage

Home Runs Allowed:

No. 365, September 9, 1954, at Boston

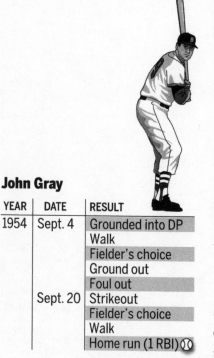

John Gray

YEAR	DATE	RESULT
1954	Sept. 4	Grounded into DP
		Walk
		Fielder's choice
		Ground out
		Foul out
	Sept. 20	Strikeout
		Fielder's choice
		Walk
		Home run (1 RBI)

I CAN REMEMBER FACING Ted Williams nine times. But I don't remember striking him out one time; I thought I struck him out four times. That's one thing I always remembered.

You see, Ted was a friend of mine. I used to run into him a lot. He used to run up and play golf with me from the Keys, and we used to have big discussions about why he never got any base hits off me to speak of.

He said something to me about it . . . I wish I could remember exactly what it was. When he came up to Kendall Lakes one time to play golf, he made some kind of remark about it. He was such a good person and very sincere. He said something like, "How come you don't ever throw the ball over the plate to me?"

And the one he did get off me was one of the craziest stories you've ever heard in your life, and if you were at the ball game, you probably would have jumped out of your seat. It was one of those runaway ball games, and Kerby Ferrell was the manager, who was an absolute dunce.

We go up to Boston to play, and I had real good luck against Ted. I never threw a fastball over the plate to him. I never got a ball over the plate. I bet I didn't throw three fastballs that ever hit that plate. And I had a pretty good fastball. But there isn't a man in the world that can throw a fastball by Ted Williams . . . nobody. I don't think there was ever a man born that could do it.

Anyway, I just kept pitching him in and out, in and out, and then I'd throw in my breaking ball where he'd have to [reach] after the ball. It was hard to get him to go after that one. He had the best eyes I've ever seen on a hitter. Shoot, if you were standing out there on the mound . . . I can remember him staring at me; it felt like I was being X-rayed; watching every move you made.

But how he got the home run: They had a runaway ball game, I don't know who was pitching that day. And they had the bases loaded or something—I can't exactly remember what it was—but Kerby asked me to go back in. Well, I didn't care. Back in those days, hell, I'd go in there every damn day if they asked me to pitch. We weren't prima donnas like they are today.

Anyway, I go out there and they kept calling [for the] fastball. Catcher says you have a great fastball. I said no. I'm standing out on the mound—you know how a pitcher will shake off a pitch with his left hand? I'm right-handed, so on my left hand was a glove, and I'd hang the glove down my side and shake it. Kerby was trying to call pitches.

So I got a strike on him or something, and they said throw the fast-ball, throw the fastball, got to get out of here. So he kept it up and I kept throwing the damn slider and the curveball, and then I'd waste the fastball because I was ahead of him. They come in with a fastball and I shake the glove off. I get down there and fastball again. I shake it off again. Finally he put the fastball down there again and I knew it had to be Kerby, because the catcher wouldn't fight with me. So I put my hand straight up in the air—my left hand—and I'm shaking in the middle of the stadium.

Kerby Ferrell comes running out, "What's wrong? What's wrong?" Well, I said, "To tell you the truth Kerby, I think my catcher's blind. I've been shaking him off down here and he didn't see it, so I thought if I stuck my hand way up in the air he might be able to see I was shaking off the pitch."

So finally he goes back in. I turn around and here comes the fastball again. I think I had a 3–2 count on him, I'm not sure. But I was so goddamn mad, I said, "Ah, fuck it," and I hauled off and threw the damn fastball.

We had Vic Power playing out in right field. Now Vic Power turns around and he runs back about three feet and stops, and he's hitting his glove hand—you know, hitting his fist in his gloved hand like he's going to catch the ball—then he backs up about four or five more feet, and he's hitting his gloved hand, thinking it's a big pop fly.

Well, in about another five or ten seconds, Vic Power is up against the fence, still pounding his glove, and that ball is still going up. I've never seen a ball hit that far or that high in my life.

And that's the only base hit he ever got off me.[56] It was comical, really. The crowd was going wild when I had my glove up in the air. I think that's the only fastball I threw him over the plate.

---

[56] Williams indeed did have just one hit off Gray, but Williams' hit—a home run off Gray—occurred September 20, 1954, when Gray was a member of the Philadelphia Athletics. The manager of that team was Eddie Joost. Gray started that game and allowed a leadoff homer in the seventh inning to Williams, with the score prior to the homer being 2–0 Red Sox. The right fielder in that game was Vic Power. Gray allowed just one home run as a member of the Indians in 1957, when his manager was Kerby Ferrell. It was a game on August 4 at Yankee Stadium against another left-handed Hall of Famer, Enos Slaughter. It was a two-out, three-run homer in the fourth inning to make the score 5–1. The right fielder in that game was Rocky Colavito.

I had watched him hit so many times, and like I said, any man that's got everybody on one side of the field 90 percent of the time when he's up to bat . . . how in the hell are you going to get a fastball by him?

He had the greatest eyes on any hitter I've ever seen. And you know what? He hit the golf ball like he hit that damn baseball. Boy, could he club it. He didn't score well, but he could hit it.

To me, he's the greatest hitter who ever walked out onto a baseball field. I couldn't imagine what he was like when he was younger before he went into the service, but I'll tell you, he was the greatest.

Dick Hall

Right-handed pitcher

1952–57, 1959:	**Pittsburgh Pirates**
1960:	**Kansas City Athletics**
1961–66:	**Baltimore Orioles**
1967–68:	**Philadelphia Phillies**
1969–71:	**Baltimore Orioles**
Career Statistics:	**93–75, 68 saves, 3.32 ERA**

Ted Williams vs. Dick Hall

4-for-8, 1 double, 1 home run, 5 RBI, 1 walk, 1 strikeout, .500 batting average, .556 on-base percentage, 1.000 slugging percentage

Home Runs Allowed:

No. 506, July 3, 1960, at Boston

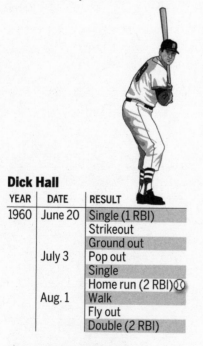

Dick Hall

YEAR	DATE	RESULT
1960	June 20	Single (1 RBI)
		Strikeout
		Ground out
	July 3	Pop out
		Single
		Home run (2 RBI)
	Aug. 1	Walk
		Fly out
		Double (2 RBI)

I CAN REMEMBER A lot of at-bats that Ted Williams had against me in 1960, the only year I faced him, because he was so noteworthy. I don't remember the double or the walk (maybe it was intentional).[57]

I started against Boston three times, first in Kansas City and then two times in Fenway. The first at-bat in Kansas City, he hit a fastball down and away for a line drive over the shortstop for a single. The next time up, I got two strikes on him and then threw my slider (the first I had

---

[57] The walk on August 1 was not intentional.

thrown him, all the other pitches the first two times up were fastballs) and backdoored it to the low outside corner (which is where I aimed it 99 percent of the time to left-handers—the slider was hard, with only a little break, and probably more resembled what is referred to these days as a cut fastball). Anyway, it was the first time he had seen it, and he just stood there and took it for strike three.

As for Fenway, the theory was that he was a little past his prime, so I started each at-bat with a high fastball and hoped he would swing at it and fly out to center field. Like Yogi Berra, I felt that the more pitches he saw off me in an at-bat, the better chance he had of getting a hit.

Well, in the later innings of a game in Boston, I started him again with a high fastball, but missed with it, as it was over the middle of the plate but up about even with his chin. He was famous for never swinging at bad pitches, but this time, because he was obviously (by hindsight) looking for a high fastball, he swung at it. *Problem*: He hit it into their part of the bullpen for a home run.

It was probably in the third game that I had faced him that for the first time I threw him my changeup (my changeup was good, though I didn't have control of it like I had of the other two pitches) and he was fooled and just took it for a strike. A couple pitches later, I threw him another one, and he was way out in front and dribbled a little foul roller toward the dugout. I threw him two or three fastballs low and away, which he fouled off. I then decided to throw the third changeup to him in that at-bat. He just calmly stroked a line drive into right field for a single. At that point, I decided throwing him three changeups in one at-bat was not a very good idea.

At the end of the season, I can remember thinking about having faced him and feeling that I had had pretty good success. Then I went through the at-bats and figured out that he had hit an even .500 against me. Oh!

He was known to study opposing pitchers, but what impressed me was that he had taken the time to try and figure me out. I wasn't over-powering at all, as I relied on good control and a funny delivery, but he had still taken the time to remember my pitch selection.

He was friendly with the other players to the extent he had contact with them. I remember an incident in Kansas City where he had just doubled, and we made a pitching change. We looked out at second and while the new pitcher was coming in, there was Williams, obviously giving a hitting lesson to Dick Howser, our rookie shortstop, which impressed all of us.

Jack Harshman

Left-handed pitcher

1948, 1950, 1952:	New York Giants
1954–57:	Chicago White Sox
1958–59:	Baltimore Orioles
1959:	Boston Red Sox
1959–60:	Cleveland Indians
Career Statistics:	69–65, 7 saves, 3.50 ERA

Ted Williams vs. Jack Harshman

5-for-35, 1 double, 3 walks, 7 strikeouts, 2 double plays, .156 batting average, .229 on-base percentage, .188 slugging percentage

WE BOTH GREW up in San Diego. Of course, he's older than me, and I didn't really get acquainted with him there, but I did know of him. The very first time I ever had a chance to talk with Ted was in 1954, in our first meeting with the Red Sox in Chicago. He came and asked one of our players under the grandstand, where we both used the same entry out on the field—we'd stay down there and talk with the other players if we had an opportunity to—and he came to one of the White Sox players and asked about me, because he knew I had come from San Diego, but he obviously did not know me. And the player introduced me to Ted at the time. We stood there and talked, and he was as gracious as you could possibly be, and I really did appreciate his time, to take time out to talk with me. He didn't have to, but he certainly was nice enough to do that.

Then, as far as how I was able to pitch against him, as far as my strategy was—if you can have one—let me say this: Of all the hitters I watched hit, in a category of 1 to 10 with Ted being a 10, I think the next best hitter would be an 8 or 8 1/2. To me, there was no real comparison to being naturally good hitters and hitters that could either hit with a great deal of power or could spray the ball around and get on

Jack Harshman

YEAR	DATE	RESULT
1954	June 2	Ground out
	July 25	Grounded into DP
		Single
		Walk
		Strikeout
	Aug. 3	Ground out
		Single
		Fly out
		Fly out
	Sept. 1	Fly out
1955	July 22	Fielder's choice
		Line out
1956	June 26	Strikeout
		Strikeout
		Ground out
		Ground out
	July 12	Foul out
		Walk
		Fly out
		Fly out
	Sept. 12	Foul out
		Single
		Fly out
		Double
1957	June 27	Walk
1958	May 10	Single
		Grounded into DP
		Strikeout
		Strikeout
	May 17	Strikeout
		Ground out
		Fielder's choice
		Strikeout
1959	May 30	Fly out
	Aug. 23	Ground out

base and that kind of thing. There was a difference, and Ted could do it all. And that's what I think made the difference.

I would come out of my own clubhouse during batting practice between the two teams, go sit on the bench, and specifically watch him hit. There was something so unique about it and so much value in the way he approached hitting; it was just a joy to watch him.

As far as my being lucky against him, that's what it is. I mean, nobody actually outpitched [Ted]; he was just that good a hitter. I was just fortunate enough to be that lucky against him. You have the statistics here—which I did not know until I read this—that he only hit .156 against me. I did remember, though, that he never hit a home run and he only had one double.

As far as pitching against the other guys—[Mickey] Mantle, [Al] Rosen, and so on—those fellas were obviously good hitters, and Al Kaline was one of the better natural hitters that you'd ever want to watch. Mickey Mantle was just brutally strong and obviously a good hitter and could run like a deer, but Ted just was something out of the ordinary.

Who was my toughest out? Well, it wouldn't be Ted, because he didn't work out to be my toughest out. He was probably the toughest hitter I ever faced; it just worked out to where he didn't do that well against me. My toughest out my first year or two was a catcher with the Washington Senators, Eddie Fitz Gerald, believe it or not.[58] That was just because he was able to hit the ball solidly in-between the outfielders.

But anyhow, as far as me and Ted talking when I was with the Red Sox, I did talk about how I would do this or do that against some of the better American League hitters, and my answers from his questions seemed to coincide with what he thought, so that made me feel pretty damn smart!

Of course, as a high-schooler, he was more interested in pitching than he was hitting. He really wanted to be a pitcher, and I think that's why he looked at hitting from that direction. Anyhow, it was interesting to do that with him and see that in most cases my theory of pitching against certain hitters kind of went along with the way he thought.

Then later on when he was a batting coach with the Red Sox and I was pitching for the Indians—I guess he was still playing, yeah, he was still with the Red Sox—but he and Herb Score both lived in Florida. When they flew to spring training, which were both being held in Arizona, Ted and Herb sat together, and of course, the conversation went to hitting, as it always did. And he said, you have a pitcher on your ballclub this year, and if you want to know how to pitch against the better hitters in the American League, all you have to do is ask him and he'll know. Of course, he was referring to me again. Herb told me that; it didn't come from Ted.

Anyway, it was a pleasure knowing him, and we seemed to have gotten along great as far as personal friendships were concerned, and he treated me just as well as you could [have] hoped that he would.

---

[58] Fitz Gerald was 18–66 (.273) lifetime vs. Harshman. But in 1955—Harshman's second full season—he was 5–12 (.417) with 4 walks.

He never really did pal around too much with the other players. He was friendly with them, but he sort of seemed like he was unto himself individually off the field, I think. One of his closest friends was the clubhouse boy at the time—of course, he wasn't a boy, he was a man—but they seemed to have gotten along very well. But as far as going out and buddying with him, Ted didn't do that much.

But in the clubhouse, that was a different thing. He was very, very congenial. He had stories written about how standoffish he was and how unfriendly he was with the media and the sportswriters, but I think he was a guy that didn't want to "yes" a man just because the guy wanted him to say it. He would say exactly what he thought, and sometimes it would be in complete contradiction to what the guy wanted him to say. And, of course, that made him standoffish and unfriendly, but that was just not Ted at all.

I had an opportunity one time to go to his home when he still had a house in Islamorada, Florida. Mickey McDermott and I went out to visit him and we spent a lovely day at his home. Like I said, he was just a real nice guy, and, of course, the best hitter that I ever saw.

As far as pitching against him, my strategy against Ted was just . . . I guess you could say, I just wanted to make a variety of pitches: Either a fastball or a slider or a screwball or whatever, not necessarily on any particular pitch count. You couldn't let him figure out what you were going to throw, because if he figured right and you threw a strike, he was going to hit it.

Something else about Ted that was outstanding was that I honestly [cannot] recall him *ever* taking an awkward swing. When he made his mind to swing, it was a fluid, good, solid, balanced swing. So many of the other hitters that were considered good very often would be totally fooled and would look awkward, but he never did. I never saw him do that. I think that could be attributed to his superior eyesight. I guess it's been pretty much documented that he had tremendous eyesight, and he said he could actually pick up the spin from the time it left the pitcher's hand. Well, that's something you can't believe, because you can't see that well, but he said he could and I'm not going to call him a liar—because he probably could!

He never swung at bad pitches. The day I struck out 16 in Boston,[59] I had him struck out a second time, but the umpire so often would give him the benefit of a close pitch. That particular pitch, it was on a 3–2 count, and I made a really good pitch on him. It was low and away on the strike zone. I mean, I know it was a strike. And I think—when he turned to throw the bat down and go to first base or turn and carry the bat back to the bench—he looked at it and the umpire said ball four, and he kind of gave me that little sly grin on his face. He was something else, he really was.

It says here that I struck him out seven times. I don't remember that I did that, but if it's there, it's probably true. Like I said, I had outstandingly good success against him; not necessarily because I was that good a pitcher, but it just worked out that way. There are other hitters that were not near as good as him that probably hit me much more consistently than Ted ever did, so it's just a matter as much of being lucky as it is being good.[60]

I think I probably considered myself a four-pitch pitcher who could throw those pitches at any count with some consistency. That made it easier for me to do things like that to Ted. Because if you're only a two-pitch pitcher—like so many in the big leagues were and are—it made it too easy for him to have a pretty good idea of what was going to come. That was just not going to happen too often with him; you were going to get it hit hard somewhere. But anyhow, I threw good pitches to him a lot, and I got him out pretty regularly, but it was more a matter of luck than me being that much better than him by any means.

---

[59] On July 16, 1954, in the first game of a doubleheader, Harshman struck out 16 at Boston in a 5–2 White Sox victory, breaking the club record of 15, set by Ed Walsh (twice in 1908 and 1910) and Jim Scott (1913). He struck out every starter at least once, including leadoff hitter Billy Consolo four times. Through the 2012 season, Harshman still is the White Sox record-holder for strikeouts in a game.

[60] Actually, the player with the highest batting average against Harshman (minimum 10 plate appearances) was Reno Bertoia, who went 9–17 with 1 home run, 4 RBI, and a .529 batting average. During his ten years in the big leagues, Bertoia had a .244 career batting average.

With me being left-handed, we didn't move that much to right field. We of course favored him to right field, but I don't think we put the second baseman out in short right field and the shortstop playing second. I don't think we did that. They would have shifted on a right-hand pitcher, but not with a left-hand pitcher. And that one double he got off of me was a double to left-center, believe it or not. He hit it hard, but it was to left-center, as opposed to pulling it down the line, or that sort of thing. [Ted] kind of felt like it was a battle between him and the other guys. He, by God, was going to prove that he could do it, and he did, what the hell.

I don't recall just sitting down with the other guys on the pitching staff and saying let's do this or let's try that or what do you do; I think that's kind of an overblown sort of conversation among pitchers. Now a pitcher has his abilities that he can do this or he can do that, which is sometimes quite different than another pitcher in that they deliver from a little bit different angle or they have a little bit different kind of fastball . . . so they have to pitch their own game. They go out there with the intention of using their best stuff at any one best count. So you can't really put a plan into action, so to speak. You can't say we're going to do this and that because it just doesn't work out that way. Pitchers are very independent and separate from one another in the way they pitch, even though it looks like there's a great deal of similarity, which there is because, let's face it, they have to throw pitches over the plate. In that respect, they're very similar, but in the manner in which they do it has a lot to do with how you will pitch against any one hitter.

I think [coming up as a first baseman] it did do me a lot of good, in that when I started pitching, I had a hitter's mentality. In other words, I looked at pitching from a hitter's viewpoint: What the hitter might be expecting or looking for or that sort of thing. So instead of me just thinking, "I'm going to throw a strike here or there," I would have a little bit more understanding about why. What would be their thought process as a hitter? And I did think—at least early on—when I first started to try to learn how to pitch. That's how my thought process was, as opposed to just try to throw it over the plate.

When we first met that day under the stands in Chicago, he didn't know me other than that I was from San Diego, and I did not know him other than he was from San Diego and was respected as an extremely good man, player-wise. When he spoke to me, we didn't have a whole lot of common subjects to speak about, but he did mention several names that were prominent in and around San Diego baseball—sandlots and so on—or coaches or what he thought I would know. So he brought their names up to me and some of them I had recognized but was maybe not acquainted with. He tried to be as friendly as he could with someone that he didn't know at all, and that's kind of an outstanding remembrance to me.

I have one more [memory] about him. After I had been out of baseball for about twenty years I guess, I was working for a company in San Diego that had been buying many season tickets in small packages, and they wanted me, because I had been in baseball, to go down and see if I could improve their location, which I did. I tried to go down there; I wasn't dressed in nice clothes at all, just in my work clothes. When I went near the general offices, I looked down the hall, and there was a group of guys standing around the doorway to one of the offices. So I got my nose stuck up there, I wanted to take a look myself to see what was going on, and when I got to this back of this group of guys, I could see over their heads into the room, and here's Ted Williams sitting on a desk in there, and he's carrying on a conversation about hitting. So what else, you know? Anyhow, I'm standing there for a matter of a few seconds, really, and I guess he saw me as I walked up, and it came to him, and he jumped down off that desk and came pushing out of there, and he put his arms around me and said, "How you doing, Lefty?"

And these guys around me, they looked at me like, "Who the hell is this guy?" But I thought it was a real tribute that he would have all those years remembered that's who I was. He came to say hello to me, and I thought that was real nice of him.

He used to come into San Diego on a rare occasion. I think that time he was there for the San Diego Hall of Fame presentations. He'd come in for that once in a while. He'd come in rarely other than that to maybe say hello to his mother. He didn't stay in San Diego for any longer than he had to. I think maybe it was because of his brother's reputation. He couldn't get along with his brother at all, and, consequently, didn't come in for more than a couple of days at a time.

I think he was the greatest hitter of all time. I've had this in mind. I've said it over and over again. If Ted Williams had not had to spend those two periods of time in the service and played his entire career in Detroit, he would have probably hit 1,000 home runs. I'm not joking. I'm serious.

Right field in Detroit was a *great* deal shorter than in Boston, and he was a high fly-ball hitter, and that's all you had to do in Detroit. And I'm serious now; he lost about five years when he was averaging close to 40 home runs a season. Well that's 200 home runs in Boston if he had played.

So I honestly believe that if he had played his entire career— uninterrupted in Detroit—he might very well have hit 1,000 home runs.

It was [the fences] shorter in New York then Boston, no question about it; *particularly* down the line in both fields. Both fields were short down the line, but it went down rapidly in both fields. New York was not quite as long in dead right field as Fenway Park. Ted hit a lot of home runs in the bullpen direction, which is kind of like dead right field but shading slightly toward center. In New York, that was still pretty short there. So he might very well have hit more home runs in New York than he did in Boston, and, of course, Yankee Stadium was a tough right-handed hitter's home run park. It was longer in dead left field than Boston is, obviously. Everywhere was shorter. He certainly would have hit a whole lot more had he not lost those years.

John James

Right-handed pitcher

1958, 1960–61:	....	New York Yankees
1961:	....	Los Angeles Angels
Career Statistics:	....	5–3, 2 saves, 4.76 ERA

Ted Williams vs. John James

0-for-0, 0 RBI, 1 walk, .000 batting average, 1.000 on-base percentage, .000 slugging percentage

John James

YEAR	DATE	RESULT
1960	July 10	Walk

I DON'T RECALL A clubhouse meeting to discuss how to pitch to Williams or any of the Bosox. I would like to think we had one and that I was in on it, but nothing comes to mind. Generally speaking, as I recall, Williams rarely swung at the first pitch, especially against pitchers he hadn't seen before. So [in my first appearance against him] I figured I could get a quick strike on him. My recollections of that at-bat are very clear as far as him being at the plate, however, I don't recall the inning or which team was ahead.[61]

I probably had the same thing going through my mind as any rookie pitcher who ever faced Williams for the first time. You are thrilled to be doing it, and you don't particularly care if you get him out. Take that with a grain of salt because you *do* want to get him out, but the

---

[61] James entered in the sixth inning with the Red Sox leading the Yankees, 7–5. He faced Williams with one on and one out. (Willie Tasby singled and Pete Runnels struck out.)

main thing is that you want to face him in Fenway Park so you can tell the story to all the guys you played ball with when you were younger, "How I pitched to Ted Williams in Fenway Park."

My undoing as far as walking him was the umpire behind the plate, Ed Hurley. He was known to be tough on rookies, and he [most certainly] was this day.

My side of the story is that I walked him on five strikes. I think he swung at one pitch for the only strike. I recall very vividly that Yogi [Berra] was going nuts behind the plate every time Hurley called a ball, which to the two of us appeared to be a strike. I also recall that Casey [Stengel] was on the top step yelling at the umpire in his distinctive voice. That may have been the only time he stuck up for me.

When I get questions about the toughest hitter I ever faced, I'm somewhat stumped for an answer. I wasn't up there long and pitched mostly in short relief, so I didn't face any hitter, let alone the Williams type, very many times. I will tell you he was the second most impressive hitter I ever faced.

I faced [Mickey] Mantle twice while pitching for the Angels after being traded in '61, and he was by far the most physically imposing person who ever walked up to the plate [that I faced]. I'm happy to report that I struck him out both times. He yelled at me after the second K that if I'd have pitched like that when I was there [with the Yankees], I would still be there.[62]

I'm sure you're aware that Williams' remains are in a facility where they are frozen in hopes that he can come back some day. That place is within a couple of miles of where I live and I go by it frequently. I always say, "Hi Ted" when we do, because he was my hero when I was a young boy wanting to be a ballplayer. My wife of course thinks I'm nuts and she's probably right. She usually is.

---

[62] On June 11, 1961, just over a month after being traded by the Yankees to the Angels, James struck out Mantle twice—caught looking in the fifth inning and swinging in the seventh.

Bob Kelly

Right-handed pitcher

1951–53:	**Chicago Cubs**
1953, 1958:	**Cincinnati Reds**
1958:	**Cleveland Indians**
Career Statistics:	**12–18, 2 saves, 4.50 ERA**

Ted Williams vs. Bob Kelly

2-for-3, 0 extra-base hits, 0 RBI, 2 walks, 0 strikeouts, .667 batting average, .800 on-base percentage, .667 slugging percentage

Bob Kelly

YEAR	DATE	RESULT
1958	May 4	Walk
		Single
		Single
	May 20	Fielder's choice
	June 3	Walk

EVERY ONCE IN a while around my town in Connecticut, they ask me to talk at baseball banquets and little leagues and so forth. And I've always taken great distress in watching kids on the bench during the ball games, eating everything from popsicles to talking to somebody else and not paying attention to what is going on in the field. So when speaking, I use an incident when I pitched against Ted as a prime example of that.

The first time I faced him was in Boston—it was the only time I faced him in Boston when I was with Cleveland[63] and I was pitching

---

[63] Kelly actually faced Williams twice in Boston: on May 4, 1958, which is the game he is referring to, and on June 3, 1958.

against a hitter—I'm not sure who the hitter was up in front of him[64]— and I was pitching against him, I noticed a presence watching me from the on-deck circle.

I got through that hitter and Ted Williams [came up to bat]. At that time, I had developed a palm ball, and it was a pitch that really benefited me getting back to the majors in 1958. I was very, very successful with it in Nashville the year before. I had won 23 games[65] down there with that thing, and I got called back up to the majors. It was a great changeup, and I think a predecessor to what they now call the split-finger. It was a pitch that you threw with all your might, and no matter how hard or what effort you put into it, it was a dead fish getting up there.

And sure enough, I got ahead of Ted and threw him this palm ball, and he was way out on his front foot and extended himself and just got the bat on the ball and hit it right on the plate and bounced over my head, dropping dead between the mound and second base, and he trotted to first with a single.

That was the first time I faced him. And sure enough—and this is what I tell the kids—the next time I faced him, he was in the batter's box and was just staring holes into me, trying to figure out what the pitch was, where I picked it up, and anything I did in my delivery I think to tell him what was coming.

And sure enough, the next time up I got ahead of him again and I come up with that palm ball. He just literally switched his feet waiting for that pitch to come up and dumped it into left field and trotted into second for a double.[66] It was one of the rare times I saw him do that, to hit to the opposite field. He just nonchalantly poked it out there.

---

[64] Williams actually led off in this at-bat, in the fourth. Kelly walked Williams in the first, after retiring Don Buddin and Pete Runnels.

[65] Actually 24; Kelly had been out of the majors since 1953.

[66] Retrosheet.org lists the hit as a single to left field.

And he picked up the pitch. He knew what I was throwing him before I threw it.

So I tell these kids that, if you spend time on the bench watching the game, no matter what position, you can learn something every minute.

You talk about going over him in the meetings beforehand and where to pitch him, sometimes you're better off walking him rather than getting in trouble with the ball going [out of] the ballpark.

Russ Kemmerer

Right-handed pitcher

1954–55, 1957 ....**Boston Red Sox**
1957–60: ....**Washington Senators**
1960–62: .... **Chicago White Sox**
1962–63: ....**Houston Colt .45s**
Career Statistics: .... **43–59, 8 saves, 4.46 ERA**

Ted Williams vs. Russ Kemmerer

4-for-15, 1 home run, 1 RBI, 6 walks (2 intentional), 1 strikeout, .250 batting average, .455 on-base percentage, .438 slugging percentage

Home Runs Allowed:

No. 496, June 10, 1960, at Boston

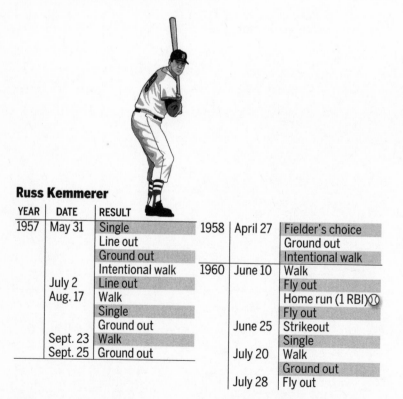

Russ Kemmerer

YEAR	DATE	RESULT			
1957	May 31	Single	1958	April 27	Fielder's choice
		Line out			Ground out
		Ground out			Intentional walk
		Intentional walk	1960	June 10	Walk
	July 2	Line out			Fly out
	Aug. 17	Walk			Home run (1 RBI)
		Single			Fly out
		Ground out		June 25	Strikeout
	Sept. 23	Walk			Single
	Sept. 25	Ground out		July 20	Walk
					Ground out
				July 28	Fly out

I WROTE A BOOK in 2002 titled *Hey Kid, Just Get It Over the Plate*, which was basically taken from when I was a high school senior. The Red Sox came into Pittsburgh, where I lived, to play a fundraising game with the Pirates. Since they had the brass along, they wanted to see me throw.

Anyway, I was pitching batting practice—of course I found out later that major-league ballplayers don't like to hit while high-schoolers pitch, but I was doing okay. I got through the reserve lineup pretty well and turned around to get some resin and there was Ted Williams. I think I described it in the book as my larynx was in full tilt. And he just pointed the bat out to the mound and said, "Hey kid, you're doing a good job, just get it over the plate."

I've had a lot of really, really great experiences with Ted. He took me in after the game—he came into the clubhouse as I was getting dressed—and he said, "You're going to play ball?" and I said, "That's all I've ever wanted to do." He said, "Well, I don't know what you have inside you, but from what I've seen tonight, you can play."

And he went on to encourage me to sign with the Red Sox. He said, "Who else is looking at you?" I said, "Pirates, of course, the Giants, Cincinnati, and Brooklyn." He said, "Well, all of those teams have about thirty farm clubs, and you can get lost down in those things." He said the Red Sox only had about eight and "if you can make it, and I think you might, you can move [up] much faster." Well, if he told me to sign with the Kokomo Brown Bears, I guess I would have.

But anyway, it was a little over two years later, and Ted came back from the service, and I had been called up to go to spring training with the team. I walked in and he said, "You're the kid from Pittsburgh, aren't you?" I said yeah, and he said, "I knew you'd make it." So that was my first meeting with Ted.

Every pitcher had an idea of how he could get Ted out. It was a combination of his best pitch, game situation, men on base, inning, and score of the game. In my case, my strategy was to stay away from him. My best pitch to a left-hand hitter was to keep the ball down and away. I had a good sinking fastball about 95 miles-per-hour. When I felt them moving closer to the plate, I tried to jam them with a hard slider in on their hands. I felt I did well, but remember few umpires called a knee-high fastball on the outside corner a strike on Ted. Ted was 4–16 against me; certainly not bad against *the greatest.*

Each pitcher has his best pitch against Ted. Game situations are always taken into consideration. The pregame advice was, "Ted's going to get his hits. With men on base, hope for a hard grounder at somebody. Outside of that, keep it in the ballpark." The White Sox and Senators moved the second baseman back on the grass and the shortstop closer to second. When Ted ripped it, unless it was right at the fielder, it got through.

[Mickey] Mantle, [Roger] Maris, and [Al] Kaline were all great hitters. The difference was that Ted had no apparent weakness. Mantle had a weakness: high and tight, provided you had a good fastball and you could keep it inside. If you got it high and away, he could lose it to left field. This was tough for me, because I was a low-ball pitcher. Maris was tough upstairs. The year he hit 61, he hit No. 15 and 39 against me. Kaline hit to all fields. He could handle the bat. He hit to the hole on the right side of the infield, bunt if the third baseman laid back, and drive the ball to left field if it was open, and seldom chased a bad pitch.

Any discussion with Ted always found its way to hitting and pitching. He remembered everything about pitchers because he studied them and would talk to other hitters about them. As a result, he had an idea once he faced them. We never discussed facing each other except the one homer he hit off me. Ted was the best hitter I ever faced. Willie Mays, [Hank] Aaron, Monte Irvin, Luke Easter, Hank Bauer, and [Roberto] Clemente were some of the greats I played against.

Unfortunately, from the standpoint to pitching against him, the Red Sox traded me to the Senators, and I didn't get to pitch against them very much, for no particular reason.[67] But when I was with the White Sox, I remember a particular game when we were in Fenway Park and were ahead 8–0.[68] One thing about Ted; I used to sit around and listen to him talk. Pitchers like myself, who were starting at that time, used to sit there and bone his bats. I always had Ted's bat to bone. I'd sit and listen to him talk so much that, if you ever threw a 2–2 slider for example, and got him out on it, next time or in that next series, don't ever throw him the same pitch again, because he was waiting for it. Just things like that. Listening to him talk about hitters and pitchers, what to do and what not to do. Anyway, in that particular ball game, I got him out—I don't remember, let's say a sinker and a slider—first two times he came to bat. He came to bat in the eighth inning and I was thinking about what I just told you. I'm thinking, okay, I got him out on this, I got him out on that, I'm going to throw him a slow breaking ball . . . and he hit that sucker about forty rows up in the seats.

If you've seen film of him running, [you'll notice that] he never really ran, he loped. He was going around first base and he was clapping. Of course the sportswriters don't know what he's saying; neither does the press or anybody else. But when he got to first base, he looked at me and said, "Hey bush, I got you in my book." He called everyone bush-leaguer. "You're in my book, I got you in my book, baby." He clapped all the way around. He was really laying it on me good. So the next day I was hitting fungos to left field, and I could hear him saying, "Hey, bush, you're in my book, baby." I turned around to him and said, "I haven't thrown a slow breaking ball to you in like two or three years, and you hit the damn thing like you knew it was coming." And he said,

---

[67] Kemmerer faced the Red Sox six times in 1957, but only once each in '58 and '59, which were his top two seasons in terms of innings pitched in his career.

[68] The game he refers to was one played June 10, 1960. It was the bottom of the sixth inning, and the White Sox were up 8–2 with one out.

"I did." Curious to find out how he knew, I asked him, "You want to tell me?" "Yeah, I'll tell you. When you got right to the top of your windup, you did a little something that you don't normally do, and I knew you were going to throw me an off-speed pitch."

He and Johnny Pesky became my mentors and [we] remained good friends. I was fortunate enough [to be invited] when they had the 60th anniversary of when Ted came into the league—the Mets were playing the Red Sox in the interleague games at Shea Stadium. He invited me, not just me, but Mel Parnell, Johnny Pesky, and Tommy Lasorda were there, because they were always close friends of Ted's. That was a magnificent evening.

Virgil Trucks and I had a talk about Williams one time, and he was kidding that he only hit one home run off him. I said I didn't play against him very much. I was with him the first years I was in the majors and didn't get to pitch against him too much after that.

In those days, Virgil said it was your best against his best. Virgil had a tremendous fastball, and he was going to throw his fastball. He said, well he hit 12 home runs off of me. I guess I wasn't ready to challenge him that much.

Marty Kutyna

Right-handed pitcher

1959–60: ....**Kansas City Athletics**
1961–62: ....**Washington Senators**
Career Statistics: ....**14–16, 8 saves, 3.88 ERA**

Ted Williams vs. Marty Kutyna

0-for-1, 3 walks, 0 strikeouts, .000 batting average, .750 on-base percentage, .000 slugging percentage

Marty Kutyna

YEAR	DATE	RESULT
1960	May 4	Walk
	June 20	Fly out
	Aug. 1	Walk
	Aug. 4	Walk

THE FIRST TIME I faced Ted Williams in 1960 was as a pinch-hitter on May 4. I came in relief with men on first and second and one out to face three left-handed hitters in the bottom of the eighth inning in Boston.

I got Vic Wertz on a fly ball. Then Ted Williams came up.[69] Harry Chiti was my catcher that day. He called for a slider, which I threw over the plate, and Ted had a good cut and fouled it off. Chiti came out to me and said, don't throw another one there, or he will hit it 400 feet. He told me to throw him inside. The next two pitches I did, and one of them was a strike, but umpire Nester Chylak called them [both] balls.

---

[69] With Boston trailing 5–3, Williams hit for Lou Clinton.

I took two steps forward and told the umpire they were strikes. The umpire came out to me and said next time you come toward me, you'll be out of the game. The next two fastballs I threw were again inside and called balls. I walked Ted.

I shook my head and looked at Williams at first. Ted looked at me from first base and shouted, "They were all strikes, rookie!"

The next hitter was Marty Keough, and I struck him out to end the inning.

Photo courtesy of Marty Kutyna

Don Larsen

Right-handed pitcher

1953:	St. Louis Browns
1954:	Baltimore Orioles
1955–59:	New York Yankees
1960–61:	Kansas City Athletics
1961:	Chicago White Sox
1962–64:	San Francisco Giants
1964–65:	Houston Colt .45s/Astros
1965:	Baltimore Orioles
1967:	Chicago Cubs
Career Statistics:	81–91, 23 saves, 3.78 ERA
World Series MVP:	1956

Ted Williams vs. Don Larsen

14-for-54, 3 home runs, 8 RBI, 18 walks (6 intentional), 4 strikeouts, 2 double plays, 1 sacrifice fly, .259 batting average, .438 on-base percentage, .426 slugging percentage

Home Runs Allowed:

No. 349, July 19, 1954 (game two), at Baltimore
No. 387, August 16, 1955, at New York
No. 449, August 14, 1957, at New York

THOUGHT HE WAS the best hitter in the American League at the time I was playing. They say his eyesight was superb. The only thing I didn't like was no matter what you did, if you threw the ball down the middle of the plate and he didn't swing, it would be a ball. So he more or less umpired his own game and I didn't appreciate that. Being what a hitter he was and with the few breaks he got could be devastating.

Don Larsen

YEAR	DATE	RESULT
1954	July 19	Walk
		Intentional walk
		Home run (1 RBI)
	Aug. 8	Single
		Intentional walk
		Line out
		Ground out
	Aug. 28	Walk
		Fly out
		Walk
		Intentional walk
1955	Aug. 10	Ground out
		Walk
		Strikeout
		Fly out
		Fly out
		Intentional walk
	Aug. 16	Single
		Ground out
		Home run (2 RBI)
		Ground out
	Sept. 23	Strikeout
		Single
		Single
1956	April 22	Single (1 RBI)
	April 27	Fly out
	May 29	Fly out
	July 4	Walk
		Single
		Walk
		Ground out
	Aug. 7	Fly out into DP
		Ground out
		Fly out
		Walk
	Aug. 16	Line out
		Foul out
		Fly out
		Fly out
	Sept. 22	Foul out
		Fly out
		Walk
		Strikeout
	Sept. 28	Ground out
		Grounded into DP
		Grounded into DP
1957	April 20	Fly out
	April 28	Walk
	May 28	Pop out
		Walk
		Pop out
	July 4	Foul out
	Aug. 14	Home run (3 RBI)
		Ground out
		Single
1958	April 21	Strikeout
		Fielder's choice
		Single
	May 31	Fly out
		Line out
		Intentional walk
		Single
	July 6	Single
		Single
	Aug. 16	Sacrifice fly (1 RBI)
		Line out
		Pop out
		Fly out
1959	July 8	Walk
	July 13	Fly out
	Aug. 15	Fly out
		Walk
	Sept. 20	Intentional walk

I liked to pitch against him. I didn't care about him hitting the home runs; it was better than a walk. At least it keeps the ball in [the stadium] for someone to make a play on it. He hit a few home runs off me, but he never beat me in a game.

The years I played against him, he never had great luck in Yankee Stadium, which you think he would have, with right field that way. There was no park too small for him. I don't know why, but he never had good luck in Yankee Stadium.[70] Of course, we had a good staff,

---

[70] In his career, Ted Williams hit .309/.484/.543 at Yankee Stadium. That slugging percentage is his third worst among stadiums he played in.

too. It was a good rivalry; I liked that. It was nice, good competition, and I enjoyed that very much.

It was a challenge, you know, and I'm glad I had a little luck against him. He was a little bit of a character in a way because everybody asked him about hitting and he always volunteered something. So he was a big asset to the players who came up during his time, too. I didn't think to [ask him about hitting], but maybe if I was playing regular I would [laughs].

He wasn't a small guy, either. He could tonk the ball out of any place. So it was a good time facing him, and you just tried to do the best you could in getting him out in certain occasions—or anytime. If he got a hit, so what? I didn't mind that a bit. Didn't want to walk him. Then you got no chance if you walk people. I did have some luck with him, and I appreciated that, too. I was happy when I got him out . . . very happy.

You had to be careful with any of the [great] hitters, it wasn't only him. You wanted to get those guys out when you really needed it. You didn't want them to beat you in a ball game, like in the eighth or ninth inning on a home run or something like that. I wasn't fond of walking him, but I did so a few times. But it's a challenge and we came up to it, and I enjoyed that competition with him.

I relied on Yogi [Berra] a lot, because I joined later, and Yogi faced these guys many, many times. Yogi knew *all* the hitters. Maybe they might change something, but he'd noticed that kind of stuff. Ted didn't change. He was a natural.

He wasn't a bad fielder in Boston, either, with that wall. He could play that wall pretty good. He wasn't noted for his fielding, but he did a good job for them.

I never played against [Stan] Musial, only one time, and that was in the National League. I spent most of my time in the American League. They had some good hitters in the National, too, like Musial. But Ted was the best I ever saw in the American League.

We may have used [the Williams shift], but I don't recall that part of it. I know a lot clubs did. Of course he'd challenge them anyway. He didn't care. He was going to go after it!

He would talk baseball to you all day long if you wanted to do that. He was very accommodating. Everyone looked up to him and tried to needle his brain. He and I became pretty friendly because he's from San Diego, where I grew up. I got to be with him at several functions in San Diego, and we had a nice relationship. More after, when we had more time to spend time leisurely. Not so much during our playing years. We weren't supposed to mingle too much, but we did anyway. That's much baloney, anyway. I liked him very much, the family and stuff. Of course, he never came back to San Diego. He spent most of the time in Florida; you know how he loved his fishing and stuff. He was the head honcho for Sears for quite a few years. He designed a few things, including making his own flies. I understand he was pretty damn good, top in the country in fly-fishing.

I saw him a little bit in San Diego when we were both retired. I didn't appreciate what happened *after* he passed away, but I don't think anyone liked that.

Bobby Locke

Right-handed pitcher

1959–61:	Cleveland Indians
1962:	St. Louis Cardinals
1962–64:	Philadelphia Phillies
1965:	Cincinnati Reds
1967–68:	California Angels
Career Statistics:	16–15, 10 saves, 4.02 ERA

Ted Williams vs. Bobby Locke

1-for-7, 0 extra-base hits, 0 RBI, 1 walk, 4 strikeouts, 1 hit by pitch, .143 batting average, .333 on-base percentage, .143 slugging percentage

HE WAS ALMOST out of baseball when I was pitching against him. He was still hitting a lot of home runs, though. I remember a guy I played with in Cleveland, Wynn Hawkins, I think he gave up the 513th home run.[71] So we was still hitting home runs in 1960.

Well, he was a great hitter, that's for sure. Anybody that faced him would tell me that. When I first faced him they said he's a great hitter. And he was. I just had some good success against him. Maybe it is because I hit him. You never know, right?

The best thing that I [heard] . . . Jimmy Piersall was my teammate. He came in and told me, he says "I had struck him out twice in one game, you know," he says "[Williams] very seldom ever strikes out twice in a game." So, also, that day I hit him,[72] Jimmy Piersall says, "Boy, he never gets hit by a pitch." He says, "What are you doing?"

He was glad I hit him, Jimmy Piersall was. He was a great ballplayer, a great teammate, and he didn't care for Ted Williams. They were

---

[71] Hawkins actually allowed Williams' 500th career home run; teammate Johnny Klippstein allowed No. 513.

[72] This happened in Locke's major-league debut on June 18, 1959.

teammates at one time, but he always felt [Williams] got away with everything, he was like a prima donna.

That's probably why I struck him out so many times, I hit him once.

Well, I don't know, he was like any batter to me when I was pitching. What can I say? I was successful against him I guess. I threw him the same pitches I everybody else - fastball, slider, curveball.

I don't think we put the shift on him, I think we played him regular like everyone else. Not like baseball today. You see how they play three or four guys in the infield, they put them all in right, right-center. You got guys way out in right field almost.

Bobby Locke

YEAR	DATE	RESULT
1959	June 18	Hit by pitch
	July 17	Walk
		Fly out
		Ground out
1960	July 24	Strikeout
	Aug. 10	Strikeout
	Aug. 23	Single
		Strikeout
		Strikeout

The only thing I remember I got from him one time, I had a sore arm and I got sent to Indianapolis—Triple-A ball—and we were at the airport together and he told me, "Ah, don't worry about it, Bob, you'll be back in a short time." And I was. I was only there like a month or two and came back.

Oh, yeah, yeah, I talked to him. He made a good comment about me. He said I was the hardest pitcher for him to hit on the Indians staff in '59. That was a good comment. He said it to the sportswriter. Sportswriter put it in the paper, there was a good write up about it. So that was good.

As far as a person is concerned, I thought he was a great guy, you know. He'd talk to an Ordinary Joe, he'd talk to anybody. He was, as a player, respected by everybody. I know all the pitchers on our team respected him. They didn't want to see him come up to bat! Not with the bases loaded or something like that. Because he didn't strike out that often, you know, he had a good eye.

First time I ever pitched against him, I pitched against him in spring training in Mesa, Arizona, and I struck him out the first time. I got out of the service—I was in the service and got out in '59—and they told me, "You know who you struck out, Bob?" And I said no. "Ted Williams." I said, so? That's what I was supposed to do.

You know what, some of the best batters I ever faced, like Mickey Mantle and Roger Maris, I believe I got them easier out than I got some of them punch hitters. Really. Maybe I bared down on them more.

Ralph Lumenti

Left-handed pitcher

1957–59: ....Washington Senators
Career Statistics: .... 1–3, 0 saves, 7.29 ERA

Ted Williams vs. Ralph Lumenti

1-for-4, 0 RBI, 1 walk, 0 strikeouts, .250 batting average, .400 on-base percentage, .250 slugging percentage

Ralph Lumenti

YEAR	DATE	RESULT
1957	Sept. 23	Single
		Walk
1958	May 14	Fly out
		Fly out
1959	Sept. 27	Pop out

IT WAS QUITE an experience to suddenly find yourself face-to-face with the guy you idolized growing up.

It wasn't nerve-racking, but it was a situation in which you were in awe. I faced him—it was the third game that I pitched in the major leagues, or at least participated in, not a full game. I started against the Red Sox, I think it was a season-ender in 1957. I believe I was out of the game by the third inning.[73] But the thing that stands out most in my mind was that I was caught in the streak where Ted Williams had gotten on base sixteen straight times in a season. I was a victim. That was my major contribution.[74]

---

[73] It was September 23, 1957, Lumenti's third appearance in the majors and his second start. He would last only 1 1/3 innings.

[74] Williams holds the modern major-league record by reaching base sixteen straight times, from September 17–23, 1957.

He singled to left field and I walked him in the other two times that I faced him when I was in there.

And subsequent to that, I think two years later in 1959, I pitched two innings of relief, I believe, against the Red Sox in Boston and faced him again. Got him out. I felt good about it because in the times I faced him, he wasn't able to pull the ball. I just don't think he could get around on me.[75]

I was wild. That was my problem in my time with the Senators. . . . And it was my undoing. Well, 1–4, if I had that as an average, it would have been great. I had a record for thirty-five years or so until Rob Dibble broke it—wildest pitcher![76] I had what amounted to a couple cups of coffee in the major leagues back then.

I talked to him kind of on a "hi" basis. When I got out of baseball, I was helping a friend coach a team in Johnstown, Pennsylvania, in the Johnstown tournament, and I ran across him down at the Norfolk prison in Massachusetts, and he remembered me. I of course remembered *him*. While he didn't mention specific at-bats, he did remember that I threw hard and said I had a good arm and he remembered batting against me. He was quite a guy.

Based on what he put up there for numbers, he was up at the top of the list. I think one of the toughest hitters I ever faced was [Carl] Yastrzemski. Another Boston hitter, left-handed, and I was a left-handed pitcher.[77]

Just determination, I guess, made him so good. Concentration. Very tough hitter.

---

[75] The detailed listing of Williams' at-bats vs. Lumenti on baseball-reference.com shows that every time Williams hit the ball against Lumenti—including his only hit—it went to the opposite field, with a single to left, two fly-outs to left, and a pop out to third.

[76] Lumenti walked 42 batters in 33 1/3 innings in his career, including 36 in 21 innings (15.4/9 IP) in 1958. Dibble walked 15.7/9 IP in 1995.

[77] Lumenti faced Yasztremski in the minors.

Morrie Martin

Left-handed pitcher

1949:	**Brooklyn Dodgers**
1951–54:	**Philadelphia Athletics**
1954–56:	**Chicago White Sox**
1956:	**Baltimore Orioles**
1957–58:	**St. Louis Cardinals**
1958:	**Cleveland Indians**
1959:	**Chicago Cubs**
Career Statistics:	**38–34, 15 saves, 4.29 ERA**

Ted Williams vs. Morrie Martin:

8-for-20, 2 home runs, 7 RBI, 2 walks, 0 strikeouts, 1 hit by pitch, .400 batting average, .478 on-base percentage, .700 slugging percentage

Home Runs Allowed:

No. 316, August 9, 1951 (game one), at Boston
No. 412, September 1, 1956, at Boston

YOU HATED TO get up there and face him, I know that. But I did my best and I had good luck against him. I had that luck because I pitched him right down the middle and up. Don't ever pitch him low because it's gone. I did that a couple of times. Once that I remember, I think that's the only home run that he hit off of me.

[He had the] best eyes I've ever seen in my life. He could take a pitch that was half an inch inside and wouldn't even bat an eye. He was great, and a good guy to go with it. I talked to him a lot of times.

The only time he hit a home run off of me was in Boston. I knew when I threw it; I said, "Uh-oh, too low," and it was gone.[78]

---

[78] Martin actually allowed two home runs to Williams and both were in Boston. The first occurred on August 9, 1951, in the first game of a doubleheader. Williams hit a solo home run in the first inning of an eventual 6–5 Philadelphia victory. On

Anyway, the next day he called me out into the outfield. I wondered what in the heck he wanted with me. So I go out there and talked to him, and he says, "Morris, it took me longer to hit a home run off you than any pitcher I've ever faced in my life." And he said that after the game was over, he'd leave something in my locker ... and he left one of his rod and reels— that's when he was with Sears, you know—he left me one of his rod and reels engraved in gold. Unfortunately, I've since lost it and can't remember what I did with it.

It just said Ted Williams, home run, you know.

He told me that as soon as it [the ball] leaves your hand, he knew what it is going to be. I said, how the heck can you miss one then? And he said, well, you don't miss them—he didn't miss them either, very seldom—but he said it is just the idea of rotating the bat and getting the bat on it right.

Morrie Martin

YEAR	DATE	RESULT
1951	April 22	Ground out
	April 29	Walk
	June 27	Single
	July 4	Fielder's choice
	July 5	Fly out
	Aug. 9	Home run (1 RBI)
		Line out
		Ground out
	Sept. 7	Single
		Fly out
1954	May 25	Fielder's choice
	May 26	Fly out
	May 31	Ground out
		Hit by pitch
	July 25	Single
	Aug. 5	Fly out
	Sept. 1	Fly out
		Single
1955	Aug. 3	Walk
		Fly out
	June 27	Single
		Single
	Sept. 1	Home run (2 RBI)

September 1, 1956, Martin relieved for the Orioles in a 2–2 tie in the bottom of the eighth, after George Zuverink allowed a leadoff single to Billy Klaus. Williams followed with a two-run home run, and the Red Sox went on to win 4–2. It was the last time that Martin would face Williams.

He was a great hitter; one of the best I've ever seen in my life. Remember Gil McDougald of the Yankees? I could not get him out! But he was not a long-ball hitter, he was just a good hitter.[79] Stan Musial was another good one . . . one of the greatest.[80] I'll tell you, Williams had better eyes than Musial. You could actually fool Musial, but not very often. Not very often at all.

I knew I had to get it over the plate [against Williams]; I didn't want to walk him, you know. Oh yeah, I wanted to make him hit it. Always did, always did. Yup.

I had a fastball, curveball, slider, and changeup. I had different pitches, and he could read them all. The fastball was more effective. You couldn't throw him a slow breaking ball; he'd kill ya. You couldn't get him out very often. When I played against him, they put that shift on him, you know, and the second baseman would go out in the outfield and pick it up and throw him out. I had to [like it]. He was strictly a pull-hitter, and he defied you to hit it the other way. He wouldn't do it. He was that good a hitter. [We used the shift] all the time and he still got his hits, doggone right.

I talked to him all the time, great guy. He loved people. I'll tell you one thing—he didn't like sportswriters. I don't know why; I guess maybe they said something against him, I don't know what, but he just didn't like them. Didn't want to talk to them. He did most of the talking with his bat.

I remember once I intended to hit him—and really hit him—and I hit him right in the rear end, and he laughed. He said at least you hit me where it didn't hurt. I thought what the hell; I'm getting tired of him wearing me out.

He was the greatest hitter I ever faced. And a great guy with it.

---

[79] While some statistics are missing, of what is known, McDougal was 16–39 (.410) with 4 doubles and 1 home run off Martin.

[80] Martin played on the Cardinals with Musial from 1957–58.

Bill Oster

Left-handed pitcher

1954: .... **Philadelphia Athletics**
Career Statistics: .... **0–1, 0 saves, 6.32 ERA**

Ted Williams vs. Bill Oster

1-for-3, 1 home run, 2 RBI, 1 walk, 1 strikeout, .333 batting average, .500 on-base percentage, 1.333 slugging percentage

Home Runs Allowed:

No. 363, September 5, 1954 (game one), at Philadelphia

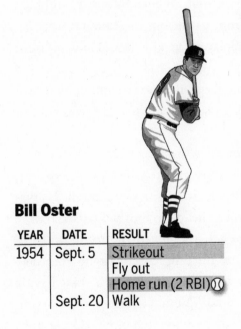

Bill Oster

YEAR	DATE	RESULT
1954	Sept. 5	Strikeout
		Fly out
		Home run (2 RBI)
	Sept. 20	Walk

IT WAS THE biggest thrill of my life.

I came in relief in the fifth inning, and he was my first hitter.[81] To make a long story short, I struck him out on four pitches. That's the God's honest truth.

I tell a couple of people that, and they look it up, like this guy can't be telling the truth. And they look it up and say, you really did, didn't you?

I couldn't wait to pitch to him. I had a lot of confidence.

---

[81] On September 5, 1954, in the first game of a doubleheader, Oster was brought in to begin the third inning. Williams would actually be the fourth batter he faced that inning.

I had nothing to lose. I'm a kid, twenty-one years old, and I could throw 96–97 miles-per-hour.

The first three were fastballs. I got two strikes on him immediately—he swung and missed. And then I shook off a curveball. You know, if I got him on the fastball, I wasn't going to fool him with the curveball [laughs]. The next pitch was high—just under his chin—and then he [the catcher] came back with the curveball again, so I threw the curveball and I guess I fooled him, because he missed it completely. It's in the record books, but that's my biggest claim to fame in baseball.

[I remember that] he commented on every pitch to the catcher. That ball was moving, blah, blah, blah, blah. When he came up a second time that game, he said, "He's starting to tire." And I was, because I gave it my all. And he hit a fly ball [out to center field].

Then the third time he got up, he said, "The kid's lost it" and hit a home run. So I went the route: from a strikeout to a home run.

He was the most respected ballplayer I've ever seen. He was just in his own class and a decent guy.

To be where I was, right out of college, that was a thrill in itself. But to face him, my first hitter, in Boston, I couldn't wait. I had a lot of confidence.

I watched him during batting practice shagging balls in the outfield, and he was all by himself. You'd see three guys together when they were shagging flies and stuff like that, but he was always by himself. He was a loner. I did observe that. I said like "hello" to him as I passed him.

I'll tell you another quick story. I just joined the team, and I'm sitting out in the bullpen with my pitching coach, Rollie Hemsley, and he says, "I want to go over these hitters with you. You have a good chance of getting in this game." Vern Stephens[82]—I can still remember all the things he said—you have to pitch him breaking stuff, low and away, blah, blah, blah. [Billy] Goodman got up and said you got to pitch to this guy. He said he gets a lot of walks, so he's not going

---

[82] Stephens actually was on the Baltimore Orioles in 1954.

to help you out. So Ted Williams gets up [laughs], and he didn't say anything. So I said, "So, Rollie, where do you pitch this guy?" He says, "Son, you just throw it and duck." That was his exact words [laughs]; you just throw it and duck.

About that same time when we played the Red Sox in Boston, we got there and we're dressing up for the game while the Red Sox were taking their batting practice. So the bat boy was hanging around and one of our players told the bat boy to let us know when Ted was taking his batting practice. So about ten minutes later, the kid came in and said he's taking his batting practice now. With that, the *whole* dressing room cleared out and went up on deck to watch him. That told me everything, you know. It was amazing.

The next trip we went into New York to play the Yankees. Mickey Mantle got up and maybe one guy went up to watch him. It tells you everything. Wow, what a respected guy.

Duane Pillette

Right-handed pitcher

1949–50: ....New York Yankees
1950–53: ....St. Louis Browns
1954–55: .... Baltimore Orioles
1956: .... Philadelphia Phillies
Career Statistics:............................ 38–66, 2 saves, 4.40 ERA

Ted Williams vs. Duane Pillette (data incomplete)

6-for-15, 2 home runs, 3 RBI, 12 walks (1 intentional), 0 strikeouts, .400 batting average, .667 on-base percentage, .800 slugging percentage

Home Runs Allowed:

No. 315, August 1, 1951, at Boston
No. 347, July 18, 1954 (game two), at Boston

WHEN I FIRST made the majors, it was with the Yankees. I never pitched against [Ted] while being with New York. I began my career as a long reliever and I wasn't very good at it. They sent me back to Newark—their farm team. In June of '50, I was traded to St. Louis [Browns]. I pitched a couple of years against him, but he hit me like he hit everybody. I thought he was the best hitter I ever saw. I'm not sure how well he did against me the two and a half years I was with the Browns. I only know that for me, St. Louis was tough on me.

You see, I'm a ground-ball pitcher, and St. Louis had both the Cardinals and the Browns playing on the surface—which seldom has grass—because the weather and the two teams using it constantly caused ground balls to go through much faster than the other parks. When the Browns played their last game ever in 1953, who lost that game? Me! We lost 2–1 in eleven innings. But then the Browns became the Orioles and I had another chance to have a better year.

Duane Pillette

YEAR	DATE	RESULT
1950	Sept. 15	Single
1951	May 23	Walk
		Walk (1 RBI)
	Aug. 1	Home run (1 RBI)
		Fly out
		Walk
		Walk
	Sept. 15	Walk
		Intentional walk
		Single
		Fly out
1953	Sept. 11	Ground out
		Fly out
		Ground out
		Ground out
1954	July 18	Walk
		Home run (1 RBI)
		Foul out
		Walk
	Aug. 8	Walk
		Walk
		Fielder's choice
		Single
		Walk
		Ground out
1955	July 8	Single
		Walk

Getting back to Williams, it seemed as though I became a real pitcher—Ted will tell you so in the article a fan sent me. He actually said it himself.[83] Yes, then Ted was mine; he couldn't do anything good. Even went 0–4 once.

---

[83] An article Pillette sent along from the website Urban Shocker's Weblog reads: "Yankees manager Casey Stengel chose Pillette to throw batting practice for the American League All-Stars [in 1954], and the junior circuit's best went on the [sic] rack up a record (at the time) 17 hits in the contest. At the game, Red Sox great Ted Williams told Pillette he was the toughest pitcher he'd faced all year, and Al Rosen of the Indians—the reigning MVP—rated him one of the league's best fastball pitchers."

I also found out that Ted has said to umpires that he played with my father[84] on PCL San Diego when he was eighteen [in 1937]. He said my dad taught me how to cheat, but that's not true!

---

[84] Herman Pillette, who pitched in the majors in 1917, and from 1922–24.

Tom Qualters

Right-handed pitcher

1953, 1957–58: .... **Philadelphia Phillies**
1958: .... **Chicago White Sox**
Career Statistics: .... **0–0, 0 saves, 5.64 ERA**

Ted Williams vs. Tom Qualters

1-for-2, 0 extra-base hits, 0 RBI, 0 walks, 0 strikeouts, .500 batting average, .500 on-base percentage, .500 slugging percentage

Tom Qualters

YEAR	DATE	RESULT
1958	May 25	Fly out
	July 10	Single

I HAD JUST JOINED the ballclub[85] and didn't expect to be seeing any action. So they called down and I got hot, and I couldn't quite understand why they were using me. It was my lack of experience. I came in the game, and Al Lopez, who was just a great manager—you couldn't kid him on anything—I met him at the mound and he handed me the ball and said, "How you going to pitch this guy?" And of course that guy happened to be Ted Williams. I'm walking in there, and I'm thinking he's going to give me all kinds of advice on what to do and what not to do, but he just asks how you going to pitch this guy.

---

[85] Qualters was traded from the Phillies to the White Sox on April 30, 1958. He faced Williams for the first time on May 25, his fourth appearance for Chicago.

I threw a natural sinking fastball and I had a curveball that every-body raved and knew about. So I said to him that I was going to try to miss low and away on the outside and try to hope he goes for it . . . and if he doesn't, I'm going to go with breaking balls the rest of the way. He said okay and walked off the mound.

As I threw my warm-ups, Williams, he moves up close to get a good view of what you're doing. So I didn't throw the ball very hard. I just threw four-seam fastballs, which don't move at all, and just laid them up there at about three-quarter speed. I [also] threw some curveballs. I threw them all like changeup curveballs, off-speed curveballs, so he didn't have a chance to see what I threw.

So the first pitch I was lucky enough that I got the ball down and away. The thing is that the bases were loaded and there was a *huge* crowd. I don't know what the occasion was, but the place was packed.[86] I luckily made the pitch I was trying to make and he swung. He went after it and just hit a short pop fly to center field, so it worked out pretty well.

Some years earlier I was in a situation—I played half a year at B-ball and this new Triple-A club was going to be in Miami, Florida. I just wanted to make that club so bad and I never thought I could. But as spring training went through day after day, I was still on the team, but we still had too many players. Opening day comes and there were a lot of ex-major league players on the team, and we had a bunch of really great young pitchers who all went to the major leagues; but here it is, opening day, big crowd and I'm still there. All of a sudden—Bill Veeck was our general manager, and he was really a wild and crazy guy—here comes a helicopter over the stadium and it lands besides the pitcher's mound. And who gets out but Satchel Paige.

So maybe the first or second or third game, I don't know what, I enter in a pretty tough situation late in the game—men on base and all that—and I get out there, and from the time I was a little kid, as long

---

[86] It was a Sunday doubleheader in Chicago. According to ballparks.com, the atten-dance was 19,121. The Comiskey capacity in 1958 was 52,000.

as I had a baseball or a rock or anything in my pocket, I wasn't afraid of anything. So here I am, I get out there on the mound and I'm taking my warm-up pitches, and I get the shakes. I never had that in my life, I tell ya, I was shaking all over. Somehow or other I got them out, I don't know how the hell it happened.

I went home that night and I thought 'you can't bullshit another player.' Probably, in my mind, every player on that team knew I was gutless. I was trying to figure out what the hell to do. I was so fearful that these guys knew I didn't have the courage to play the game.

So I'm down in the bullpen the next night, I'm just sitting there and I guess I was pretty quiet. And Satch, as early in the season as it was, we had become close friends. He sat behind me, and he bumped me on the leg and said, "What's the matter son?" I didn't know what to do, so I told him what happened.

He just laughed and said, "I'm going to tell you something, son. Them sons a bitches can beat you, but they can't eat you." And damned if that same night I wasn't back in another close game. I went out there and got the shakes again. I just said to myself, "you sons a bitches, you can beat me, but you can't eat me," and I got over it and sailed through and from that day on, I could hardly wait to get out there in those situations.

The way you think of it—at least the way I do—when you come into that situation [against Williams], I was flabbergasted in the fact that I was even in that situation and he brought me in.

You look at it as an opportunity; you don't look at it negatively. You look at it as a positive, because here's the great Ted Williams. Well, hell, everybody knows he should hit me, so if I can get him out, then that's a plus for me. If he gets a base hit, that's Ted Williams.

So I learned early on because of Satchel Paige that you go out there and you do the best you can do. You win some, lose some, and some are rained out.

I knew it was Ted Williams, but to me it was just another hitter. I just think he was a special hitter, and if I get him out I get him out, and if he gets a base hit, it won't be his first one.

Hal Raether

Right-handed pitcher

1954:	**Philadelphia Athletics**
1957:	**Kansas City Athletics**
Career Statistics:	**0–0, 0 saves, 6.75 ERA**

Ted Williams vs. Hal Raether:

0-for-0, walk, .000 batting average, 1.000 on-base percentage, .000 slugging percentage

July 4, 1954, bottom of the eighth inning, led off with a walk.

Hal Raether

YEAR	DATE	RESULT
1954	July 4	Walk

THAT WAS MY first major-league game.[87] I had just graduated from the University of Wisconsin when they still had baseball. I completed my eligibility in June and signed that month with the Philadelphia Athletics. They kept me after I signed with them, which I felt was a little bit unusual. Of course, they were not very good, so I suppose they needed all the talent they could find.

What was probably the highlight of the whole thing was that I had a friend from high school who was stationed in Newport, Rhode Island, and when I got to Boston, I thought, gee, I ought to really give him a call and let him know I'm with the Athletics. So I did call him and got him a ticket, and he came to the game with his wife and little daughter.

---

[87] July 4, 1954

He and I have remained friends ever since, and for him to have seen me pitch in the big leagues in the first place, and then against Ted Williams, was kind of a unique thing for our friendship.

Well, anyway, I don't recall what inning I got in, but I know we were [laughs], well, behind in the game.[88] I can remember standing out on the mound and looking out at the crowd—obviously the biggest crowd I'd ever played in front of—and saying to myself, "Here you are, what are you going to do about it [laughs]?"

I think it was in the second inning that I pitched in which Williams came up—I don't think it was the first inning—and I'm trying to remember some of the other ballplayers that the Red Sox had. Jimmy Piersall might have been playing at that time. I think he might have been in center field.[89] Anyway, all of a sudden, gee, there's Ted Williams swinging a bat, getting ready to face me, and I'm saying to myself, for a guy from Lake Mills, Wisconsin, this is pretty big stuff. I had never seen him play in person before, and all of a sudden, I'm playing against him.

I'm trying to remember who was catching for us at the time. Possibly Billy Shantz? Joe Astroth probably would have been the catcher.[90] Anyway, I think I had him 3–2 if I'm not mistaken, and then on the [next] pitch, I walked him on what I thought was a pretty good pitch. I'm kind of reminded of the fact that most umpires probably realized Ted Williams had better eyes then them, so if he didn't swing, it had to have been a ball.

Well anyway, he gets on first base and I was as nervous, of course, as you can imagine. What I was doing was—I had my foot on the rubber and in my nervousness, I take the ball out of my glove and throw it

---

[88] Raether entered the game in the seventh inning with the A's trailing, 7–0.

[89] Raether faced Williams in his second inning of work. Piersall did play, but came in mid-game for Jackie Jensen and played right field.

[90] Shantz started at catcher, but was replaced by Astroth, who was behind the plate when Raether entered the game.

back into my glove. Take it out, throw it in. Take it out, throw it in. And in the definition of the rules, that's a balk.

I was warned by the umpire not to do that. In the meantime, Ted Williams, who was on first base after I walked him, asked Lou Limmer, who was our first baseman, to come over and tell me to relax and that things would be okay. So I thought that was rather noteworthy. I somehow or other ended up getting out of the inning. I think I gave up one run in the two innings, if I'm not mistaken.[91] But basically that was my experience facing Ted Williams.

What's really been neat about it is that I've been able to tell my grandchildren about it—and anybody else who wants to listen to me— that I pitched against Ted Williams. It was a very proud moment of my life.

The next spring—I had a big-league contract, so I took spring training with what was then the Kansas City Athletics—and if you recall, Eddie Joost was fired, and the team was sold, and they brought over Lou Boudreau, who had been the manager for Boston that previous year. And he brought over his pitching coach. I remember they were telling stories about Ted Williams—meaning the coaches— of his extreme, acute eyesight. One of the stories they told us was that when he got out of the service, he rejoined the Red Sox and he was taking batting practice. He said, you know, something is wrong with the pitching rubber. He said that the pitcher, when he throws to me, seems to be out of whack a little bit. The rubber must be wrong. They put a transit on it apparently, and found out that, I think, the rubber was like an inch off or something on one end. It wasn't square with the plate. So he had great eyesight.

Another story they told was that—you know, most ballplayers do go to a lot of movies because they have time on their hands. And they'd step out of the hotel they were staying at, and Ted would come out and they'd say, Ted, what's playing in that theater down there four blocks

---

[91] In two innings of work, Raether gave up 1 run on 1 hit with 4 walks.

down from the hotel? And apparently, he'd—according to what they said—he could tell not only what the movie was, but who was playing in it.

They also said that he'd—when they were on the road and in a hotel room—he'd spend a lot of time with his bats, swinging and looking at his swing while looking at the mirror. So apparently he worked very hard at what he did, or was good at. That's just another story, whether it is true or not, I don't know. Those are the things I heard.

Phil Regan

Right-handed pitcher

1960–65:	Detroit Tigers
1966–68:	Los Angeles Dodgers
1968–72:	Chicago Cubs
1972:	Chicago White Sox
Career Statistics:	96–81, 92 saves, 3.84 ERA
National League All-Star:	1966

Ted Williams vs. Phil Regan

0-for-0, 0 RBI, 1 walk, .000 batting average, 1.000 on-base percentage, .000 slugging percentage

I ONLY FACED WILLIAMS one time—threw six pitches down and away—he never swung at one.

The 3–2 pitch was good, down and away. Catcher[92] said to me, "Phil, that is a strike to everyone else—not to Ted Williams."

Phil Regan

YEAR	DATE	RESULT
1960	Aug. 6	Walk

---

[92] Regan's catcher was Harry Chiti.

Marv Rotblatt

Left-handed pitcher

1948, 1950–51: ....Chicago White Sox
Career Statistics: .... 4–3, 2 saves, 4.82 ERA

Ted Williams vs. Marv Rotblatt:

2-for-7, 1 double, 0 home runs, 4 RBI, 0 walks, 0 strikeouts, 1 grounded into double play, .286 batting average, .286 on-base percentage, .429 slugging percentage

Marv Rotblatt

YEAR	DATE	RESULT
1948	July 23	Fly out
		Double (3 RBI)
1951	June 3	Fly out
		Grounded into DP
	June 22	Foul out
	June 24	Single
	July 12	Fly out

I SIGNED WITH THE Sox in 1948, and they told me they were going to put me right in the majors, or else I would have signed with the Dodgers, which I would have anyway. But it worked out because I'm short-sighted. I'm thinking, "wow, they offered me a chance to play right in the majors. I have to do it. I might never have this opportunity again." So I took it.

I'm there about three days—it was in June of '48[93]—and they finally put me in a game against the Tigers on a Sunday. The guys on the bench are all telling each other "Hey, put Marv in the game," so I heard about it.

---

[93] Rotblatt made his major-league debut on Sunday, July 4, 1948, in the first game of a doubleheader.

They bring me in the game in the eighth inning—two innings to go, we think. The first pitch I threw was up against the screen . . . I was a little nervous. So Mike Tresh, our catcher, comes out to me—this is true—he looks at me and says, "Marv, this is a ball. That's a glove. That's the mound. Now get the fucking ball over the plate." I believe he used the *f* word, but he might not have. He was a real gentleman. And I think I told you his son was Tom Tresh.

So I get all six guys out on ground balls. I don't know what I'm doing, but I get out of it. I can tell you an aside that happened. Bob Elson was our radio announcer, The Commander. He said he confronted Rogers Hornsby—a drunk and a boozer and a gambler who hangs out at the ballpark in the Bard's Room—that's where he drinks and eats. You know, the media room. So Elson went up to Hornbsy and says, "Rog, what did you think of that left-hander we brought up from the University of Illinois?" And he said [with a straight face], "Bob, if they turned the lights out in ballpark, I'd go 3–4 off of him." Which is a very funny remark for a guy like Rogers Hornsby to come up with.

The next game we're on the road in Fenway Park, bases loaded in the bottom of the eighth inning, and we're losing, 2–0. Bill Wight is pitching a very good game. They get the bases loaded with nobody out, and Ted Lyons brings me in. Wight was a lefty, why he was bringing me in—another lefty—I don't have the slightest idea. He wasn't exactly a genius manager, but Ted Lyons was a hell of a nice guy and a great pitcher. He was a competitor. You lose a game, a close game, he'd break down half the lockers. But on the surface was a real pleasant guy.

He brings me in the game, and again, I don't know what the hell I'm doing. I get Stan Spence, who led the league in hitting the year before for the Washington Senators.[94] The Red Sox got him, of course, to see if he could help them buy a pennant. I get him to 3–0—way

---

[94] Spence hit .279 for the Senators in 1947, which did not place him in the top ten of the leading hitters. Spence was 10th in hitting in the American League in 1946 (.292), 5th in 1944 (.316), and 3rd in 1942 (.323).

to get ahead of him, Marv. Fastball, 3–1, takes it. Fastball, 3–2, takes it. Three-and-two pitch, he hits a pop fly to the first baseman. I don't know what I'm doing, but I've got the out.

The next hitter is Vern Stephens. Good power hitter. I get him 3–0. I don't know how I'm getting the ball over the plate, but I am; I got guts. Then I get a strike, 3–1, then another one, 3–2, then he hits a pop fly to the shortstop for the second out.

I now have two outs and here comes Ted. I get him 3–0. I like to get ahead of these guys because I feel sorry for them—making a facetious remark, why didn't I. So the count is 3–0, and then I get a called strike, 3–1. Now, you tell me on God's earth, why Ted Williams, the greatest hitter of all time, is going to take a fastball off a little Jewish kid who is five-foot-six. With the count 3–1, he takes it right down the pike, 3–2. The next pitch ends up about four or five inches inside; I know that because I got it there. But he swings and pops it up to the second baseman for the third out, which if we count correctly, now means a one-two-three inning. And the crowd kind of gives me a nice standing ovation . . . and that was my first experience against Ted.

I came down from our dressing room to our ballpark and Joe Dobson, who pitched with us . . . I have a picture of us when we won twelve in a row on the road in 1951, which is damn hard to do *anywhere*. We won twelve in a row and I saved Dobson's game, as a matter of fact. He's holding me up in the picture.

Anyway, he said, "Hey, kid, how'd you throw that atom ball?"

"What do you mean?"

"Well, you throw it and they hit it at 'em."

It's a baseball joke. Never going to be funny anywhere.

So the next game he brings me in again. Think lightning can strike twice? Bases loaded, nobody out, and Ted Williams is the first guy I'm facing. First pitch, he's not taking a strike. He doubles off the monster; hit it hard. He just hit it out and got it up on the ball, no big deal. That was it for the time being. That was 1948. He [usually] pulls the ball, but he didn't pull it against me. My 110, 140 mile-an-hour fastball, he couldn't get around on it.[95]

The next time I faced him was 1951, and I faced him a couple of times. I got him out, but he beat me in a game in Fenway Park; it had to be in August. We were in first place at the time, barely, against the Yankees. He brings me in the game—but my fault though—first guy up, I walked. You don't do that in a tie ballgame, bottom of the ninth inning. My fault.

Next batter was bunting. Bob Dillinger comes in from [third] base, no one was covering third base. It was Dom DiMaggio, beats it out.

John Pesky comes up next, first and second, nobody out. And I'm a good fielder—I actually started a triple play.[96] So he bunts it down third, and I grab it right off the mound. After he bunted, I'm there, I'm ready, picking up the ball, ready to go to third base, and here's this schmuck, Bob Dillinger, standing next to me again. He was a good hitter, but a nitwit. A flake.

So now I have the bases loaded, nobody out, and of course I'll embellish the statement and say I looked into the dugout, and what are they doing? They're packing up their bags. They weren't really packing up the bags, but it's a good logical idea to get a head start.

So the first pitch to Ted, I throw him a fastball—extra fastball—I threw it by him, I know I did. So he turns and says something to Phil Masi, who after the game tells me he said, "What'd that kid do,

---

[95] Rotblatt pitched twice against the Red Sox in 1948, and they did come on back-to-back days—July 22 and 23. However, Williams did not play in the game on July 22. Rotblatt relieved Bill Wight on July 23, and pitched three innings, facing Williams twice in that game—flying out to left field in the fifth inning and doubling with the bases loaded in the seventh inning. Stan Spence played on July 22, but not on July 23. Also, Vern Stephens batted after Williams in the lineup on July 23, not before.

[96] On May 13, 1951, Rotblatt caught a pop bunt off the bat of Cleveland's Jim Hegan before it hit the ground, then threw to Chico Carrasquel to catch the runner off second, and Carrasquel threw to first to complete the triple play.

take something off that pitch?" I threw my best shot! I know damn well I threw it right by him—swing and a miss. Unless he just missed the ball, and Williams doesn't miss many fastballs down the middle.

The next pitch was a curveball—swing and a miss. I got him 0–2, and my changeup at that time was my best pitch. When I throw [my changeup] to right-handers, it tails away from the hitter. Mickey Mantle hit the ball off me three times—twice to the first baseman on spin jobs off the end of the bat. He was way out in front of it. It would tail in to the lefties, which was a little dangerous because you can get away with it; you can fool them and they can get wood on the ball if they're able to.

So sure enough, I got him 0–2, and we call a changeup. I tried to get it way outside, you know, try to get it on the outside corner and end up there. It went on the outside corner initially, and I fooled him on it, he was out in front. He hit a little ground ball, a dribbler past me, beats it out, ball game.

The next day I see him in the outfield. "Hitter my ass," I tell him.

"Marv, it looks like a line drive in the books." Can't argue with that![97]

The couple of times I met him—I'm selling insurance now. One time, I did a crazy thing. We were doing an insurance course in Boston. My home office was New England Life. It was actually the oldest charter company in America. We had a school there. So we go to school, and there's a buddy of mine who played a little pro ball, played in Class C, one of the agents. I said let's go out to the ballpark, I want to throw batting practice. Out of the clear blue! I'm going to throw fucking batting practice to the Red Sox—like I can get away with it!

So we go out there, and fortunately [for us] it rained, so they didn't have batting practice. We go to the dressing room. I'm trying to

---

[97] On June 24, 1951, Williams hit an RBI infield single off Rotblatt in the bottom of the seventh inning to give Boston a 6–5 lead in an eventual 8–6 Red Sox win, in which Rotblatt would suffer the loss.

remember the right-handed pitcher who played at Fenway Park the year before, when Pinky Higgins was the manager of Birmingham. He was now the manager of the Red Sox. Real nice guy, real nice guy.

We go into his dressing room—I can't think of the name of the guy; it wasn't Denny Galehouse; it wasn't Tex Hughson; it was a good right-handed pitcher with the Red Sox, and I'm sorry I can't think of his name.[98] Well, he recognizes me in street clothes!

He says, "Marv Rotblatt, what are you doing here?" Bah-ba-ba-dum. He says, "Come in and say hello to Pinky Higgins, he'd like to see you." Now why would Pinky Higgins like to see me? Rhetorical question.

So I go in there and the first thing he says is, "Hey, remember Marv Rotblatt?" And Pinky Higgins says to me, "Changeup my ass." That's what he says. First three words to me, because I had beaten Birmingham—when I won 22 in 1950. I was there at school in like 1957 or '58; I was out of baseball. He remembered. That year I was 6–0 against Birmingham.

So I see Ted and tell him that I'm in the insurance business. He says who you with? I say New England, and he says, "Oh, I have a policy with them. I got a policy with about ten companies." Probably can't say no to an offer. I didn't have the guts to say, 'Ted, let's make it eleven,' but he was friendly as hell.

I saw him two more times after that. I saw him when I was playing semi-pro ball and selling insurance in 1959. That was the year the [White] Sox won the pennant. I'm pitching batting practice with them; I'm also pitching with the Cubs because I'm playing semi-pro ball. I was 12–0 that year! They were riding the hell out of me. Get the old guy off the field, bah-bah-bah-dum. But I was tough and a good competitor.

---

[98] The player Rotblatt refers to likely was Frank Sullivan, who played for Higgins in Birmingham in 1950, and pitched for the Red Sox from 1953–60.

So after batting practice, I wanted to go get an autographed ball for one of my clients from Ted. The dressing rooms were next to each other in Chicago those days. I walked into the dressing room because I knew the clubhouse guy—it was a guy named Sharky Colledge. Ted is on the rubbing table and I go up to talk to him. He says, "Marv, I want to tell you a story about the ball game last night. I'm up, we're losing by a run, top of the ninth inning, and they bring in Gerry Staley." Staley was a relief pitcher that year and helped them win the pennant. "I'm in the batting box, and he throws *nine straight* knuckleballs warming up. What's his first pitch going to be, Marv?"

I said, "Fastball."

He says, "Right. I looked for the fastball, and I got the fastball, I was so anxious, I hit a one-bouncer back to him, I broke the fucking bat. I was so pissed because I was way in front of it and I guessed right."

See, you'd say the average guy would say, he threw nine knuckleballs warming up, he's going to throw a knuckleball, right? He was setting him up. I knew that because I would do the same thing, having pitching experience and so on.

Then in batting practice a couple of times, when I was still playing ball, I'd do my wind sprints and then come back down on the field and watch him hit because he was a pleasure to watch. He'd be behind the cage talking to Nellie Fox or Eddie Robinson about hitting and helping them. They had a second baseman named Bobby Doerr, who hit around .300, .310 with the Red Sox in those days. Ted once said of Bobby Doerr in an article, "I could have made him a .350 hitter if he'd have listened." That's the kind of rapport he had with ballplayers.

The last time I saw him—alive of course—was when he became the manager of the Washington Senators for a year after he retired from ball. He didn't exactly work at it very hard—you might say hardly working. I didn't have a lot of experiences with him, but enough to remember.

Nobody talks about this and it was a big happening. It was the last game of the year [in 1948], and they're [the Red Sox] playing us at Comiskey Park. And Cleveland, who they were tied with, had already lost, so they were half a game ahead going into the last game of the year. Williams is up and we're ahead by a run, first and third, two out. And they warned John Pesky, he was on first base. The coach at first base must have told Pesky to be aware of his [Bill Wight's] move, because he had the best move I'd ever seen in baseball, and I'm counting all the great moves like Warren Spahn, Whitey Ford, guys like that. He had a move that was dynamite. One split second and he'd already have the ball at first base.

So sure enough, on the first pitch, Williams has the bat on his shoulder, ready to hit, and Bill Wight picked him [Pesky] off. End of ball game. That's the way the ball game ended with the Red Sox, with Williams hanging with the bat in his hand. They walked off the field and I said, "They're beat." And the next day in the playoff game at Fenway Park, Boudreau hit two home runs, a double, a single, and drove in about five runs, and that was it. But they never talk about it. Imagine getting beat with a guy getting picked off first base and Ted Williams with a bat in his hand. They never talk about it. To me, it is a very important story about Ted Williams.[99]

There's an article from 1988 in *Sports Illustrated* called "Nemesis." That's a funny article. Army has Navy. Muhammad Ali has Joe Frazier.

---

[99] It is unclear which game Rotblatt is talking about, but the Red Sox actually ended the regular season with four straight wins over the Indians and Yankees. Boston lost eight games to the White Sox in 1948: A pair of 4–3 games to the White Sox in a May 23 doubleheader in Chicago; 5–3 at Fenway on June 12; 3–1 in Chicago on June 24; lost three of four in early August in Chicago (4–3 on August 6; 5–1 on August 7; 2–1 in game two of a doubleheader on August 8); and 17–10 in Chicago on September 15.

Oklahoma has Nebraska. Ted Williams has Marv Rotblatt, with a question mark. Great article. We don't know who started the rumor; it must have been by Rotblatt. That's how it ends, which is funny.

I had no idea. One of my son's buddies told him about it back in 1988: Hey, your dad is in *Sports Illustrated*. It's an honor to have gotten in there.

He was the best. I enjoyed watching him play. After a workout, we'd come downstairs and hang around the dugout by the batting cage just to watch him hit, because he had such great control of the bat.

Bob Shaw

Right-handed pitcher

1957–58:	Detroit Tigers
1958–61:	Chicago White Sox
1961:	Kansas City Athletics
1962–63:	Milwaukee Braves
1964-66:	San Francisco Giants
1966–67:	New York Mets
1967:	Chicago Cubs
Career Statistics:	108–98, 32 saves, 3.52 ERA
National League All-Star:	1962

Ted Williams vs. Bob Shaw:

4-for-14, 2 doubles, 1 home run, 3 RBI, 3 walks (1 intentional), 0 strike-outs, 1 sacrifice fly, 1 double play, .286 batting average, .389 on-base percentage, .643 slugging percentage

Home Runs Allowed:

No. 509, July 27, 1960, at Boston

I THINK I WAS very fortunate against Ted Williams, but I consider him probably the best hitter that I ever faced. And then when I looked at the statistics, I realized that I did fairly well [against him]. I got a real swollen head.

In '59, he said in some article that I was the third-toughest right-hander for him to face. Well, woooo. That kind of blew my mind. But he was outstanding. The things that stick out in my mind are things that you've probably heard already.

If you were warming up in the bullpen, he would just watch every move you made. He studied you. I also did some lecturing, and I was on the dais with him, and he was very intelligent. If you were talking about fishing, he knew what he was talking about. If he was talking about baseball, he knew what he was talking about.

He believed in that four-degree upstroke. He was trying to get that ball out of the park. Now, you could argue—Joe Gordon used to teach hitting down on the ball, [Hank] Aaron, I think, hit down on the ball—but he really knew what he was talking about. He was a student of the game and a very impressive individual.

I do remember the home run. Bad news, yeah, I remember that. He hit it in Fenway Park way out there where that wall is. He hit it to right-center field. I can still see it going.

I had to keep the ball down, and that's the way I pitched. Now I'll tell you one thing, you didn't want to knock him down. There's a few guys in the league that you knew that if you knocked him down, he'd get pissed and be a better hitter. Because back in those days, you know, you'd loosen up some guys pretty good. But you didn't want to do that with Williams. We would talk about that, because he would just became a better hitter. Now that doesn't mean you don't pitch in, but you don't want to try to intentionally knock him down because the results were not going to be good.

Bob Shaw

YEAR	DATE	RESULT
1958	June 18	Sac fly (1 RBI)
	July 27	Intentional walk
1959	May 13	Fly out
		Fly out
		Single
		Ground out
	Sept. 13	Ground out
1960	May 12	Fielder's choice
	June 12	Walk
		Line out
		Double
	June 24	Line out
		Walk
		Double (1 RBI)
		Fly out
	July 27	Ground out
		Grounded into DP
		Home run (1 RBI)

When [I think about my] toughest out . . . if I had to name a couple guys, I'd mention Jackie Brandt, Tito Francona, Bob Lillis—a little shortstop for Houston. Now [Mickey] Mantle, he hit some gigantic home runs off of me, but I could still get him out.

I would have to say I was extremely fortunate [against Williams]. I mean, when I look at the stats—4–14, .286—hey, that's not too damn bad against him, someone I consider probably the best hitter I ever saw.

He would not swing at a bad ball. No matter what the score was, what the situation, he was not going to swing at a bad ball. But you still had to pitch to him carefully. Now when I look at it, I see where I did give him three walks. You had to be careful. He would not swing at a bad ball, which of course makes it more difficult. Some guys you can get them to go after a bad pitch, but not him.

I would pitch him low and away—because my ball sank—was probably my best bet. As I look back and reflect on it, I know that if I had to throw a strike, I had to throw it low and away to him. He was a very good breaking-ball hitter, so you had to be very, very careful about that. For me, my best shot would be low and away.

He'll hit the high ball, too. But my point is that I wasn't very effective high. Even if that's his strength, I had to go my strength against his strength because I was not effective up, as the ball would straighten out. I was not really overpowering, with a great fastball. The ball moved well; I had a good slider, a good sinker, but for me, reflecting back, if I gotta throw a strike, I still would rather throw the sinking fastball.

I don't know whether it was in Chicago [the last time I saw him], if it was a big clinic and I can't remember, Spokane or wherever it was, but he was there. They had him lecturing on hitting and they had me lecturing on pitching, and then for some reason or other, they got me and him and somebody else up there answering questions that the coaches might ask. But I got a chance to meet him personally, and he was a very dynamic person. If he walked into a room, he kind of electrified the room. He had quite a presence.

George Spencer

Right-handed pitcher

1950–55:	**New York Giants**
1958, 1960:	**Detroit Tigers**
Career Statistics:	**16–10, 9 saves, 4.05 ERA**

Ted Williams vs. George Spencer

0-for-1
May 2, 1958, bottom of the eighth inning, led off by lining out.

George Spencer

YEAR	DATE	RESULT
1958	May 2	Line out

WE WERE IN Boston and I was sitting out in the bullpen with my buddies. It was the first time I had ever been in the American League, and we were just talking naturally about Ted Williams, and they were good enough to tell me that if he hadn't seen or faced you before, he would not hit the first pitch. Well this is pretty good information for a pitcher to have, or at least you'd think.

Anyway, I get in the ball game—I think it was the eighth inning or so—and here's Ted Williams as the first hitter I'm going to face. I get my warm-up pitches in, and while I'm warming up, he's about halfway between the on-deck circle and home plate . . . and he's watching me like an eagle.

I finally finish up my warm-up pitches and I look up, and Dick Gernert was in the on-deck circle, and he hollered at Williams, and Ted walks back over to talk to Dick. Now I know exactly what Dick is telling Ted, because I had pitched against Dick in the American Association a couple of years [earlier].

Ted then comes back up to the plate and here we go. I was a sinkerball pitcher, and I knew Dick Gernert was telling him that he's a sinkerball pitcher, so watch for it low and away. But my buddies out there in the bullpen, they'd also told me that he won't hit the first pitch. Now I'm more inclined to go along with my own team.

I throw the first pitch, which was low and away. Good pitch. It was either a strike or just off of the plate. And he swings at it and hits a line drive to Ray Boone, who was playing first base. Boone thought the ball was going to carry and started to jump after it, and it was a sinker. Boonie caught it just about waist-high. If he hadn't jumped, he might have ended up in right field, the ball was hit that hard.

On how I came out of the experience on pitching to Williams . . . well thank God he didn't hit that ball back through the box! But that was my experience with Ted Williams. There's not much to it. I should have told Boonie to charge that ball, but it was quite an experience. It was one of the highlights, I think, of my career.

It was interesting to find about my teammates; those guys didn't do me any favors. Apparently they were giving me some good information, but I think the fact that Dick Gernert was in the on-deck circle and called Ted over and explained to him what he thought the kind of pitcher I was, gave Williams the edge. Because he was looking for a pitch and he got it. He didn't pop it up, I'll tell you that.

I can't remember what year it was, but I was in the Red Sox organization and went to spring training. I had hurt my arm in the winter time and was trying to rehab. You know, I can throw, and I'm starting to come around in the strengthening of the arm, and I'm doing halfway decent. The Red Sox go on the road, and they leave Rico Petrocelli.

Left him at home and Ted was one of the coaches who stayed at home. Anyway, I'm going to throw some batting practice to Rico. I get all warmed up and there we go, and I'm on the mound throwing batting practice. Now when I throw batting practice, I wasn't one of those guys who tried to lay the ball in and see how far the hitters could hit it. I'm trying to help the hitters; at least that's the way I felt. I won't say that I'm wide open, but I'm putting some pretty decent stuff on the ball. I threw two different fastballs—a cross-seam fastball and a sinking fastball. So we're in the process of taking the batting practice and Ted is behind the cage and I could hear him. I would throw a cross-seam fastball and hear him say, "Did you see it, did you?" Then I would throw the sinker, and he wouldn't say anything. I was mixing up the pitches, and I'm saying to myself—and I'm an older pitcher and I'm saying to myself, "What in the world am I doing that he can call every pitch that I'm throwing?" And I'm only throwing the two fastballs, I'm not throwing a breaking ball or anything. But, anyway, I didn't ask him what I was doing. I should have, but as smart as I am, I guess, why would you want to know what you're doing that he's reading? But that was another experience with Ted.

In that spring training, it was interesting to me—he had a voice that was absolutely explosive. We would be in the ballpark, and he was great with the fungo. He could lay that ball—where you're running the pitchers or something like that—he'd lay that ball out there, just off to where you couldn't quite catch it. Somebody would do something out there, teasing him or something like that, and you could hear him and his favorite thing to say was: *"Is that right?"* And it would just fill the ballpark. I don't think I've ever been around anybody who had a voice like he had in that ballpark. But he'd wear those pitchers out.

We were in the dressing room one day after the main part of the club had gone on the road. We were in the clubhouse and of course, when you're around Ted Williams, you have to be discussing baseball. So at one point, he looks over at me and said, "Spencer, you're an older guy, why does a baseball curve? When you throw a curveball, why does it curve?" I said, "Well, I think what happens is when you put the spin on the ball, there's some aerodynamics involved there that the spin of the ball causes the ball to curve."

And he didn't say too much, but he walked over to a trash can that was there, and he grabbed a big piece of cardboard that was in there and grabbed a marking pen. And he drew a wing, with, of course, the upper part of the wing was the curvature on it, and the lower part was flat. He had been in the Air Corps doing the war, and he went through the technicalities of why an airplane can fly. The fact that the air underneath goes straight, and the air up above has to go up above the wing. That was his explanation of why the curveball curves. And who am I to argue with him?

I always thought he was very interesting. It was a great experience being around him . . . one of the highlights of my career, and I'm glad I had the opportunity.

Dick Stigman

Left-handed pitcher

1960–61:	Cleveland Indians
1962–65:	Minnesota Twins
1966:	Boston Red Sox
Career Statistics:	46–54, 16 saves, 4.03 ERA
American League All-Star:	1960

Ted Williams vs. Dick Stigman

0-for-2, 1 RBI, 1 walk, 1 strikeout, .000 batting average, .333 on-base percentage, .000 slugging percentage

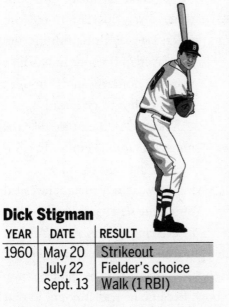

Dick Stigman

YEAR	DATE	RESULT
1960	May 20	Strikeout
	July 22	Fielder's choice
	Sept. 13	Walk (1 RBI)

SINCE WILLIAMS WAS at the end of his career, I can't really say my success against him was all that great. I just felt privileged to have pitched to him. My best memory is a game on May 20, in Cleveland, when I struck him out on three pitches, probably all perfect; he never swung the bat, but just whirled around and walked back to the dugout.

Al Kaline was the toughest out because I faced him more than Williams (no discredit to Williams, having only faced him three times).[100]

Obviously pitching to someone so famous made your heart beat faster, and would bring your adrenaline to its peak.

---

[100] Kaline had 54 plate appearances against Stigman, going 9–43 with 9 hits, 2 home runs, 5 RBI, 10 walks, 6 strikeouts, and a .209 batting average.

Wes Stock

Right-handed pitcher

1959–64: .... **Baltimore Orioles**
1964–67: .... **Kansas City Athletics**
Career Statistics: .... **27–13, 22 saves, 3.60 ERA**

Ted Williams vs. Wes Stock

0-for-1, 1 strikeout
August 21, 1960, bottom of the ninth inning, led off by striking out swinging.

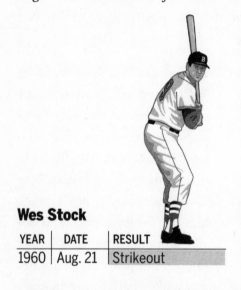

Wes Stock

YEAR	DATE	RESULT
1960	Aug. 21	Strikeout

TO START OFF, I only pitched against him one time. I saw his last home run when I was with Baltimore, and we played in Boston, and he hit a two-run homer[101] in the bottom of the eighth to go ahead.

Then, in the top of the ninth—I think Pinky Higgins was the manager—and when the inning was ready to start, he called time and sent Carroll Hardy in to exchange places with. And he [Williams] ran all the way hard, ran right into the dugout and down and up the runway, and for ten minutes they could not start the game because he would not come out and take a bow. Because he had announced that was his last game. So that's the only thing I know about Ted.

I was in bullpen [during the game]. He almost hit one in the at-bat before. When you're a kid coming up, you don't realize all the history to it, you know.

---

[101] It was actually a solo home run.

The slider was one of my best pitches. So I mean, coming up, I wanted to be successful, so I went with my best stuff. But I had very good control and I just struck him out on a slider [swinging]. I don't think he took too many pitches.

I did strike him out. He was forty-five and I was twenty-five, I think, and I struck him out on a slider. Paul Richards was the manager, and as soon as the inning was over, he said to me—and I don't know what day it was, but it might have been the day before. I wasn't in that ballgame [Williams' last]. Anyway, he said to me, "Hey son, you better get that baseball." And I didn't know what he was talking about. I think he was the last out of the inning for me; I struck him out on the slider, which I guess he didn't like. I heard later on that he didn't like the slider in baseball. I never knew what Paul Richards was talking about. Of course, now, after I realize it and everything . . . because he would have signed it. Ted was that kind of a guy.

I can remember when he was managing the Washington Senators and being in Baltimore . . . what was the last year of his home run, his last year playing? 1960? See, I had just come up. We had to come over earlier, because we just took a bus over there, and the guys got out, and he had both clubs down there and was teaching them how to hit! And the umpires came out there and said, "Ted, the gates are about ready to go open, you can't do this!" He said, "These guys want to learn something about hitting, I'm going to teach 'em." Both clubs. He didn't care. That's just the way Ted was.[102]

---

[102] Williams managed the Senators from 1969–71. Stock's final year in Baltimore was 1964, and his last year in the majors was 1967. However, Stock was the pitching coach for the Milwaukee Brewers from 1970–71, so this is likely when the incident took place.

I met him, talked to him a couple of times after his career was over, and he was a big fly fisherman and stuff like that. You'd mention your name and he'd say, "Oh, yeah, I know who you are." Whether he did that on purpose or not I don't know, but he'd sit and talk to you. But he didn't like the press; he wouldn't talk to the press.

I think the next year [after he retired], we happened to be up there [in Boston], and they had a day to honor him the next year, and we were there for that, but I can't remember much from that day. But he would not come out and take a bow for that [his last] game. No way. I don't know what it was. But of course, I didn't see him in his real great career. I saw [Mickey] Mantle and, to me, he was the greatest player I ever saw.

At that age—1960, it was—I had just been called up in June or July, and I'm just up there wanting to make the big leagues. I came up for about a month and had to go back down, and then I got called back up in June or July. It must have been July, because my son was born the night before I won by first ball game. No, he was born the next day; I won my first ball game on July 31, 1960, and my first son was born on August 1.

When you just come up to the big leagues in those days, you were just in awe of every player, so it didn't make any difference. I can remember Jimmy Piersall in one of my first games. He talked up there while he was hitting. Things like that you remember. I became more in awe of him as I got older in the game and realized what he [Ted] did and what people talked about the things he had done.

I did get an autographed ball from him; I was smart enough to do that. I can't remember when I got it, because he came to a big clinic out here in Washington [that] I was involved in. I probably got it then, but I can't remember exactly. You know, when you're in the big leagues your first year, and you're a big country boy, any of the ballplayers . . . was in awe of them all.

Now that I think about it, as a young guy, I wish I observed more of those guys. But Ted, the only time I pitched against him; at least I got to pitch against him and I was lucky to strike him out. But again, he was forty-five and I was twenty-five. He was over the hill [laughs].

Virgil Trucks

Right-handed pitcher

1941–43, 1945–52: ....Detroit Tigers
1953: ....St. Louis Browns
1953–55: .... Chicago White Sox
1956: ....Detroit Tigers
1957–58: ....Kansas City Athletics
1958: ....New York Yankees
Career Statistics: .... 177–135, 30 saves, 3.39 ERA
American League All-Star: 1949, 1954

Ted Williams vs. Virgil Trucks (data incomplete)

32-for-92, 6 doubles, 1 triple, 9 home runs,[103] 17 RBI,[104] 20 walks (2 intentional), 9 strikeouts, 1 hit by pitch, .348 batting average, .469 on-base percentage, .728 slugging percentage

Home Runs Allowed:

No. 108, June 24, 1942, at Detroit
No. 115, August 2, 1942 (game two), at Detroit
No. 146, April 26, 1946 (game two), at Detroit
No. 174, May 19, 1947 (game two), at Boston
No. 189, August 2, 1947, at Boston
No. 226, May 4, 1949, at Detroit
No. 236, June 5, 1949, (game one) at Detroit
No. 243, July 16, 1949, at Detroit
No. 320, August 29, 1951, at Detroit

---

[103] Of the known available box scores, Williams hit 9 home runs off Trucks. But the data is available for all of Williams' 521 career home runs, and he ended up with 12 off Trucks, the most he hit off any pitcher.

[104] Retrosheet.org has more data of Williams vs. Trucks, but does not include RBI. Baseball-reference.com lists Williams with 17 RBI in 74 at-bats (93 plate appearances) vs. Trucks.

No. 342, June 3, 1954, at Boston
No. 437, June 23, 1957 (game two), at Boston
No. 444, July 16, 1957, at Kansas City

Virgil Trucks (data incomplete; missing 1946-47)

YEAR	DATE	RESULT
1948	May 5	Ground out
		Strikeout
		Fly out
		Single
	May 18	Grounded into DP
		Strikeout
		Double (RBI)
	July 29	Fly out
		Pop out
		Ground out
		Ground out
	Sept. 1	Fly out
		Strikeout
		Double
1949	May 4	Ground out
		Strikeout
		Home run (1 RBI)
		Single
	May 22	Walk
		Fly out
		Double
		Ground out
		Ground out
		Grounded into DP
	June 5	Home run (2 RBI)
		Hit by pitch
		Walk
		Walk
	July 16	Home run (2 RBI)
		Fly out
	Aug. 8	Triple
		Single
		Fly out

YEAR	DATE	RESULT
1950	May 9	Fly out
		Fly out
		Fly out
1951	May 3	Walk
	July 21	Ground out
		Walk
		Reached on error
	Aug. 5	Single
		Walk
		Fly out
	Aug. 29	Strikeout
		Home run (3 RBI)
		Walk
		Single
1952	April 30	Single
		Strikeout
1953	Aug. 27	Single
		Ground out
		Ground out
		Fly out
	Sept. 13	Ground out
1954	June 3	Strikeout
		Fly out
		Walk
		Home run (3 RBI)
		Fly out
	June 27	Strikeout
		Ground out
		Single (1 RBI)
	July 23	Fly out

YEAR	DATE	RESULT
1955	June 2	Walk
		Walk
		Fly out
	July 23	Single
		Strikeout
	Aug. 3	Fly out
		Intentional walk
	Aug. 30	Single
		Walk (1 RBI)
1956	June 5	Fly out
		Pop out
		Ground out
	July 20	Ground out
		Line out
		Walk
	July 30	Fly out
		Ground out
		Walk
		Ground out
1957	May 1	Ground out
		Fly out
		Walk
	May 18	Double (1 RBI)
		Walk
	June 23	Home run (1 RBI)
	July 16	Walk
		Walk
		Ground out
		Home run (1 RBI)
	July 23	Walk
		Fly out
		Out (unknown)

THERE'S NO ONE today better than him. He's the best hitter I ever saw or ever will see. He just had that great hand-eye coordination; you couldn't fool him on pitches. I never even tried to fool him, because it would just be wasting a pitch anyway. So I just pitched him power against power. He liked that because he knew he had the over power. He could hit anybody, I don't care who they were.

He [Ted] always wanted to play in Detroit, but really, the right-field fence in Boston was not bad as it went out, but down the line it was only 300 feet or something . . . less than 300. That was the smallest ballpark in the major leagues when I played. I would have rather faced him in Detroit any time. Oh yeah, he could pull the ball. He'd pull the ball all the time, just like I said, the second baseman—when you're talking about the shift—he'd hit balls between the first baseman and second baseman, and they could almost shake hands. He'd hit a line drive right past him. I never ever saw him hit a ball to the left of second base. Never. It didn't work. You could put the whole infield over there, and it wouldn't work. And you know [how] they talk about always wanting him to try to go to left field? He said no, I'm not going into my batting stance to try to go to left field. They pitch me out there; I'll pull the ball anyway. And he could. He could pull it off anybody on the outside corner. So he didn't worry about them putting [on the shift]. He wasn't going to change his batting style.

I tried to throw him some sliders inside and he'd just lay off those because they were balls. If I threw the fastball and it was over the plate, it was a goner. He was just phenomenal, that's all. His hand-eye coordination was terrific and he would always figure out a pitcher. Facing him two or three times, he'd know ten times later if that same pitcher pitched against him, he knew everything he threw. And he knew *the way* he threw it, too.

You'd try to hide the ball from him, and he would still pick it up. He'd see that ball and he could see those seams and he knew what you were throwing. If you showed him that ball at all—just up here before you release it—he could pick it up right there. He could see a gnat on a gnat's nest from 100 yards.

He was absolutely terrific and was a good friend. He was good to me and I was nice to him. I think I was too nice to him on the mound.

I faced him for fourteen or fifteen years. That's still not one [home run] a year. I know one time in Detroit I was going into the game, and it was 0–0 in the seventh, and he hit a home run off me, and they won the ball game, 1–0—because we didn't score any runs![105] It seemed that way every time I pitched, we didn't get any.

He just liked me, I guess, and he put me and Gaylord Perry in there [to his Hitters Hall of Fame] as the last two guys to go in [before his death], and we were both pitchers. He thought we were great enough to go in as pitchers. He had several pitchers, I don't know how many were in there, but there were quite a few. We were just the last ones.

He told me when he came back from the service [in Korea] and we were in Boston—it was the first time I had seen him since he got out of the service—and I went over and told him that I was glad to see him back and wished him luck. And he told me later that I was the only player from the opposition that ever mentioned that to him. And that's a true story, because I know I was there when he told me.

I know if he had not gone into the service, he'd probably be leading the home run circle. I think he would have had 800 or 1,000. If you look at the amount of at-bats he missed, I guarantee if you figured it out, you'd see he'd hit at least 800 home runs or more.

There was no way that they [other good hitters of that era] could touch him. Of course, [Mickey] Mantle was a great hitter. After all, he was a switch-hitter, and the first real good switch-hitter that came up. Another good switch-hitter nobody knew about was Roy Cullenbine. Now Cullenbine was the best switch-hitter before Mantle. I've not seen one since who has been better than Mantle. I don't know how great Williams would have been if he were a switch-hitter. If he could hit like he did left-handed—jiminy—it would have been something awesome.

He was great. There's just none greater, and I'm glad I got to know him personally and been able to pitch against him. I got to know him

---

[105] On June 24, 1942, Williams homered off Trucks in the top of the seventh inning of a 1–0 game. It was Williams' 108th career home run and his first off Trucks.

[well], oh, the last ten years he lived. I would talk to him at least once or twice, maybe more, a month. I lived only about 200 miles from him. I would go up to see him and he had a golf tournament every year that I played in. And his museum was there, too. I got to know him, I guess, as well as anybody. We would sit and talk when I would visit. I would to go his house . . . he had an electronic gate on his yard where you couldn't get in, and the gate was probably 100 yards from the house; they had to let you in and out. I went in his house, had pictures taken with him in his kitchen, and spent quite a bit of time with him. We talked about everything. We talked about our days of playing, players, he would talk about pitchers he hit against, and he had me there to back up everything he said.

Oh, he loved to face me. He [looked forward] to hit against me. He loved to hit against the Detroit staff, Newhouser and Trout; mainly because we all threw hard, and of course, Newhouser had a pretty good curveball, and he would throw that to him. But he hit Newhouser right on. I bet you Newhouser didn't strike him out much. I only remember one time that he did.[106] I can only recall one time striking him out myself. And that upset him. He turned and walked away, and on the way back to the bench, he hit the bat on the ground with the little knob—and his handle wasn't bigger than a finger—and it just snapped in two. I said, I hope he doesn't have any more. I hope he had to use somebody else's bat. I don't know what would happen if he were playing today with all those bats breaking up like they do. Jiminy. I didn't want to agitate him in any way. He hit me well enough. If I had agitated him, there's no telling. I probably never would have gotten him out.

He was just a great guy and a great hitter and not appreciated as much as he should have been in Boston. But of course, he wasn't very good to the fans there. In that field, they booed him all the time, espe-

---

[106] Retrosheet.com has incomplete data of Williams vs. Newhouser, but lists 6 strike-outs in 64 at-bats.

cially the fans sitting out in left field right near him. I'll never forget one day we were playing them and I wasn't pitching, but the ball was hit to left field. It was a ground ball between third and short, and it went between his legs. He turned around to go back to the fence to get it—he didn't have a long ways to go—but he went back and then he made a bad throw and the fans booed him . . . especially the ones in left field. Then he came up to bat in that half of the inning, and they booed him when he came to bat. And he just politely hit a home run. As he rounded the bases, when he got to first, he gave [the fans in right field] them the middle finger; then he got to second and gave it to the [fans in the] bleachers in center field; then he got to third and gave it to those bunch around the third-base line. And when he got to home plate, he gave it to the press box.

They fined him $5,000 for that. What happened was, the fans took up the $5,000 to pay the fine, but that wasn't permissible. You had to pay your own fine if you were fined. So he took that money and he couldn't keep it, so he gave it to the Jimmy Fund. That was his big organization. He originated that.

Another time we were playing Boston and [Joe] Ginsberg was catching and Williams came up and [walked on] four straight pitches, and Joe's questioning the umpire about it. On the last one, he said, "Bill"—Bill Summers was the umpire. He said, "Bill, don't you think that ball was a strike?" And Bill said to Joe, "Mr. Ginsberg, Mr. Williams will let you know when it is a strike." And that's about the sum of it. He could umpire his own ball game. I never, ever saw a bad pitch called on him, but I never saw him *swing* at a bad pitch, either. If it wasn't a strike, he'd just put the bat on his shoulder and let it go by. But he was always set to swing if it happened to be over that plate, and especially to his liking. You see, pitchers knew that they couldn't just throw balls. If they did, he was going to walk every time. They knew they wanted to get him out. All of them wanted to pitch against him, naturally, or they wouldn't have anything to talk about the rest of their life if they didn't.

It's really amazing and too bad that everybody couldn't have seen him play. The same way with me; I would have loved to have seen [Ty] Cobb and those guys play. They were great, too. I'm not taking away from them. The players today think they invented the game. They don't even know who [Abner] Doubleday was. Some of them don't know who Ted Williams was. If they don't, they don't care about base-ball, because I always cared about Cobb and [Babe] Ruth and [Lou] Gehrig and all those guys. They set the stage for us. We tried to set the stage for these guys. We did for 'em to make more money.

His swing was as fluid as you can get; that's why he was such a great hitter—his timing, his swinging. I never saw him hold on a pitch, like some hitters will part-swing. Not once. Of course, I didn't see him every game, but I saw quite a few. I never saw him do anything close to that.

Pitching him low and behind would hold him to a double. That's about the sum of it, too. I'll tell ya, the infield didn't play close up. The second baseman was almost out there with the right-fielder. The shortstop was on that side of second base, and the third baseman was right back of second base. There was nothing on the third-base side. Even the outfielders were shifted, but not as much as the other players, the infield. But the outfield shifted as well. When you got a hitter like him, you have to try to play some shift or something to try to get him out, and that wasn't easy.

Oh, I got him out a few times, and I felt good about it, being able to get him out at all.

Ozzie Van Brabant

Right-handed pitcher

1954: .... **Philadelphia Athletics**
1955: .... **Kansas City Athletics**
Career Statistics: .... **0–2, 0 saves, 7.85 ERA**

Ted Williams vs. Ozzie Van Brabant

*1-for-4, 0 RBI, 1 walk, 0 strikeouts, .250 batting average, .400 on-base
percentage, .250 slugging percentage*

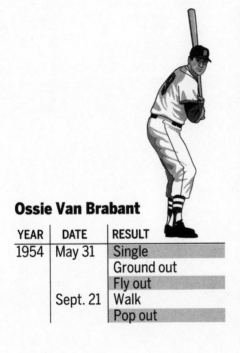

Ossie Van Brabant

YEAR	DATE	RESULT
1954	May 31	Single
		Ground out
		Fly out
	Sept. 21	Walk
		Pop out

HE WAS AN incredible
hitter. He knew the strike
zone as well as anybody and,
you know, he had a heck of
a lot of base on balls. A lot of
people didn't want to give him
anything good.

[I remember when] I pitched
against him that he hit one
dead center. I thought it was
gone, but luckily it wasn't. The
ball was against the center-
field fence, you know, the flat
fence in dead center field [in
Fenway]. The guy was right
to the track. It wouldn't have
gone over, but that's the kind
of hitter he was.

I faced him maybe three or four times, but he always hit the ball
well. The thing is, I started too late and ran out of gas too soon. No
excuse about it.

FACING TED WILLIAMS

Well, they gave him a lot of wrongs, I tell you, because he was a nice person. They [the media] always had something [negative] to say about him. I'd seen him one time going around third base, looked up at the press box, and spat at them. That's how bad it was. They just hounded him continuously.

Vito Valentinetti

Right-handed pitcher

1954:	**Chicago White Sox**
1956–57:	**Chicago Cubs**
1957:	**Cleveland Indians**
1958:	**Detroit Tigers**
1958–59:	**Washington Senators**
Career Statistics:	**13–14, 3 saves, 4.73 ERA**

Ted Williams vs. Vito Valentinetti

3-for-10, 1 triple, 1 home run, 3 RBI, 3 walks, 1 strikeout, .300 batting average, .462 on-base percentage, .800 slugging percentage

Home Runs Allowed:

No. 480, September 26, 1958 (game one), at Washington

YOU'D LOVE TO face these guys, because if they hit a ball out of the park, well, that was their job. They're good and they're known for that; like [Mickey] Mantle, [Willie] Mays, and the rest of them.

I had pretty good luck against Ted. I just see that he had one home run off me. Of course, I didn't pitch against him that much. I was in the American League and the National League. In the American League, I was with Detroit, Cleveland, and the old Washington Senators. When I was with Washington, I was a reliever and a starter.

I remember one game up in Boston against Ted and his buddies when I pitched a two-hitter, although I lost the ballgame, 2–0. [I remember that] I had two hits [in that game]. I hit one off the Green Monster, but Ted held me to a single, which was fine, as I didn't run that fast

Vito Valentinetti

YEAR	DATE	RESULT
1958	June 9	Ground out
		Walk
	June 12	Lined into DP
	Aug. 6	Triple (1 RBI)
	Aug. 7	Ground out
	Aug. 11	Strikeout
	Sept. 20	Fly out
		Walk
		Fly out
		Ground out
	Sept. 26	Single
		Walk
		Home run (2 RBI)

anyway. I had two hits and the rest of the team only had one. Our old catcher, Clint Courtney, pinch-hit for our second baseman, John Schaive, and he got a base hit.[107]

But it was fun pitching to Williams. Here's a guy, he's supposed to beat your brains in, you know? So after that game—it was a Saturday or Sunday— the next day we're standing on the sidelines and I start talking with him. Because he hit a ball I thought was going out in center field. He says, "Nah." Our center fielder caught it in front of the monument.

Then he said, "I'm 3–13 off of you, Vito." So he counted those three walks as times at-bat. He was probably 3–13 because he wanted to hit the ball four. But anyway, that's what he said to me.

He walked a lot and had one home run off me. It's like I say, pitching to those guys was like . . . what are you going to be nervous about? It's the .220 hitter that you got to worry about if he gets a base hit or a home run. The other guys—[Mickey] Mantle and Williams—that's what they're supposed to do!

---

[107] The game was September 20, 1958, and the Senators actually had four hits, as Bob Allison had the other. The Red Sox only had three hits, but one of them was Jackie Jensen's two-out, two-run single in the bottom of the eighth. Ted Williams was 0–3 with a walk.

He had a great batting eye. I remember striking him out once in Washington. He had a bad wrist, his wrist was taped up and he just took the pitch, you know. Got a called third strike on him.[108] It was just a fastball, but the lights weren't that great in the old Washington stadium; maybe that had something to do with it. Normally when he took [a pitch], the umpire called it a ball. He had great eyes, being a pilot and all. He probably would have broken all kinds of records [had he not gone off to war]. The guy didn't have any weaknesses. I mean, your best bet was maybe a changeup and to just mix it up [against him].

I don't [remember the home run], I really don't. I don't know if it was in Washington or Cleveland. I'd like to know what ballpark it was in, because that Washington ballpark was a big park. In the old days, it was pretty big, and then they shortened center field.[109]

Was he the best? I think he was the best power hitter, but I think [Stan] Musial . . . well, I was a right-handed pitcher and Musial was left-handed, and so was Williams. But Musial, one day pitching to him—that son-of-a-gun—I could see him switch his feet like he was going to hit the ball over the third-baseman's head . . . and he did. I pitched him outside and he hit the ball over the third-baseman's head. So he was a pretty good hitter, a cagey hitter. Well, the records show, right?[110]

I mean you're going to get them out once, maybe, once out of four, twice out of four? But you're not going to get them 0–3 or 0–4, not those guys. But they're going to hit the ball hard someplace.

I'd hardly see him hit the ball to left field. He was going for the home run; he was going for the downs on every pitch he could pull. I

---

[108] The strikeout occurred in the seventh inning of a 6–3 Senators win on August 11, 1958, at Griffith Stadium in Washington.

[109] The home run occurred in the fifth inning of Boston's 6–4 win on September 26, 1958, at Griffith Stadium in Washington. It would be the last time Valentinetti would face Williams.

[110] In seven plate appearances against Valentinetti, Musial went 4–6 with 4 hits, 1 home run, 2 RBI, 1 walk, 0 strikeouts, and a .667 batting average.

think he was, yeah. He was a power hitter. What else could you expect from a power hitter? Hit one out of the park, hit one off the Green Monster, or hit one to deep center field? He enjoyed that, I guess, hitting home runs off of people.

The coaches did that [watch Williams during batting practice] a lot. Sometimes a pitcher was pitching that day and would sit down with the coach on the bench. This guy likes this ball here and that ball there. Then they'd have meetings in the clubhouse. And half the time [laughs] they'd tell you to pitch one way and the ball don't always go where you want it to. You don't have that kind of stuff. I didn't have a good curveball, but I had a good slider, a good changeup, and a pretty good fastball and sinker. They tell you to pitch him one way, and if you can, fine.

[From what I remember], he was kind of a loner. You never saw him outside the ballpark. I knew where he would stay, but you never saw him around a restaurant or a bar. He was a good boy.

Jerry Walker

Right-handed pitcher

1957–61: .... Baltimore Orioles
1961–62: ....Kansas City Athletics
1963–64: .... Cleveland Indians
Career Statistics: .... 37–44 13 saves, 4.36 ERA
American League All-Star: 1959

Ted Williams vs. Jerry Walker

4-for-6, 1 home run, 3 RBI, 1 walk 0 strikeouts, 1 double play, .667 batting average, .714 on-base percentage, 1.167 slugging percentage

Home Runs Allowed:

No. 483, May 30, 1959 (game two), at Boston

I REALLY DON'T REMEMBER the first time I faced him, but I remember the first game I was ever in where he was supposed to be the first hitter. It ended up being a lopsided game, and they pinch-hit for him. I know it was his spot in the order and he would have been the first guy that I faced.[111]

I remember the first game that I lost; he hit a home run in that game. It was my first major-league loss.[112] It wasn't the first home run I had ever given up, but it was the first game I lost [in the majors]. It was a game in Boston, and he hit it right down the right-field line. A lot of 'em hit home runs off me.

------

[111] Jerry Walker made his major-league debut at eighteen years old on July 6, 1957, for the Orioles at Boston. Walker began the seventh inning; Williams had been the final out in the sixth.

[112] Williams hit a two-run homer off Walker in the seventh inning to give the Red Sox a 4–3 lead in an eventual 8–3 win over the Orioles in the second game of a doubleheader on May 30, 1959. Walker had been 1–0 in thirteen appearances in 1957, and had no decisions in six games in 1958.

You just had to make the pitches that would be the safest ones to throw him. You know, obviously the charts that told how much he hit at different places, you tried to pick out one of 'em where he hit in the .200s and .300s. And that didn't mean he wasn't going to get hits off of you, it just meant you had a little better chance of getting by without him hurting you too bad.

I never really talked with him. Pretty much in those days, hitters and pitchers didn't do a lot of talking. To some extent, you didn't spend a lot of time dealing with some hitters on your own club.

Jerry Walker

YEAR	DATE	RESULT
1959	May 30	Single
		Ground out
		Walk
		Home run (2 RBI) ⓧ
1960	July 4	Grounded into DP
		Single
		Single (1 RBI)

Looking at what he had done in the past and what he did in his last couple of years, you could certainly see that there wouldn't be too many hitters better than him. In fact, I was in the park the day he hit his last home run. Baltimore, Jack Fisher. It was late in the season and the rumor was if he hit a home run, he wasn't going to go to New York. He did not want to go to New York and have to hit a home run and have to walk off the field from that. So—I think it was the last home game; I think they were going on the road the next day[113]—the wind was blowing in from right field about 15–20 miles-per-hour, and he went up there and he, you know, he was trying to hit a home run every

---

[113] It was September 28, 1960, and Boston's final home game of the season. The Red Sox finished up the season with three games in New York against the Yankees from September 30–October 2.

time. He hit some balls in the air that got up and just didn't . . . he didn't hit them solid enough to get them past the wind.[114] But that last one, there was no doubt about it. He ran the bases, kept his head down, and ran right into the dugout and right down the runway to the clubhouse. And the manager made him go back to left field to start the next inning, and then he sent a replacement out for him.

That's just a part of the game. You pitch against a guy . . . my understanding is at some point he contacted Jack and thanked him for challenging him and not walking him, but that's just part of the game. Those kinds of hitters are going to get hits off you. You feel worse about a guy who hits one a year hitting a home run off you than someone like Williams. You don't think anything about it at the time. Looking back several years later, and even just a few years later, you realize the significance of the player and what happened. You were kind of glad you were there and saw it happen, just like a no-hitter, perfect game, or someone hitting for the cycle; you remember those things, and you especially remember them if it's a guy of the caliber of Ted Williams. I think he probably was [the greatest hitter], you know, because of his ability to hit for an average, he didn't strike out a lot . . . he was just a good hitter.

---

[114] Williams had flied out in his two previous at-bats. He also walked in the first inning.

George Zuverink

Right-handed pitcher

1951–52:	.... **Cleveland Indians**
1954:	.... **Cincinnati Reds**
1954–55:	.... **Detroit Tigers**
1955–59:	.... **Baltimore Orioles**
Career Statistics:	.... **32–36, 40 saves, 3.54 ERA**

Ted Williams vs. George Zuverink

2-for-20, 1 home run, 3 RBI, 2 walks (2 intentional), 3 strikeouts, 1 hit by pitch, 2 double plays, .100 batting average, .217 on-base percentage, .250 slugging percentage

Home Runs Allowed:

No. 305, June 10, 1951 (game two), at Cleveland

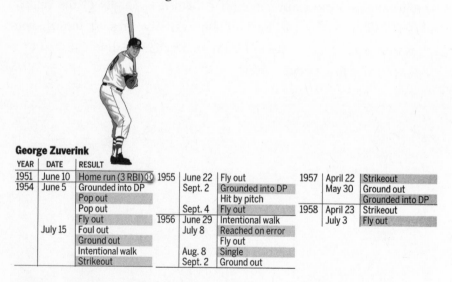

George Zuverink

YEAR	DATE	RESULT	YEAR	DATE	RESULT	YEAR	DATE	RESULT
1951	June 10	Home run (3 RBI)	1955	June 22	Fly out	1957	April 22	Strikeout
1954	June 5	Grounded into DP		Sept. 2	Grounded into DP		May 30	Ground out
		Pop out			Hit by pitch			Grounded into DP
		Pop out		Sept. 4	Fly out	1958	April 23	Strikeout
		Fly out	1956	June 29	Intentional walk		July 3	Fly out
	July 15	Foul out		July 8	Reached on error			
		Ground out			Fly out			
		Intentional walk		Aug. 8	Single			
		Strikeout		Sept. 2	Ground out			

THE FIRST TIME I faced him was in Cleveland in 1951. He welcomed me to the major leagues by hitting the ball over the center field fence!

He was a terrific hitter. Before each game against Boston, as he took batting practice, we would all stop playing catch and admire this star.

His next hit against me was in 1956, and he hit a single to right field. I had good luck against him; most of the time was while I was a reliever. I changed speeds so that no pitch was alike.

In 1961, when the Red Sox had spring training up in Scottsdale, Arizona, and I was retired, I went to the ballpark and introduced myself to him. He said, "George, I think you could still get me out!"

What a compliment!

INTERVIEWS

Chuck Churn

Right-handed pitcher

1957:	**Pittsburgh Pirates**
1958:	**Cleveland Indians**
1959:	**Los Angeles Dodgers**
Career Statistics:	**3–2, 1 save, 5.10 ERA**

Ted Williams vs. Chuck Churn:

0-for-1, .000 batting average, 1.000 on-base percentage, .000 slugging percentage

May 5, 1958, bottom of the eighth inning, led off by grounding out to shortstop with the Williams shift in effect.

Chuck Churn

YEAR	DATE	RESULT
1958	May 5	Ground out

Q. What was your strategy against Williams, and how do you think you fared?

A. Only faced him one time! Pitched him [on the] low outside part of the plate.

Q. Did your teams use the "Williams shift," and if so, did you like that and how did it fare? If not, do you wish they did?

A. I liked the shift!

Q. Was he the toughest hitter you faced?

A. For me, Gil Hodges was tough to pitch to!

Jerry Davie

Right-handed pitcher

1959: ....Detroit Tigers
Career Statistics: .... 2–2, 0 saves, 4.17 ERA

Ted Williams vs. Jerry Davie

0-for-0, 1 RBI, 2 walks, 0 strikeouts, 1 sacrifice fly, .000 batting average, .667 on-base percentage, .000 slugging percentage

Q. What was your strategy against Williams, and how do you think you fared?

A. Move the ball around, in–out.

Q. Recollections of any specific at-bats vs. Williams.

A. 3–2, threw the ball, and I knew it went down the middle, belt high. He took the pitch, and I thought I had a strikeout, but the ump called it ball four.

Jerry Davie

YEAR	DATE	RESULT
1959	May 17	Walk
		Walk
	June 9	Sac fly (1 RBI)

Q. What was the talk among other pitchers, pitching coach and/or catchers on how to face Williams in pregame meetings or just in general?

A. Just hope he screwed up.

Q. Did your teams use the "Williams shift," and if so, did you like that and how did it fare? If not, do you wish they did?

A. Yes we did.

Q. Was he the toughest "out" you faced?

A. Him and Minnie Minoso.[1]

---

[1] Minoso was 3–6 with a double, home run, and walk vs. Davie.

Sonny Dixon

Right-handed pitcher

1953–54: .... Washington Senators
1954: .... Philadelphia Athletics
1955: .... Kansas City Athletics
1956: .... New York Yankees
Career Statistics: .... 11–18, 9 saves, 4.18 ERA

Ted Williams vs. Sonny Dixon

5-for-10, 2 doubles, 1 home run, 3 RBI, 1 walk, 0 strikeouts, 1 double play, .500 batting average, .545 on-base percentage, 1.000 slugging percentage

Home Runs Allowed:

No. 329, August 23, 1953, at Washington

Q. What was your strategy against Williams, and how do you think you fared?

A. Keep the ball away from him. The first pitch to him he hit for a home run.

Q. Recollections of any specific at-bats vs. Williams.

A. Ted hit a double down the left-field line. I went to second base mad, because he got a double. Ted said, "Sonny, you threw the ball by me." I told him that was all I wanted to know.[2]

---

[2] On July 10, 1954, Williams doubled to left field off Dixon in the top of the tenth inning to score Jimmy Piersall and break a 2–2 tie in an eventual 5–3 Red Sox win in eleven innings.

Q. What was the talk among other pitchers, pitching coach and/or catchers on how to face Williams in pregame meetings or just in general?

A. Was not too much chatter.

Q. Did your teams use the "Williams shift," and if so, did you like that and how did it fare? If not, do you wish they did?

A. Yes. Most of the time it worked.

Q. Was he the toughest "out" you faced?

A. No, Nellie Fox.[3] He was tougher; I never got him out.

Q. Can you compare how it was to face Williams vs. hitters like Al Kaline, Larry Doby, and Harvey Kuenn.

A. I was lucky with Ted. He always was kidding me that I was his "out man." He signed a picture for me and put, "Your out man."[4]

Sonny Dixon

YEAR	DATE	RESULT
1953	Aug. 23	Home run (1 RBI)
1954	July 4	Fielder's choice
		Single
	July 10	Double (1 RBI)
	Sept. 5	Double
		Grounded into DP
		Fly out
		Ground out
	Sept. 21	Single (1 RBI)
		Walk
1956	Sept. 29	Single

---

[3] In 11 at-bats, Fox went 4–11 with 2 RBI, 1 strikeout, and a .364 batting average against Dixon.

[4] It might seem strange that Williams would say Dixon was his "out man," but Dixon allowed just one single and one walk to Williams in the last six times he faced him.

Bubba Harris

Right-handed pitcher

1948–49, 1951: .... Philadelphia Athletics
1951: .... Cleveland Indians
Career Statistics: .... 6–3, 8 saves, 4.84 ERA

Ted Williams vs. Bubba Harris (data incomplete)

2-for-8, 1 home run, 2 RBI, 4 walks, 0 strikeouts, .250 batting average, .500 on-base percentage, .625 slugging percentage

Home Runs Allowed:

No. 259, September 3, 1949, at Boston

Q. What was your strategy against Williams, and how do you think you fared?

A. Don't throw strikes. Pitch low and behind.

Q. Did your teams use the "Williams shift?"

A. Yes

Q. Was he the toughest hitter you faced?

A. Yes

Bubba Harris

YEAR	DATE	RESULT
1948	May 31	Fly out
	Aug. 18	Single
1949	April 27	Walk
	May 30	Fly out into DP
	July 8	Ground out (1 RBI)
	July 9	Walk
	Sept. 2	Fly out
		Walk
	Sept. 3	Home run (1 RBI)
	Sept. 10	Foul out
1951	April 21	Walk
	April 29	Ground out

Don Johnson

Right-handed pitcher

1947, 1950:	New York Yankees
1950–51:	St. Louis Browns
1951–52:	Washington Senators
1954:	Chicago White Sox
1955:	Baltimore Orioles
1958:	San Francisco Giants
Career Statistics:	27–38, 12 saves, 4.78 ERA

Ted Williams vs. Don Johnson (data incomplete)

4-for-16, 1 triple, 1 home run, 6 RBI, 3 walks, 0 strikeouts, .429 batting average, .529 on-base percentage, .786 slugging percentage

Home Runs Allowed:

No. 291, September 15, 1950, at St. Louis

Q. What was your strategy against Williams, and how do you think you fared?

A. Good

Q. Recollections of any specific at-bats vs. Williams.

A. None

Q. What was the talk among other pitchers, pitching coach and/or catchers on how to face Williams in pregame meetings or just in general?

A. Throw it down the middle and poof.

Q. Did your teams use the "Williams shift," and if so, did you like that and how did it fare? If not, do you wish they did?

A. No shift

Q. Was he the toughest "out" you faced?

A. Yes

Don Johnson (data incomplete; missing 1947)

YEAR	DATE	RESULT
1950	April 18	Walk
	Sept. 15	Ground out
		Single
		Fly out
		Home run (3 RBI)
1951	May 23	Walk
	Aug. 12	Ground out
		Reached on error
		Single
		Single
	Aug. 18	Triple (2 RBI)
1954	June 26	Single (1 RBI)
		Ground out
		Ground out
	July 25	Ground out
		Fly out
		Walk

184

Don Lee

Right-handed pitcher

1957-58: ....Detroit Tigers
1960: ....Washington Senators
1961-62: ....Minnesota Twins
1962-65: .... Los Angeles/California Angels
1965-66: ....Houston Astros
1966: .... Chicago Cubs
Career Statistics: .... 40–44, 11 saves, 3.61 ERA

Ted Williams vs. Don Lee

2-for-7, 1 home run, 1 RBI, 2 walks, 0 strikeouts, .286 batting average, .444 on-base percentage, .714 slugging percentage

Home Runs Allowed:

No. 517, September 2, 1960 (game one), at Boston[5]

Q: What was your strategy against Williams, and how do you think you fared?

A: Change speeds—yes

Q. Recollections of any specific at-bats vs. Williams.

A. Ted Williams hit a home run off my father and one off me (it's a trivia question)—the only player to hit a home run off of a father and son. My father was Thornton Lee, who pitched for Cleveland and the Chicago White Sox from 1933 to 1946. Ted Williams has called my father one of the toughest left-hand pitchers he ever faced.[6]

---

[5] In the listing with his statistics, Lee wrote in under the one home run that it was No. 518 (it was actually Williams' 517th career home run).

[6] In four at-bats against Thornton Lee, Williams only had one hit and struck out once.

Don Lee

YEAR	DATE	RESULT
1960	June 2	Walk
	Sept. 2	Ground out
		Fly out
		Pop out
		Home run (1 RBI)
	Sept. 18	Ground out
		Single
		Walk
		Line out

Q. What was the talk among other pitchers, pitching coach and/or catchers on how to face Williams in pregame meetings or just in general?

A. Pitch around him—don't give him anything good to hit.

Q. Did your teams use the "Williams shift," and if so, did you like that and how did it fare? If not, do you wish they did?

A. Yes, and we fared well.

Q. Was he the toughest "out" you faced?

A. Yes, even though I only faced him one season.

Q. Can you compare how it was to face Williams vs. hitters like Mickey Mantle, Roger Maris, and Carl Yastrzemski?

A. Mantle and Maris were no real problem for me. Yaz was somewhat a problem. Williams was feared more.

Bob Savage

Right-handed pitcher

1942, 1946–49: ....Philadelphia A's
1949: ....St. Louis Browns
Career Statistics: ....16–27, 9 saves, 4.32 ERA

Ted Williams vs. Bob Savage (data incomplete)

6-for-15, 3 doubles, 2 home runs, 5 walks, 2 strikeouts, .313 batting average, .476 on-base percentage, .875 slugging percentage

Home Runs Allowed:

No. 166, April 18, 1947, at Philadelphia
No. 178, June 29, 1947 (game two), at Philadelphia

Q. What was your strategy against Williams, and how do you think you fared?

A. No particular strategy

Q. Recollections of specific at-bats vs. Williams.

A. I remember one game I had three strikeouts the first three at-bats. Homer and double the last two at-bats.[7]

Q. What was the talk among other pitchers, pitching coach and/or catchers on how to face Williams in pregame meetings or just in general?

A. No discussion

---

[7] Savage allowed 2 home runs to Williams: April 18, 1947, in which Williams went 1–3, and June 29, 1947 (game two), with Williams again going 1–3.

Q. Did your teams use the "Williams shift," and if so, did you like that and how did it fare? If not, do you wish they did?

A. No

Q. Was he the toughest hitter you faced?

A. Joe DiMaggio

Bob Savage (data incomplete; 1942, 1946-'47)

YEAR	DATE	RESULT
1948	April 22	Ground out
	April 29	Walk
	July 9	Fly out
		Walk
	Aug. 18	Ground out (1 RBI)
		Fly out

Carl Scheib

Right-handed pitcher

1943–45, 1947–54: .... **Philadelphia Athletics**
1954: .... **St. Louis Cardinals**
Career Statistics: .... **45–65, 17 saves, 4.88 ERA**

Ted Williams vs. Carl Scheib (data incomplete)

6-for-30, 1 home run,[8] 2 RBI, 9 walks, 2 strikeouts, .200 batting average, .385 on-base percentage, .300 slugging percentage[9]

Home Runs Allowed:

No. 179, July 2, 1947, at Boston
No. 192, August 31, 1947, at Boston
No. 234, May 30, 1949 (game two), at Boston

Q. What was your strategy against Williams, and how do you think you fared?

A. Pitching to Williams, I tried to pitch him low and inside, maybe on curveballs. I think I fared pretty well against him.

Q. Recollections of specific at-bats vs. Williams.

A. Specific game against Williams, I pitched him curveballs low and inside and got him out three times at-bat. A story later was that he told

---

[8] Of the known available box scores, Williams hit 1 home run off Scheib. But the data is available for all of Williams' 521 career home runs, and he ended up with 3 off Scheib.

[9] Retrosheet.org has more data of Williams vs. Scheib, but does not include RBI. Baseball-reference.com lists Williams with 2 RBI in 25 at-bats (31 plate appearances) vs. Scheib.

Carl Scheib (data
incomplete; missing 1947)

YEAR	DATE	RESULT
1948	Aug. 18	Single
		Single
	Sept. 3	Strikeout
		Fly out
		Walk
		Fly out
1949	April 27	Fly out
		Walk
		Walk
	May 30	Ground out
		Ground out
		Ground out
		Home run (2 RBI)
	July 8	Strikeout
	Sept. 11	Fly out
		Fly out
		Walk
		Fly out

YEAR	DATE	RESULT
1950	April 30	Pop out
		Grounded into DP
	June 29	Fly out
1951	April 22	Walk
		Fly out
	June 27	Ground out
		Single
		Fly out
	July 4	Ground out
		Walk
		Fielder's choice
	Aug. 14	Single
	Sept. 9	Foul out

the guys on the bench, if I started him again on curveballs, he would hit a home run . . . and he did. It beat me in the ball game.[10]

---

[10] Scheib likely is talking about the second game of a doubleheader between the Red Sox and A's on May 30, 1949, in which Williams hit career home run No. 234 in the bottom of the eighth inning of a 4–3 Boston win, a two-run home run that provided the final score. Williams had been hitless in his previous three at-bats in that game.

Something you learn, not to start a good hitter four times the same way in a game.

Q. What was the talk among other pitchers, pitching coach and/ or catchers on how to face Williams in pregame meetings or just in general?

A. First of all we were a second-division club[11] and therefore not many pregame meetings were held. You pitched Williams the way you thought was best for you.

Q. Did your teams use the "Williams shift," and if so, did you like that and how did it fare? If not, do you wish they did?

A. We did not use the shift.

Q. Was he the toughest hitter you faced?

A. Each pitcher has a few hitters which were tough for him, not saying they were better hitters. Williams was probably one of the toughest hitters to face, but some other hitters gave me more trouble. But overall, I would vote Williams as the best hitter ever.

---

[11] In Scheib's ten seasons with the A's, Philadelphia finished in the second division eight times and in fourth place the other two occasions.

Bobby Shantz

Left-handed pitcher

1949–54:	Philadelphia Athletics
1955–56:	Kansas City Athletics
1957–60:	New York Yankees
1961:	Pittsburgh Pirates
1962:	Houston Colt .45's
1962–64:	St. Louis Cardinals
1964:	Chicago Cubs
1964:	Philadelphia Phillies
Career Statistics:	119–99, 48 saves, 3.38 ERA
American League All-Star:	1951, 1952, 1957
American League MVP:	1952

Ted Williams vs. Bobby Shantz (data incomplete)

15-for-49, 4 doubles, 2 home runs, 8 RBI, 13 walks (2 intentional), 9 strikeouts, .306 batting average, .452 on-base percentage, .510 slugging percentage

Home Runs Allowed:

No. 287, June 27, 1950, at Philadelphia
No. 403, July 26, 1956, at Kansas City

Q. What was your strategy against Williams, and how do you think you fared?

A. My strategy was to make him hit breaking balls and try to keep the ball in the ballpark.

Q. Recollections of any specific at-bats vs. Williams.

A. All of his at-bats were tough because he made me throw strikes and had a great eye.

Bobby Shantz

YEAR	DATE	RESULT
1949	May 30	Grounded into DP
		Walk
		Ground out
		Walk
	July 10	Walk
	Sept. 2	Strikeout
		Ground out
1950	April 30	Walk
		Fielder's choice
		Pop out
	June 27	Double
		Home run (2 RBI)
		Double
		Walk
		Foul out
1951	Aug. 9	Strikeout
	Aug. 16	Ground out
		Line out
		Single
		Fly out
	Sept. 9	Ground out
		Fly out
		Single (1 RBI)
		Ground out
1955	June 3	Single
		Ground out
		Ground out
	July 21	Single
		Walk
		Ground out
		Ground out

YEAR	DATE	RESULT
	Sept. 13	Ground out
		Ground out
1956	June 2	Line out
	June 23	Strikeout
		Single
	July 17	Walk
	July 25	Strikeout
	July 26	Home run (2 RBI)
	Aug. 26	Strikeout
1957	April 20	Single
		Strikeout
	April 27	Single (RBI)
		Walk
		Fly out
		Ground out
	July 4	Strikeout
		Ground out
		Ground out
		Walk
1958	July 6	Walk
	Aug. 17	Double (1 RBI)
		Single
1959	July 8	Ground out
		Single
		Strikeout
	Aug. 11	Double (1 RBI)
	Aug. 14	Walk
1960	June 3	Fly out
	June 5	Intentional walk
	Sept. 5	Intentional walk
	Sept. 23	Strikeout

193

Q. What was the talk among other pitchers, pitching coach and/ or catchers on how to face Williams in pregame meetings or just in general?

A. We never talked that much about him to get him out because he was that good.

Q. Did your teams use the "Williams shift," and if so, did you like that and how did it fare? If not, do you wish they did?

A. Yes, we used the shift, but it didn't do much good. He could have gotten a hit every time up if he wanted to push the ball down the third-base line. Of course, he didn't do that!

Q. Was he the toughest "out" you faced?

A. Yes, he was the toughest hitter I ever faced.

Q. Can you compare how it was to face Williams vs. hitters like Al Kaline, Rocky Colavito, and Minnie Minoso.

A. I would rather face Minoso, Kaline, and Colavito before Williams anytime!

Dave Sisler

Right-handed pitcher

1956–59: ....Boston Red Sox
1959–60: ....Detroit Tigers
1961: ....Washington Senators
1962: ....Cincinnati Reds
Career Statistics: ....38–44, 29 saves, 4.33 ERA

Ted Williams vs. Dave Sisler

1-for-3, 1 home run, 1 RBI, 0 walks, 0 strikeouts, .333 batting average, .333 on-base percentage, 1.333 slugging percentage

Home Runs Allowed:

No. 485, June 23, 1959, at Detroit

Q. What was your strategy against Williams?

A. No pattern

Q. How do you think you fared?

A. Bad

Q. Recollections of any specific at-bats vs. Williams.

A. He hit a home run on a day I shouldn't have been pitching.

Dave Sisler

YEAR	DATE	RESULT
1959	May 17	Fly out
	June 10	Fielder's choice
	June 23	Home run (1 RBI)

Q. What was the talk among other pitchers, pitching coach and/ or catchers on how to face Williams in pregame meetings or just in general?

A. Everyone said he was the best.

Q. Did your teams use the "Williams shift?"

A. Yes

Q. Did you like that and how did it fare? If not, do you wish they did?

A. Didn't face him enough

Q. Was he the toughest "out" you faced?

A. Among the best

Q. You played with Williams from 1956–59. Did you ever discuss your matchups with him and/or his theories of hitting?

A. No

Q. Did playing with him help you in preparing to face him in later years?

A. Yes, but not enough

Q. What was it like watching him hit every day?

A. Priceless—the best hitter I ever saw, though not the best player or teammate.

Section Two: Catchers

Del Crandall

Catcher

1949–50: ....Boston Braves
1953–63: .... Milwaukee Braves
1964: ....San Francisco Giants
1965: ....Pittsburgh Pirates
1966: .... Cleveland Indians
Career Statistics: .... 1,573 games, 179 home runs,
.254 batting average
National League All-Star: 1953–1956, 1958–1960, 1962

MY INTERACTION WITH Williams was very limited, since he was in the American League.

When I first went to the Braves in 1949, the Braves and Sox always played a Jimmy Fund charity game. I was nineteen at the time. Anyway, some of our veterans didn't want to take part in the home-run hitting contest before the game. Ted was in it, and the Braves asked me to be in it. As it turned out, Ted and I wound up in the finals and hit the same number in the playoff. Now that was a tremendous thrill for me, not Ted!

In the early '50s, we played the Red Sox in the Hall of Fame Game, and it was great to listen to him talk about hitting. He was very generous with his time and enjoyed talking hitting. I was part of the limited group that was talking with him. He was more than willing to share, and he just loved talking to ballplayers—I'm not sure about other people—but he was just a great guy as far as other players were concerned. And he spent as much time talking baseball as he could. I'm talking half-an-hour, forty-five minutes, maybe even an hour. I was twenty-four at the time and hadn't made much of a name for myself, so I was a listener. There's no way I can remember [exactly] what he said. We were talking about swings and that sort of thing, but no, I didn't come away with anything that was seared in my brain that I used over and over again.

Whenever I was around him, I tried to watch what he did when he was hitting. He was just one of those magical players that you just couldn't take your eyes off of. I wasn't around Joe DiMaggio much, but it was the same way [with him]. I was just there with him in spring training when he had that heel problem, I think, but whenever he was on the field, I couldn't take my eyes off of him, either.

There wasn't [an aura around Williams] because we didn't get to see him. We got to see [Stan] Musial, and we knew how great he was, but Williams had that mystique about him that he was better than the best we had in our league—although I think Musial has been *totally* under-rated over the years. But we couldn't really identify with Williams because of the fact that we really didn't see him a lot. And not during his prime, either. So we had our own stars, you know. Musial, [Willie] Mays, [Hank] Aaron, and whoever else I've forgotten.

Del Crandall was an eight-time All-Star in the National League.

I was so young [when I played in Boston for the Braves], I'm not sure I got much of an impression from all this. What I got was from the newspapers mostly, reading about his trials. But he was just a hero. He was just a guy who was the best. Once again, I had to read about him mostly and hear what people had to say because not being in his league, it was difficult to form any real opinion.

You got the sense that he was kind of a laid-back manager. I can't remember him being real aggressive in the field, I can't remember him . . . I'm sure that hitting was really his big thing. I know it was probably intimidating for hitters to go up there and do their measly little thing when you had the greatest hitter in the history of baseball—possibly—sitting over there on the bench. So I'm sure it was hard to play for him.

When I managed the Brewers, Ted was the manager with Texas. George Scott was on my club and he gave the fans the finger when they booed him when he was having a tough time at the plate. Scott was fined and went into a pout. I remember Ted also had an incident with the fans and was fined for his "obscene gesture." I asked Ted if he would talk to Scott and he did willingly. He just never hesitated [when asked to help out in the Scott incident]. He went right out and went to center field and talked to him. Scott came [into the locker room after that] and apologized and went on to have a great year with Milwaukee.

I liked him. He was a real baseball man and always had time for people in uniform.

Jim French

Catcher

1965–71:...Washington Senators
Career Statistics:............................ 234 games, 5 home runs,
.196 batting average

Note: French did not play against Ted Williams, but was managed by him in 1969 with the Senators.

THERE WAS AN awe factor to start with. I would say that he's was the most charismatic man that I ever knew personally. To give you an example, a number of years ago we had a reunion in Washington, DC, and he was in a wheelchair. And, I don't know, there had to be 600 people in there eating dinner and he came wheeling into the crowd and the whole place went silent. Just totally silent. But he was like that.

He was very charismatic. A very likeable guy at the same time a pretty nasty son of a bitch when he wanted to be. Which was quite often. Mercurial I guess would be the right word, I don't know.

Gosh, you know, you remember little things. His favorite term was bush. If you had a shirt on that was out of style or something, you were bush. This is off the field. On the field, he was not the greatest tactical manager. I don't think he had the patience to be what I would call a great manager. He certainly was a hell of a lot better hitter than he was a manager, just like I'm a hell of a lot better lawyer than I was a catcher—so that's not saying much.

He and I got along very well. We used to argue all the time about pitchers. With pitchers, he thought pitchers were stupid. And I guess because he hit .400 and a bunch of home runs he would.

We worked together pretty well. I was like a second-stringer . . . you know, back then, we called the pitches, the catchers. And he loved the slider. Loved the slider. Even if the pitcher had a shitty slider, he loved it.

It was a strange relationship that he had with all the players. Some players, I mean, *vehemently* disliked him. Vehemently. Bernie Allen was one that I can recall. And I can't remember why. I talked to Bernie about it and he did something, whatever. But I guess he was that kind of a guy, you know.

He would, I guess when I said patience, he would talk to pitchers about how to pitch and they'd they go out and get beat up, get him and then he would drop it. He didn't stay with somebody long enough to . . . he didn't know how to throw sliders, he didn't know to pitch other than strategy pitching. In other words what pitch, when, where, whatever. Hell, I was just as good as he was at that or better because I knew the pitchers. And I knew the hitters better. If I was good at anything that's what I was good at.

He thought that, I think, that pitchers should pitch to everyone like pitchers should have pitched to him. But you know in retrospect, it was a great experience to play under him. I mean, one day he'd come in and make you feel like a million dollars and the next day not speak to you and you'd wonder what the fuck you did wrong. Pardon my language, I don't talk like this when I'm a lawyer but when I get to talking baseball I regress.

Here's his biggest problem as I look back. He had a bench coach, Joe Camacho. And Joe's credentials—don't get me wrong, nice guy, really nice guy—his credentials were that he played some minor-league ball and then ran Ted's baseball camp. And Joe didn't have the respect that someone that had some experience or whatever would have had. Wayne Terwilliger, good friend of mine, Nellie Fox, God bless him good friend of mine, Sid Hudson, another coach and a good friend of mine, George Susce, I don't know how a good friend—I used to tease George too much and when I look back I say, why did I do that?—in my opinion was not the greatest coaching staff in the world.

Twig, good third-base coach, worked hard with the infielders. I don't think any of his coaches—and I may be wrong, because I didn't sit in any of the meetings—would stand up to him, and say this is stupid, you're doing this wrong or whatever. That's the impression I got. Obviously I wasn't in the meetings.

I also played under Gil Hodges and Hodges had a hell of a staff, ok. Plus, Hodges was a much, much smarter manager and handler of guys even though he . . . I guess we all have our drawbacks. And Ted lost interest at the end, no question. No question. He just lost interest. And you can't do anything, write your books, go into a case, if you don't have interest in it. You go through the motions. Plus, I guess his personal relationships were not the greatest. Who knows, who knows.

You know even though I was a college grad—I signed after I got out of college and went to grad school in the offseason—I was relatively older than most of the guys and, I won't say worldly, but educated, if that's the right word, and I was still—I don't know if awe is the right word—I was a little bit afraid of Hodges.

You have to understand I was far from a star, a pretty good ballplayer but if I screwed up enough I was gone. That's just the way it was. But I would say I was on the fringe, let's put it that way. So I was concerned, because I came up under Hodges. Hodges was a very aloof guy, very aloof. Even if you screwed up, he very seldom would say anything. He'd have Joe Pignatano tell you. And that bothered me.

Whereas Williams, I was never afraid of him like I was Hodges. Apprehensive is the better word with Hodges. And that was never the case with Williams.

I was more of what you'd call a banjo hitter when compared to him. If the fences were in 10 feet closer I would have had 150 home runs instead of four. So I can remember the first or second year of spring training, he came down in the batting cage to work with my hitting. And after about twenty minutes he gave up. Because I hit different. He had he classic turn the hips good, slightly uppercut swing. Well, shit, if I hit the slightly uppercut I had a 150, 200 fly balls on the warning track. Where I should have been hitting line drives.

He could not, in my opinion, teach somebody to hit except the way he hit. And so if you weren't like him, alright, that type of swing, that type of power . . . two differences between he and I, besides size, was that his eyesight was better than mine—because I wore contacts—and he could open up his hips at the last moment and really get around on the ball, which I could not do.

I got along really good personally with Williams. Except you'd argue long enough with Williams and he'd call you a bush dumbass and walk away. You know, because you were winning the argument. Or at least you thought you were. In his mind I don't think he ever lost an argument. He was a *very, very* strong personality and at times not a very nice guy.

I spoke to him a couple times at reunions or old-timers game, and my God, he greeted me like his long-lost brother every time.

Hal Keller

Catcher

1949, 1950, 1952: ....**Washington Senators**
Career Statistics: ....**25 games, 1 home run,**
.204 batting average

AS YOU KNOW if you looked it up, I had a very abbreviated major-league career. As I recall, I didn't play more than one or two series, and I only caught one game I'm sure of that Ted hit in.

I hit my one and only home run in Boston in the left-field bullpen, and Ted walked up and said, "Did it feel good?" And of course I said yes.

Ted was a unique individual, really, but he was a very kind person. Very intense in his opinions. I don't think [he] really appreciated the fine points of baseball, but he was consumed by the battle between the pitcher and the hitter. I doubt if he ever would attempt to instruct a middle infielder on how to make a double play, that sort of thing. His all-consuming passion was hitting.

He didn't have the best product to work with, of course, but you know, I think hitting—I've never had much faith in hitting coaches. The best they can do, I think, is help your mental approach. You can either hit a baseball or you can't, it's that simple. Whoever made George Brett into a .350 hitter did nothing for Frank White.[1]

The best hitting coach I ever worked with was an old player named Deron Johnson, who just emphasized mental approach . . . did very little with swing.

---

[1] A career .255 hitter.

I never saw Ted—the years I worked with him[2]—screw with a hitter's swing. He always emphasized two things: Get a pitch you can hit and pop your ass and turn your hips, so your body releases all this power into it. You probably read his book with the average zones; he stressed that.

---

[2] Williams and Keller worked together when Keller was the farm director for the Washington Senators, from 1969–1972.

Hal Naragon

Catcher

1951, 1954–59:	Cleveland Indians
1959–60:	Washington Senators
1961–62:	Minnesota Twins
Career Statistics:	424 games, 6 home runs, .266 batting average

IT WAS ALWAYS very interesting [facing Ted], because he was a great hitter. Of course at the time I caught behind Williams I was with Cleveland, and we had a great pitching staff, so it was always a real battle. I'm not sure how well he did against us at that time. But I was a Ted Williams fan, I can tell you that. I told this story and my wife didn't really believe it, but when he would swing and miss the ball, you could kind of smell burning a little bit. I always remembered that. And it wasn't too long ago, I was listening to an interview on one of those stations—I can't remember who said it—and they said the same thing! So I guess I really wasn't dreaming. It really happened [laughs].

I remember we had a situation once in Cleveland on a Thursday afternoon. Back in those days, the way the stadium was situated late in the day the shade would come in and the pitcher would be in the sun, and the batter would be in the shade, and the shadow would be about halfway between the pitching mound and home plate. It's kind of difficult picking up the ball. Mike Garcia was pitching, and he threw his sinker. The ball was about halfway up to the plate and Williams says, "There is something on that ball." I didn't say anything; I just caught the ball. It was a strike, but the umpire called it a ball; it was one of those close pitches. Nobody argued, and I flipped the ball back to Mike. Hank Soar was the umpire, and he walked around and said, "Mike, I'd like to have the ball." So Mike rolled the ball into him. Williams then said to me, "What was that pitch?" I said, "a sinker," and that's all that was said [laughs]. They always said he had good eyes.

I always found Ted to be very friendly towards baseball players. If you had a uniform on, he knew your name and a little bit about you; that was my opinion. He'd speak to you; if you said something, he'd talk to you. But I know this—I remember when being a rookie, my first full year in the major leagues—Kenmore Hotel was the one we stayed at in Boston. Well, we used to walk to the ballpark because it was that close, which was nice. We'd always go out early—get dressed and go out—because we always wanted to watch Ted Williams take batting practice. When Ted Williams came to bat up in Boston, I think everything stopped [laughs]. And I wasn't alone either. Half the team was out there. And we had some good hitters on that team that year, too [in 1954]. We won 111 games that year.

But what I really remember most, other than his great hitting, was—I think it was my second year in the major leagues, I'm not quite sure—I asked Ted Williams for an autographed picture. We were in Cleveland then, and he said to me, "Well, when you get to Boston, you tell the clubhouse gentleman"—his name was Vince—"and I'll make sure you get the picture." So I go to Boston and I go out to the ballpark early with other ballplayers to watch Williams, and we're just leaning against the fence there, just outside the dugout. And the truth is, I kind of forgot about the picture. But after he got through hitting, he came over and told me, "I sent that picture over to you." So I thought that was pretty good. And I still have it.

You know he served his country twice. He was in the Air Force. He did this *twice*. I wonder what his record would have been if he only had one military service instead of two. Same way with Bob Feller. Well, there were a lot of guys back then who did that playing major league baseball.

[I'm not sure if he had the benefit of the umpires]; that's probably stressing it a little. But he did have a great eye at the plate. I mean, he didn't offer at bad pitches. And I would think maybe, you know, you get a reputation of swinging at anything, and the umpire might widen your strike zone a little bit. But Williams was the other way around.

You had to throw the ball over the plate, or at least hit some part of the plate, for him to go for it. He was a disciplined hitter. That's the reason he was such a great hitter.

We had Bob Lemon, who was a good sinkerball pitcher. I read where Williams said that he thought Lemon was a tough pitcher to hit, because he had great movement on his pitches. I can't tell you exactly which one that you would throw Williams if you're Lemon. He had great pitches, so you couldn't go wrong calling any of them.

I don't remember so much about the discussion on how to pitch Ted Williams. I think it would just be a waste of time [laughs]. I think our manager, Al Lopez, who would never hold any group meetings, as far as going over hitters was concerned. He left it up to the pitcher and the catcher that day. I thought that was the way to go—I still think that's the way to go, because when you get into a group meeting, you may come out with four or five suggestions that need not be said. Where the pitcher and catcher, they're on the team within themselves. They can work it out much better and very effectively. I thought with Al Lopez, that was a great way to go.

We won 111 games [in 1954], and I think they [the entire starting staff] completed like 73 of them. I think Lemon, and Early Wynn, and Mike Garcia, I think those three—or at least two of them—completed over 20 games. That's unusual today.

We did shade him to right field. Williams, you know, he's going to hit the ball over your head and over the fence. He didn't hit to left field much. I don't know if he bunted once just for fun.

He was one of my favorite players even before he got there, and then to catch behind him and *talk* to him—it was a real thrill. He liked to talk about baseball. He would help you. If you went over there and ask him or get into a conversation about hitting, he would give his thoughts. He wouldn't back away about that. But he was a great hitter; probably the best I've ever caught behind.

Nobody hit like Ted Williams—I didn't—but he did tell me once that he liked my idea of hitting. I wasn't a power hitter at all, but he told me he thought I had a good stroke for what I was doing, which will give you a little confidence.

He seemed to be a very friendly guy in uniform, and I've talked to some of his former teammates, and they thought he was a really good teammate and very helpful when you wanted to talk to him. The players seemed to really like him.

I don't remember them [booing him in Boston]. There could have been, but I don't remember. I don't know how you could boo Ted Williams [laughs]. If they did, I don't know how long they stayed in the ballpark.

I have two pictures of Ted Williams at my home; I have the one he gave to me and then a picture of us talking when we were in Cooperstown playing the Red Sox. That's probably the time we talked more than when he would come to bat. I was probably too flustered to really talk to him [laughs].

There was a writer that was here, he was from Canton, Ohio, and I remember him telling me that he asked Ted Williams if he could have an interview. He said he was kind of timid about doing it, and Ted said, "Yeah, let's go in the dugout." He said it was just like that. He said, "We went out there and had a nice chat." He told me this a few years ago, and I said you are probably the only one [laughs]. Oh, I think he treated the press better than what they'd like you to believe.

When you have your team, like Dale Mitchell, who hit .315 lifetime,[3] and you had people like Al Rosen, Vic Wertz, and Larry Doby—we had a good team, I hate to mention names because I know I'm going to forget some—but they would go out and before the game, go early

---

[3] Mitchell's lifetime batting average was .312.

to the ballpark and watch Williams hit! Well, that's quite an honor, I think.

I remember he would hit balls to the opposite field if he wanted to [in batting practice]. But he was hitting them over the fence in right field, too [laughs]. But he was definitely the best hitter I ever caught behind, and I'm sure there are a lot of other catchers who would say the same thing.

He was a great hitter. I remember him once saying during an interview, he asked the press when they were going to have a good year!

Neal Watlington

Catcher

1953: .... **Philadelphia Athletics**
Career Statistics: .... **21 games, 0 home runs,**
.159 batting average

IT IS WITH great pleasure that I can relate what I remember about the days I played against the great Ted Williams.

As a catcher, it was very hard to call pitches when he was hitting. I think the umpires favored him because of his great eyesight. If he did not swing, they thought it had to be a ball.

Some said to call the fastball down the middle and surprise him. We, the Philadelphia A's, had a pitcher named Harry Byrd, who proclaimed that he was going to see how Ted hit laying flat on his back. He found out—the first time Byrd faced him, he knocked him down—Ted got up, brushed himself off, and proceeded to hit the next pitch nine miles out of the park.

I broke into the majors at Fenway Park in 1953,[4] and Ted was just back from the Armed Services and the Korean War. I remember that day well, too. When I came up in the latter part of the game, I hit a ball to the 380-foot marker in right field, and Jim Piersall jumped up and speared it. Ted came up in the eighth and hit a prolific blast to right that beat us.[5]

That year, when Boston came to Connie Mack Stadium, Ted and Gus Zernial staged a home run contest . . . this being the only game the stadium was filled. I was kind of thrilled to be designated to catch

---

[4] Watlington's debut was July 12, 1953, for the A's in Boston.
[5] Williams returned to action on August 6, 1953, against the St. Louis Browns. He played against the A's four times: August 11 (game two of a doubleheader), August 13, August 18, and August 19. Williams' home run in the seventh inning on August 19 at Fenway put the Red Sox ahead, 5–4, in a 6–4 win.

the contest. They were to have ten swings each. I think everyone was surprised when Gus out-hit him 4 home runs to 3.

The only conversation I ever had with him was briefly while catching the home run contest, but I did hear him talking to other ballplayers around pregame batting practice. He was eager to help players with advice and was well liked by all ballplayers.

There is one thing that stands out in my mind, and that is every time we saw him hit in pregame batting practice, everything got so quiet and [the stadium] came to a standstill. All activity stopped on the ball field and in the stands. I am privileged to say without a doubt that Ted Williams was the most pure hitter that I have ever seen.

INTERVIEWS

Bob Oldis

Catcher

1953–55: ....Washington Senators
1960–61: ....Pittsburgh Pirates
1962–63: .... Philadelphia Phillies
Career Statistics: .... 135 games, 1 home run,
.237 batting average

Q. Being a catcher, you had an interesting vantage point. What was your defensive/pitch selection strategy against Williams, and how do you think you fared?

A. High and tight, low and away

Q. Do you think Williams got the benefit of the umpires' calls and, if so, why?

A. No

Q. Recollections of any specific at-bats and/or plays vs. Williams.

A. Connie Marrero, a knuckleball pitcher for us in Washington was pitching, and Ted hit two home runs on knuckleballs. In the dugout, he said, next time he hits, we are going to give him four fast-ball pitchouts.[1]

Q. Was he the hitter you feared the most in the field?

A. He was just a good hitter—knew strike zone.

---

[1] On August 11, 1954, in the first game of a doubleheader at Boston, Williams homered off Marrero in the first and third innings. Marrero was lifted for a pinch-hitter in the fifth inning and wouldn't face Williams again that day.

Q. Did you ever have occasion to interact with Williams either when he was up at bat or off the field? If so, what kind of guy was he like?

A. In 1953, both teams came out of the Red Sox dugout, and the visitors had to walk across the field to the third-base dugout. The Red Sox were taking batting practice, and Ted stopped me and [my first time in Boston] wished me good luck and hoped [that I had a] successful career in the big leagues. After a little bit, he asked me about a rookie pitcher we had by the name of Pedro Ramos. I told him that he had a good fastball, hard curve (now slider), and good control—and when I went to our dugout, Mickey Vernon and Eddie Yost, my teammates, asked me, what did that big donkey want? He wished me good luck and congratulated me for getting to the big leagues and then asked me about Ramos, I told them. Mickey said to Eddie Yost, see, he already got a scouting report on Ramos.[2]

---

[2] In his career, Williams would end up hitting .365 with 6 home runs and a .730 slugging percentage against Ramos.

Red Wilson

Catcher

1951–54:	Chicago White Sox
1954–60:	Detroit Tigers
1960:	Cleveland Indians
Career Statistics:	2,037 games, 24 home runs, .258 batting average

Q. Being a catcher, you had an interesting vantage point. What was your defensive/pitch selection strategy against Williams, and how do you think you fared?

A. Pitch selection: Throw strikes or walk him—he didn't swing at "balls." We did okay.

Q. Do you think Williams got the benefit of the umpires' calls and, if so, why?

A. He got little if any favoritism from umpires.

Q. What was the talk among other players on how to face Williams in pregame meetings or just in general?

A. Ted Williams was respected as a player and an individual. Our effort was to concentrate on keeping his teammates off the bases, so he couldn't hurt you as much with his bat when hitting with the bases empty.

Q. Was he the hitter you feared the most in the field?

A. Yes

Q. Did you ever have occasion to interact with Williams either when he was up at bat or off the field? If so, what kind of guy was he like?

A. No contact off the field. Brief conversations about fishing in Wisconsin. He was a man of few words.

Section Three: Infielders

Dr. Bobby Brown

Third base / Shortstop

1946–52, 1954: .... New York Yankees
1984–94: .... President, American League
Career Statistics: .... 548 games, 22 home runs,
.279 batting average

WHEN I WAS playing shortstop, that shift wasn't in vogue. I think Lou Boudreau started that thing. I believe what we did is the third baseman would move over to shortstop, and then of course the shortstop went over behind second base, and the second baseman moved more towards first and a little deeper. I don't think they moved into the outfield like they do now.

I do remember that if they had a man at first base and he came up—usually [Johnny] Pesky hit second and Dom DiMaggio hit first—and if either one of them was on first, and second base wasn't occupied, the first thing Joe Collins would do is signal to the bench that he'd like to get halfway. He didn't want to be that close [laughs] when he was hitting. And he'd look over there with this look on his face, like, you've got to let me get back a little bit.

I read somewhere not too long ago that the shift never really bugged Ted too much. He'd either just hit over it or through it or whatnot, and he just whaled away [as usual]. They said that someone tried to teach him—well not teach him—but try to get him to hit to left field and [he] tried it but gave up on that. He just popped away in his usual way.

He was a swell guy. He was *extremely* popular with not only his own teammates, but with all of the opposing players, too. He'd talk to everybody if they wanted to talk. He was very, very helpful and always wanted to talk about hitting and whatnot.

One year I guess he broke his collarbone and they went in and tried to reattach the fragments. They used screws and whatnot, hoping that he'd be able to get back sooner. I remember visiting and asking him how it went and so forth, and he said, well, he was just getting his swing back. I saw him swing a few times and he knocked all the air out of the place where he was swinging, and I said, "Well, I think you're doing okay, Ted." He was very much interested in surgery. When he was in the hospital, he told me that what he did . . . I think he broke his clavicle, and then he also broke his radius in the All-Star Game.[1] He injured the head of the radius, which is a bad break, and they were very worried whether they'd be able to get a good result, but they did. But he told me that he would show up in the operating room at about six o'clock in the morning before anybody got there and they'd let him scrub in, and he'd stay in the operating room all day, watching operations. He really enjoyed that. I said, "What did you like the most?" He said, "I like the eye operations the best." So I do remember that.

Outside of the ball field, I didn't see much of him. As I said, I did see him when he was getting over those injuries, because I was a doctor or I was in medical school. I was in med school when I was playing and graduated in 1950. I was just curious of how he was getting along. Usually he was rehabbing when I'd see him.

He was done managing by the time I started in the American League [as President], but I was in Texas when he came down for his first year; he came down with the Senators. He was just here one year. I had little chance to talk with him. I might have said hello a few times, but as I recall, there was no lengthy conversations or anything.

He loved to fish. He loved to hunt, but he *really* loved to fish. As you know, he gave those exhibitions of fly casting at Madison Square

---

[1] In the 1950 All-Star Game at Comiskey Park, Williams crashed into the wall catching a Ralph Kiner fly ball, injuring his elbow.

Garden when they had the big hunt and fish show up there. He'd put [on] demonstrations of fly casting. I guess he was one of the best in the world at that. For a long time, he was the top expert at Sears in testing new equipment: camping equipment, fishing rods, guns, and so on and so forth. He was excellent at that.

We were all friendly with the Red Sox, but it was a war on the field. But they all had good guys; there was no viciousness to it. It was just guys that *really* played hard because they knew it was two tough teams that would hook up. But they were all good guys.

Ted got along with everybody. He had his deals with the press and the fans, but with the ballplayers, he was always first-rate. He missed, what, five seasons with Korea and World War II?

He was ultimately dangerous wherever he was. It didn't make any difference what ballpark he was in. There was no such thing as he'd hit better in the short fields. No, he made all fields just . . . they were all very good for him. He could just flat hit, as you know.

Joe [DiMaggio] was a more complete player. He's a guy who could run and throw and field and hit, but Ted as a hitter was probably the best hitter of that era. He and [Stan] Musial and Joe were all three right in there together. There were a couple of others that were close, like Johnny Mize and some of the others. And then Hank Aaron came on a little after I left. I think he came on the first year that I retired, and he was in the National League, so I didn't see him. But Ted was certainly the best hitter of his era.

They talked about that [the supposed DiMaggio-for-Williams trade], but Joe would have hit . . . if Joe didn't have to go into the service and played in Fenway Park, he would have hit 700 home runs. He would have! And Ted would have hit more home runs, too. But both of them would have hit better if Ted hit in Yankee Stadium and Joe hit in Fenway. Joe—I think one series up there, maybe in '49—I think he hit five home runs in three games.

That's a lot of baloney [that if Williams didn't swing the umpire would call it a ball]. That's just a lot of baloney. Obviously he was a good hitter, and good hitters have good eyesight. You watched everybody at batting practice, but you always watched him, too, because he was fun to watch.

You have to remember, in those days, they must have had maybe five dailies in Boston, and, of course, they had other New England papers, so they were always looking for angles. That put a real strain on the ballplayer because they were always trying to find some gimmick that they could write about. And the same thing happened in New York. We had, I think, maybe seven daily papers in New York at the time. They had big press corps that really tried to write about things. Of course in those days, they had to write a lot more about the ball game itself. Nowadays, they don't have to write the exact account because it's on TV. But before TV became commonplace, they had to write about the ball game. That was a good bit of their writing, but they were always looking for an angle somewhere. Especially in Boston.

He would speak his peace. Sometimes in Boston that wasn't exactly beneficial. They were irate fans—just like they are now. They lived and died with the Red Sox, and anyone else that came in there was the enemy. So you expected that. They would get on Ted, sure. One of the columnists was really hard on him—Egan, the old Colonel, I think his name was—he was always on Ted with bad write-ups and so forth. But it couldn't be too bad; the guy hit .350 every damn year.

There wasn't a big contingent of fans that were against him. They loved the guy up there, but he did some things and whatnot, and they'd get mad at him. Just like in New York; they'd get mad at DiMaggio. They'd want a perfect game every day, and of course, that's not going to happen.

Tom Carroll

Shortstop / Third base

1955–56:	**New York Yankees**
1959:	**Kansas City Athletics**
Career Statistics:	**64 games, 0 home runs, .300 batting average**

WELL, I WAS a rookie bonus player in 1955, and I pinch-ran in several games, played in the field a couple of innings, and didn't even get an at-bat until the last day of the season. We were in Boston and had clinched the pennant in '55 that day, and there was a doubleheader to end the season. So I played both games of the doubleheader the next day at shortstop.[2]

I had never played on the second-base side—in Little League or anytime else. So when Williams came up, you know, we put the shift on. I'm on the second-base side on the outfield grass, and I'm very uncomfortable. I'm not so uncomfortable just because it's *him*, but because I'm on the wrong side of second base [laughs]. But as I said, I'm on the outfield grass, so one thing I could do is really throw the ball.

Anyway, I don't remember what at-bat it was of his—it was either his first or second at-bat[3]—and he hit a line drive at me. And you instinctively know whether, you know, it's in range or not. It was definitely in range. It was about a foot or two to my left. A really well-hit line drive is *dead* at you, and maybe a little bit rising. Occasionally, you get a line drive that *knuckleballs* at you.

---

[2] Carroll pinch-ran, played shortstop, and batted twice in the first game of a doubleheader on September 25, 1955, and started and led off in game two.

[3] It was his first at-bat. Williams walked his second time up and was replaced by a pinch runner.

This didn't do any of those things [laughs]. And I stuck out my arm, you know, I've got the ball, I've got the ball. And it was *by* me! And that line drive came at me not on the dead level, not rising, and not a knuckleball. It came at me like a golf shot. Terrific overspin on the ball. I mean sort of [like]—what was the great Swedish tennis player? [Bjorn] Borg. That used to get this tremendous undercut topspin, only more so on me [laughs]. It was just amazing. I never—I mean, I did play six years of ball in Triple-A and the majors—but I never saw that. I never saw a ball come at me like that.

The most amazing thing that I saw in baseball involved Ted Williams. He was, in my opinion, the greatest hitter I ever saw—and I played with [Mickey] Mantle and [Roger] Maris. I played with Maris in Kansas City and Mantle in '55, '56, and again briefly in '59. In '59, I played two years—'57 and '58—in Triple-A, but knew I wasn't going to make the team. I was in the army that winter and got to spring training late. But to make a long story short, I went north with the team because my options were up. So I was sitting on the bench when the season began, and we began it against the Red Sox in New York.

Williams had apparently been hurt and missed most of or part of the end of the season in '58. And how old was he in '59? I think he was thirty-nine or something like that. He was born in 1918? So he was forty-one . . . forty to start the season. I don't know what kind of year he had in '58, but I understood that he banged into a wall or hurt an arm and had missed a month or two at the end of the season.

It was the first series of 1959, and Bob Turley was pitching. He was not only the Yankee player representative, but he was one of the hardest throwers in the league. A power pitcher. He first faced Williams in the top of the first. Turley was throwing him fastballs. Williams didn't get around on the ball and hit a lazy fly ball to left-center, which, because Mantle was playing [him] as a strict pull-hitter as he should have been, played him in right-center and didn't get to the ball, and Williams had a loafing double.

So, the second time he was up—and Turley was still on, throwing really hard—Jim Turner was our pitching coach. He was very aggressive . . . we used to call him Colonel Jim. He took a lot of things on himself, and Stengel gave him free reign with setting up the pitching rotation; but occasionally, Turner exceeded his brief. But he's decided that Williams, who was injured in '58, and was fairly old at this time, can't get around on Turley.

So he tells [Frank] Crosetti, who was the infield coach, to get Mantle over in center field from right-center. And Crosetti jumps up on the dugout steps in the stadium and starts whistling in this very piercing whistle at Mantle to move, waving him over. And Mantle doesn't see him for a while, so the whole game is stopped. And I don't know if you know, but Williams was famous for having rabbit ears: always looking in the other dugout, always wanted to see what was going on. He's watching all this by the way. And in fact, they used to do things when he was at-bat to try and distract him by whistling and doing all kinds of things . . . not very successfully.

So, Mantle didn't see him for the longest time. When he finally saw Crosetti waving him over, he just refused [laughs] . . . he refused to believe it or act on it, so he's sort of stuck in right-center. The game is totally stopped, but Crosetti keeps waving at him, and finally Mantle kind of stomps toward dead straight-away center field.

As I said, Williams is watching all of this. So Mantle gets positioned in dead center field, and I don't know if it was the next pitch or the second pitch thereafter, but Turley threw a fastball in on Williams' hands, and he hit into the third deck of Yankee Stadium about five feet fair. And that was the most amazing thing that I've ever seen.[4]

And you know, he was well-respected by his teammates and by his opponents. Everybody thought he was a great hitter. His being a bad guy or not a team player—that was all started by the newspaper situation in Boston and by this guy Colonel Egan, Dave Egan, who was a *drunk*. Early in Williams' career—I think Williams came up in '39, is that what it was? And you know he had terrific years right from the get-go. But he was sort of invited or commanded to an interview with Egan, who wrote for the *Boston Eagle* or something,[5] I don't remember which particular paper. And one of the problems in Boston is that they [have] six or seven papers that were all competing with each other. And Egan, who was a lush, had Williams come in for this interview. I think it was in a hotel room. And Egan was drunk, just so you know, and Williams walked out on him. So they were enemies from then on. So Egan did his level best to defame Williams. And then there were pro- and anti-Williams factions on the newspapers and stuff. But he loved to talk hitting, and he'd talk hitting with everybody, including with people on the other team. He was very supportive of me. We only had one conversation, but he was very encouraging.

He hated lousy hitters, bad hitting. Sammy White was a great defensive catcher for the Red Sox for years. He was a tall, rangy guy, and he did everything wrong at the plate. And [I believe] he was a .220 hitter for his career.[6] So much so that Williams, when White would be in batting practice, would get so upset with White not changing and

---

[4] The game Carroll is likely talking about occurred in July 4, 1955. In that game, Williams doubled off Turley in the first inning and homered in the fifth. The Yankees did open with the Red Sox in 1959, but Williams didn't make his season debut until May 12. Carroll was traded from the Yankees to Kansas City on April 12. Williams hit four other homers off Turley, but Carroll was not with a major-league team during any of those times.

[5] The paper was the *Boston Record*.

[6] White's career batting average was .262, but it was .261 and .245 in the years that Carroll was with the Yankees.

improving and doing some things fundamentally different, that he'd turn his back. He couldn't bear to watch White swing the bat [laughs]!

His book, *The Science of Hitting*, is absolutely interesting. He divides the strike zone into probably twelve squares in that book. And he shows as you wander away from the fat part of the strike zone . . . what his projected batting average would be. As you got out on the corners, his average dropped. He was a .250 hitter in some of these places, which is very interesting, and I think very accurate description of the facts of hitting.

He would do one thing very unusual; he didn't have a narrow stance with his feet. He had an average or I'd say a little longer than average stance, but as he hit in a game—I mean, for real—he'd stride forward, oh, six inches or more, which is very normal.

I saw him take batting practice a lot, and he'd spread out his feet to where his foot would be after the stride in a game and hit that way. I guess it would force his arms and his hands to be quicker, because he wasn't getting the impetus from the weight moving forward. I never talked to him or got an explanation from him, but I suspect that's what it was.

Jerry Coleman

Second base / Shortstop / Third base

1949–57:...New York Yankees
American League All-Star: 1950
Career Statistics: .... 723 games, 16 home runs,
.263 batting average

HE WAS THE best hitter in baseball, maybe one of the greatest hitters of all time. He doesn't have as many hits as [Ty] Cobb—he hit .344 and Cobb hit .367—but Cobb was a running guy and a bunting guy, and Williams . . . you know, if he had done early in his career what he did the last year he led the league in hitting—bounce the ball off the left-field wall—he'd have hit .900. But he was a power guy and in Fenway Park, the toughest part of the ballpark was to right-center field, and that's where most of his balls went.

Of course [Yankees manager Casey] Stengel pulled me in [for the shift]. I forget when it was . . . I think [Cardinals manager] Eddie Dyer was the first guy to use that shift in the World Series. They played the Cardinals in '46, and I think Dyer was the first one to have the swing-around—and of course they do it all the time now.[7] Anyway, Stengel sent me to short right field—and this is a true story. I'm out there [thinking], I've been out here for a couple years and he's never hit a line drive to me since I've been out there. So he says to me come on in. And I'm going to tell you this is the God's honest truth. The first game, a sinking line drive right over my head right where I would have been standing, but I wasn't. It was amazing. I stayed in [from then on]. See, the problem is, anytime there's a runner at first base, you have to come in for a possible double play. And so I'm trying to think, [Al] Zarilla was the number two hitter or Billy Goodman, and Dominic

---

[7] Dyer had the Cardinals play a form of the shift in the 1946 World Series, but Cleveland manager Lou Boudreau used the Williams shift earlier that season.

[DiMaggio] started it off, but there was always someone at first base [and] I had to come in. But there were probably, because of that ball-club and their hitting skills and their 1-2 hitters, I didn't get to play out there as much as I did out there normally if they had bad 1-2 hitters.

He was such a great hitter and [received] the greatest animosity of any ballplayer in history. You know, the sportswriters hated him there. The highlight of my career (and his) was when he came around and hit a home run and jumped up at home plate and spit at them at Fenway Park [laughs]. I just thought that was outstanding!

[Albert] Pujols is a good player, but Williams was a *nationally* good player, as were [Joe] DiMaggio, [Mickey] Mantle, and [Willie] Mays. These were guys that covered the entire United States. Pujols was great with the Cardinals, but not to the extent that these guys were—not from a press standpoint. There's more things going on in baseball *and* in sports these days.

But he was not a great defensive player. In fact, the reason we beat the Red Sox in one of those final two games was that he butchered a line drive that went by him. Should have been a double and it became a triple. [Phil] Rizzuto hit it. Then [Tommy] Henrich hit a 27-hopper ground ball to Bobby Doerr, and we stayed ahead in the game. That might have been the final game, I'm not sure.[8] That play Williams *didn't* make might have cost the Red Sox a pennant. It's a true story. The triple was really a double that he botched.

He wasn't bad in left field. He knew how to play that left-field wall very well, even when the ball was going to hit the wall and he couldn't get it. And he could run. You know, if you played too deep on him . . . I got a couple of ground balls back in right field and he'd beat

---

[8] On the final day of the season in 1949—October 2—the Red Sox and Yankees were tied for first place. Phil Rizzuto led off the bottom of the first with a triple, and the next batter, Tommy Henrich, drove him in. The Yankees would never trail in the game, which they would go on to win, 5–3.

them out. It was amazing. He could run quite well, I thought, for a big man. He was a thin guy, of course, but this was at the end of his career.

He basically, I think, was the greatest hitter I ever saw. He had *one* great day against us and Vic Raschi, hitting two home runs at Yankee Stadium in the upper deck. And I'll tell you, we pretty much stopped them. Now, you have to look these things up. My memory bank is dead. Now, you're talking a couple of years ago. More than a week or two [laughs]![9] Tommy Byrne struck him out twice in one game and he walked. But I do know this—Ted was a *very* sharp person. He used to stroke the umpires all the time. Sit with them and talk with them and this and that. Well, you know, umpires are human. I'm not saying they gave him the benefit of the doubt all the time, but I do think when you have that situation, you have this guy Williams, you are prone to not strike him out, if it's a marginal thing, you see. So you give him the benefit of the doubt. That might have happened, and I personally think it did happen. I know Tommy Byrne, our left-handed guy, had a fastball and a breaking ball that exploded; the trouble was that he walked 27 men a game. That's why they traded him; he walked too many people. But I know he struck him out twice and he got ball four.[10]

I roomed with Mickey [Mantle] for two years, and he was one of the finest human beings on this earth. He was a follower. When somebody said, let's go have a cocktail, he'd go with them. If they said, let's go to a movie, he'd go to a movie. Had Mickey been a guy that didn't drink, didn't smoke, didn't do all these things, he would have lived another

---

[9] On September 24, 1950, Williams hit two solo home runs off Vic Raschi in a 9–5 New York win at Yankee Stadium.

[10] On April 30, 1949, Tommy Byrne struck out Williams the first two times he faced him, then walked him the third time.

ten years. Now, Williams, he took good care of himself. Of course, for him, his goal was to be the greatest hitter that ever lived. And he might have been, if you consider average and power.

A lot of those other guys were doubles hitters or single hitters, Cobb was a bunter and runner and so forth, and even [Tony] Gwynn at .338 doesn't touch Williams' .344. But I do think this—I think it is harder to hit now than when Williams played. The pitchers are better; the bullpen has changed the game. If the guy hiccups in the fourth inning, he's gone, and you bring in a 100 mile-per-hour fastball or 98 or something like that, then two more guys just like him. And pitching is tough to hit now, that's what I think.

Photo courtesy of the United States Navy

Jerry Coleman played against Ted Williams, took his military physical in the same place as Williams, and, in his post-baseball career, saw Williams when he visited.

He lived in San Diego. The man who ran sports things in San Diego at the park—Williams was his god. And he's got Williams' bat that he hit .400 with and those kind of things. If he ever wanted to sell it— well, he's dead now—but he's got a fortune in his office somewhere. But Ted used to come all the time and we'd entertain him at our dinners. I was there the day they named the boulevard after him. In fact, I got up and made a speech and told everybody how much I hated him—no, I didn't [laughs]. I use that phrase—I didn't like Ted—because he was on the other team, that's all.

He didn't talk to banjo hitters [laughs]. The last time we met to hold hands was when we went overseas down in El Toro,[11] and they were taking pictures of these two great ballplayers going to win the war. Of course we did win the war single-handedly.

We took our physicals together in Jacksonville. And [laughs] Ted had broken his elbow or something in Chicago the year before—I don't know what happened, he ran into the fence—and the guy patted it twice and said, "You're fine." He had no chance of missing that physical, I tell you. But he went to a different place for preparation, somewhere in the East; I was on the West Coast. But we had the same gathering together when we went overseas to Korea. He went to k-3 and I went to k-6.

The only time I ever heard about Williams overseas after departing—when we went to our various squadrons—was when the Marines went on a big mission once in North Korea somewhere. And all of a sudden, "I'm hit, I'm hit! I've got a mayday, I've got a mayday!" We're listening to this. Now *that* becomes your brother, because you know it is one of your guys. And we're listening and finally someone says, "I got ya, I got ya. We'll go to 55, follow me." And the next thing I know, they get to 55, and there's no more conversation on the air. The next day I find out it was Ted Williams. He landed at k-55, I believe it was no wheels, no flaps, going about 80 knots faster than he should—you land at 150, and he was going about 220 or something. Why he didn't blow I'll never know. Usually you blow up when you get like that. When he got out of that, it was really a miracle that he survived.

What happened [laughs] . . . Ted started castigating the Marine Corps for getting him there, and they took him out of there because they didn't want the bad publicity. He did a great job over there, but he was such a prominent figure that if he said, "I didn't like this," it went all over the United States.

---

[11] El Toro is a Marine Corps air station in San Diego.

The trouble is, if you said, "Ted, what about this slider?" Thirty minutes later, he was done. One of the great things . . . he came out here to one of our dinners, and Gwynn at one time had four batting titles and missed the last one. And they're chatting and chatting and chatting. And Gwynn—what he got from Williams in that one meeting—led the league in hitting the next four years. You could look it up.[12] Late in his career as well, and Williams led the league in hitting when he was thirty-nine, I believe.[13]

He wasn't a great defensive player or a great runner or stuff like that, but his bat and knowledge of the game was unsurpassed. The more I think about it—what he did and how he did it—just incredible. We used to stack all the time against him, and we had great pitching, too. The only game where I recall where we really got nailed by Ted was when he hit the two home runs off Raschi, off hanging curveballs or something.

I'll never forget; we were in spring training in '52, and we both had our [military] call-up coming up, and they gave us a physical in Jacksonville in some hotel. So when it's over, we go into the elevator down to the bottom. The way it worked was that the garage let out onto two different streets. It went right into a through street and into the next one and then right into another one. And some little midget of a writer came up about the time we got there, and looked up [laughs] at Ted from the street, and then he [Williams] said, "You little son of

---

[12] Gwynn won three straight batting titles from 1987–89, then went four years without winning one, although he finished second in the National League in 1993. From 1994–97, Gwynn, from the ages of thirty-four to thirty-seven, won four straight batting titles with averages of .394, .368, .353, and .372. He had hit higher than .353 just twice in his first twelve seasons.

[13] Williams won his final batting title in 1958 at the age of thirty-nine, with a .328 average.

a bitch, get the hell away," and started running in the other direction [laughs]. He tried to track him.

Apparently the writers were really maliciously difficult on him . . . and because he was the one to write about. He was *the* guy. Like DiMaggio in New York, he was *the* guy. They weren't bad on Joe, but I think they burned him [Williams] pretty bad in Boston, and I think he resented it deeply over the years.

Billy DeMars

Shortstop / Third base / Second base

1948: .... Philadelphia Athletics
1950–51: ....St. Louis Browns
Career Statistics: .... 80 games, 0 home runs,
.237 batting average

IN THE MAJOR leagues we used the Williams shift. It was the best way to play him, but he still managed to get his base hits.

We all knew that he was the best hitter in the game. During batting practice before the game, we would all stop and watch him hit.

I played with him in 1945 at Jacksonville Naval Air Station, where we were 45–6. He didn't have much to do with the minor league players. We had Charles Gehringer and Bob Kennedy, and he spent most of his time with them.

Gail Harris

First base

1955–57: ....**New York Giants**
1958–60: ....**Detroit Tigers**
Career Statistics: .... **437 games, 51 home runs,**
.240 batting average

IPLAYED IN BOTH leagues, and Williams was the greatest pull-hitter of all-time. His ground balls and line drives would eat you up. I played on the outfield grass with nobody on base. We used the shift to no avail, as he was able to just hit balls through the shift.

On July 20, 1958, we played the Red Sox in Fenway. It was Vermont Day, and they were giving maple candy for base hits, extra-base hits, home runs, etc. [Jim] Bunning had retired 26 batters in a row. The last hitter was Williams for his no-hitter. I walked over to the mound, and Bunning said to me, "I could pitch around Williams and pitch to Jackie Jensen, who has never hit me. I'm going to give that big sucker all I have left. If he hits it, he hits it." Williams fouled off two fastballs. With the count 2–2, he hit a monstrous fly ball that [Al] Kaline caught for the final out. I thanked the Lord for keeping the ball away from me.[14]

He was a perfectionist. A great baseball player, a marine pilot, and an expert fly fisherman. His vision was unbelievable. Only two players said they were able to know the type of pitch that was coming to the plate—Williams and [Stan] Musial.

The greatest scene I ever saw was the reaction of the major league players when Williams came out in the golf cart at the All-Star Game.[15]

---

[14] Bunning pitched a no-hitter against the Red Sox on July 20, 1958, walking two and striking out 12. Williams went 0–4 and flied out to right field to end the game. Frank Malzone batted behind Williams, with Jensen after Malzone. In his career, Williams hit .377 with a .500 on-base percentage and .852 slugging percentage off Bunning. Malzone was .250/.293/.326 vs. Bunning, and Jensen was .165/.242/.259.
[15] At the 1999 All-Star Game in Fenway Park.

Grady Hatton

Third base / Second base

1946–54:	Cincinnati Reds
1954:	Chicago White Sox
1954–56:	Boston Red Sox
1956:	St. Louis Cardinals
1956:	Baltimore Orioles
1960:	Chicago Cubs
Career Statistics:	1,312 games, 91 home runs, .254 batting average
National League All-Star:	1952

I NEVER PLAYED AGAINST Ted and only played two years with him. Players who did play against him played short right field. Ted had no speed and infielders could play deep.

When I played with him, he liked to talk hitting with all.

Ted was a fine man and was fun on the club. He was good to young kids and signed autographs.

Randy Jackson

Third base

1950–55:	**Chicago Cubs**
1956–57:	**Brooklyn Dodgers**
1958:	**Los Angeles Dodgers**
1958-59:	**Cleveland Indians**
1959:	**Chicago Cubs**
Career Statistics:	**955 games, 103 home runs, .261 batting average**
National League All-Star:	**1954, 1955**

I WAS JUST TRADED to Cleveland from the Dodgers, and my first time up in Cleveland, I hit a triple and pulled a muscle between second and third, so I'm out again.[16]

[After I] recovered, we came into Fenway to play a weekend series. Friday night, the manager let me pinch-hit, and I hit a ball over the wall in left field. So he said, "Okay, you're playing tomorrow."[17]

So I went out there and Williams came up in the first inning. They, of course had the shift; they moved over, and I moved over from third to shortstop. And I was just standing there. This was maybe about my fourth week in the major leagues [that season], and I had only played one game because of my injuries. And I was standing there saying, you know, god almighty, this is the first time I've seen Fenway Park—I had spent all of my career in the National League—and I was just standing there saying, god almighty, here's Ted Williams [coming] up. I came out and watched batting practice just to see him hit and there he is,

---

[16] Jackson was purchased by Cleveland from the Dodgers on August 4, 1958. In his first game with the Indians, game one of an August 10 doubleheader, he tripled to lead off the bottom of the sixth, and then was replaced by a pinch runner.

[17] Jackson first returned on August 17 and struck out as a pinch hitter. On August 20, he entered in the ninth inning at third base and did not bat. On August 21 at Fenway, he hit a pinch-hit home run.

he's up at the plate and he doesn't ever hit it this way, so I can just stand here and watch him . . . and he hit a one-hopper off my shins and I didn't even have a chance to move. You talk about a big knot on your leg the next day. My leg stopped it. I can't remember if they gave him a hit or not—I'm sure they gave him a hit.[18] I don't know how long the American League insignia was on my leg, but it was there for a while.

Randy Jackson took home a "souvenir" the only time he played against Ted Williams.

But that was my first and only experience playing against Ted Williams and the only time I've ever seen him play, except on TV or something.

There wasn't much reason to talk about him in the National League because you never saw him. Pitchers weren't going to get together and say how we going to pitch Ted Williams. They're in the National League; they're not going to be pitching against him.

He just was an idol—not an idol—but had the utmost respect. Because you knew what kind of person he was

---

[18] Williams was credited with a single.

and what kind of record he had. Even though he may be in another league, you had respect for him.

I never met him. I was never around him other than that one three-game series. But you just read about him and listen to commentators. I don't think I ever asked any ballplayer who came over from the American League, "What you think of Ted Williams?" The only thing I knew is that he and Mickey Mantle were the highest-paid players in the league one year, and they made $100,000, and $100,000 was like way out of there.

You hear about people, about other ballplayers, and you've never seen them, and they're the best that there is, so why not go out there and sit in the dugout and watch Ted Williams hit batting practice? I mean, that was a thrill to me, just to see that. I don't remember if there were other guys—I didn't really care, I just wanted to do it for myself because I knew I probably wouldn't get to do it again. I don't think any ball-players lost any sleep out of going out and coming out to watch me hit.

I had a very interesting experience [with Ted Williams] and got a sore leg out of it.

Bob Johnson

Second base / third base / shortstop

1960:	Kansas City Athletics
1961–62:	Washington Senators
1963–67:	Baltimore Orioles
1967:	New York Mets
1968:	Cincinnati Reds
1969:	St. Louis Cardinals
1969–70:	Oakland Athletics
Career Statistics:	874 games, 44 home runs, .272 batting average

HIS LAST YEAR was 1960, which was my first year. The story that you hear the most is his last time up in Boston and he hits the home run and goes right to the clubhouse, never tipped his hat, decided this is it, see you guys later. And I think if I'm not mistaken, that's what happened on the last play of his career.

I got to know him a little bit. He had a good friend who was in charge of the scoreboard at Metropolitan Stadium. That fellow's name was Charlie Wilcox. Charlie was a little older, but somehow he and Ted became good friends. Charlie worked the scoreboard at the ballpark out in Bloomington. And Charlie, he'd come in and sit in the dugout and they'd talk. I think Charlie was probably one of Ted's favorite people in the major leagues. Ted wasn't going to overwhelm you with his desire to talk, but he really just made friends with Charlie. And I knew him [Charlie] quite well. Our daughter, he always took a liking to our daughter, and we used to go out for dinner a lot of the times and the conversation always seemed to come back to Ted Williams. And what a neat guy he was.

I recall one incident where Williams and Charlie decided to—he had to catch a train, I think, to go somewhere, Williams did. They had played what might have been an afternoon game. So they went to a movie and Williams had to leave to catch a train to go to Chicago, and he said, "Charlie what I want you do to is, this is a pretty good movie and it will take us a while to get down there, so as soon as this movie is over call me at the hotel and let me know how it comes out."

He had his own individuals that he talked to more than somebody else. I'm not sure where they fit in with the sportswriters, some he preferred more than others. But this Charlie Wilcox that I mentioned, he became like a brother to Charlie.

And to go back when he was playing with the Minneapolis Millers way back, and how he broke the water cooler over a called strike that wasn't a strike, as far as he was concerned. He took out his frustration on the water cooler when he went back to the dugout.

But Williams, his reputation always seemed to precede him, but he had the great eye. Joe Mauer has that kind of an eye, where if he doesn't swing at it, the umpire doesn't call it a strike. But Williams, he had that bat in his hand he was just like squeezing it and moving it, and somehow whether you're an infielder or an outfielder you need to have some kind of a way of being able to relax, and that's how Ted used to do it.

I used to go out and watch him take batting practice before the game started. I picked up his bat one time and looked, I was trying to determine where he hit the ball and it was right on the sweet spot every time. Everything else was smooth, there wasn't any detail or anything. Where he hit the ball on the sweet spot, right below the lettering, he hit it there every time. You pick my bat up and it's all over the bat! His was strictly the sweet spot and mine was whatever spot I swung at.

You know he'd be right at the top where great hitters are concerned. I think he had to learn how to play the outfield but that gave him more time to . . . he knew he'd always be able to hit, so that gave him more time to put in to be a better outfielder, too. He learned how to play left field pretty well, too, there in Boston with the Green Monster. But he was quite a guy . . . heh, heh . . . the Thumper.

What I enjoyed doing was going out and watching him hit and take batting practice. He provided a lot of thrill to watch him go out there and look for a pitch. It seemed like he never swung unless it was to his liking—not to the pitcher's liking. You get somebody like that . . . and I don't know how many walks he had, but to measure a good hitter and a guy with a great eye, he usually has more walks than strikeouts. And that would have been Ted.[19] And as probably as many or more walks that they put him on purposely.

It was a thrill to just be sitting out on the bench and hear him talking and see him play. A lot of guys didn't get a chance to see him play because his career was over in 1960.

There's some that can talk a good game but they maybe don't play it. He played it, talked it, and did everything necessary to be a great player but also somebody where you'd want to pick up the paper and see how'd he do last night.

He was a little kind of red-ass, but that was okay. I think that in his case that's just the way he was and he got by with it. But boy, when it came time to go up there and hit that ball, he just attacked it. When you have a great eye, you can wait for your pitch and you can get to a point where you'll take two pitches if you're looking for a certain pitch and aren't going to get it until the third pitch, he's probably going to get it and still hit it hard.

I had a friend that said one time, I think he kind of put it wisely, he said how'd you like to go to the ballpark every day and hit the ball three out of four times right on the sweet spot. He was referring to Williams.

It would have been nice to know him a little more, but you need those kind of guys to show you how to *play* the game. They know how to play the game, they know what it takes to be a winner and that was Williams.

---

[19] For his career, Williams never struck out more than he walked, and his season-high was 64 Ks, which was in 1939, his first year in pro ball.

Charlie Kress

First base

1947, 1949:	Cincinnati Reds
1949–50:	Chicago White Sox
1954:	Detroit Tigers
1954:	Brooklyn Dodgers
Career Statistics:	175 games, 1 home run, .249 batting average

HE HIT BULLETS. He was the greatest hitter that I ever saw. He hit line drives, I mean, you had to have your glove up. At first base, I got out as far back in right field as I could get and still get back to the bag. I would be back on the grass quite a bit.

When you had to hold a man on first base . . . to give you an illustration, we were playing up in Fenway Park, and Dom DiMaggio was on first base, and I was holding him on. When I held him on, I would just pivot around real quick and put the glove up in front of my face. I mean, I didn't run out, didn't take a step or anything. Anyway, he hit a bullet over my head, and Dom DiMaggio never moved. I turned and looked, and the ball was already bouncing in the right-field seats in Fenway Park. That's how quick it got out there. Oh, he was uncanny.

We used to pick up the bat when he took batting practice and

Photo courtesy of Charlie Kress

Charlie Kress played against Ted Williams both in the American League and the military service.

there'd be one spot, one area, which had grass stains on it from the ball. Not on the handle, not down the barrel, not down the end of the bat, not on the underside—just one spot, like he painted it there. Oh, he was unbelievable, really.

I played against him in the service, too. I was lucky to play against him quite a few times. A real nice guy, too, I really enjoyed talking with him. When I played against him in the service, we had a pitcher by the name of Homer Spragins, who pitched for the Phillies, and could throw about 95–96 miles-an-hour. One day in the gym after we played a ball game, Williams and I we were having sandwiches and stuff, and he asked me, "Would you call that fellow over that pitched today?" So I called Spragins over, and I said, "Ted wants to talk to you." So we stood there and he [Williams] said, "Now, son, I don't want you to think I'm getting cocky or anything, but, when you hold your fastball, you hold it with the seams, don't you?" And Spragins said, "Yeah, why?" And Ted said, "Well, when you hold it with the seams, I can see the rotation of the ball. If you hold it across the seams, it makes it a little tougher for me to follow." Can you imagine that?

He's the one guy—and this has been documented—that [said] when the ball hits the bat, the bat actually bends a little and the ball flattens a little bit. And they said you can't actually see that. So they took slow-motion pictures and the bat *does* bend a little bit and the ball *does* flatten. So that will tell you what kind of eyesight he had.

[While we were in the military], he was over near Pensacola, and I was at Eglin Field in Florida. They had a catcher—we were playing Tyndall Field one day, another air force base nearby—and this catcher says, "Charlie you want to look at this." He had an 8 x 12 photograph—and he wouldn't sell it to me and told me he wasn't going to make any copies because it was the only one—and it showed Ted Williams in the batter's box, and his eye was focused right on the ball, like he's going to drill a hole in it. And it's in the picture. And he hadn't moved a muscle, and the catcher said I could field the ball. We had him!

And he hit that ball over a hangar in right field about 500 feet from home plate. That's how quick he exploded. He was just uncanny.

I talked to him about everything. Herb Score was a great left-handed pitcher. Gil McDougald put him out of baseball; hit him with a baseball right in the face. But Herb Score was a terrific left-hander, real hard to hit. When we played the Red Sox, he [Williams] came over to me and said, "Have you faced Herb Score yet?" And I said, no [laughs], they don't play me against guys that good. I play against the right-handers. And he said, "What do you think he throws in the clutch?" And I said, "*Well*, he's got a hell of a fastball and he probably can get that over a little better than his curveball." And I remember Ted saying, "Well, I'll see what I can do with him." I watched the box scores and the first time he faced him, he hit one up in the seats in left-center field.[20] He made a study of hitting. He just knew what it was all about.

We had a ceremony up in Fenway Park, and they had a Ted Williams Day, and we're all lined up at home plate. Our team was on one side, on the third-base side towards home plate lined up, and the Boston Red Sox were lined up on the right side. And the microphone with Ted and the emcee was right there at home plate. And they gave him—and right next to me, I was the second guy in line [was] Joe Tipton, [who] was our catcher.[21] He was right next to Ted, and I was next to Tipton, and they gave Ted all this fishing equipment: fly rods, reels, all kinds of lures and flies, I mean, a whole bunch of stuff. And Tipton leaned over to Ted and [whispered], "Ted, if you don't need this stuff, I can use it [laughs]." And Ted just grinned at him.

---

[20] Williams first faced Score on June 7, 1955, and doubled his first time up against him. The second time Williams faced Score was June 19, 1955, and he homered off him in the fifth inning.

[21] Kress and Tipton were teammates with the White Sox in 1949.

So we're in the clubhouse after the game, and here comes the clubhouse fellow and he gave all that stuff to Tipton. The whole works. I don't know the value of that stuff, but it had to be a lot of money. And I thought, "Charlie, why in the hell didn't you say something?" But I wasn't a fly fisherman. I love to fish, and that's how Ted and I got to talk a little more because of fishing. I could talk his language, although not the kind of fishing he did all the time.

I've got pictures with him at a reunion we had down in Florida, and I remember we were all standing around waiting, and someone [whispered], "Here comes Ted, here comes Ted." And sure I saw all these guys came around. And what amazed me, the players he played with—like Walt Dropo and Mel Parnell—they all stood in line to shake hands with Ted. He just sat there on the sofa. Fortunately, I got to sit next to him and have my picture taken with him. But, yeah, I thought, here's a guy they played with all year and they're still standing in line to shake hands with him. That's respect.

He's the only player that I saw—and I played against [Joe] DiMaggio and Stan Musial and guys like that—and he's the only guy that stopped everything on the ball field when he stepped into the batting cage. Guys running in the outfield, guys playing pepper in back of the cage, guys just playing catch, talking around—when he walked in there, it was just like a curtain dropped down that field. Everything stopped. And he hit until he had enough. But he was fantastic. The ability that man had. If he hadn't put in those four years in the marines, there'd be records out there that no one would catch. Normally you'd go up there and bunt one and hit five, but he just walked in there and he hit until he was ready.

Yeah, he was a quite a hitter . . . and a good outfielder, too. I remember I hit a couple of balls off that Green Monster in Fenway Park in left field, and he held me to a single. Most of the time you can get a double out of it, but not with him. He played that wall like he knew where it was going to bounce.

I think they stole the player of the year award away from him when DiMaggio hit in those consecutive games and Williams hit .406.

I mean, who in the hell's going to hit .406? Of course, like they say, who in the hell is going to hit in 56 consecutive games? And you know the story was—and Joe Cronin was the manager—they were playing in Philadelphia, playing the Athletics in a doubleheader. And after the first game in the clubhouse, Cronin said to Ted, you're hitting .39999 or something. He said, they'll give you .400 on that, I think I'll sit you out the second game. And Ted said, no, if I hit .400, I'm going to hit .400. And he played that second game and I think went 4–6 or something like that to get him up to .406. Isn't that something? Now that's guts.

He said he did [remember me]. I'm not sure though, because I was just a humpty-dumpty. I wasn't a big-name player. But, well, he must have remembered me, because he used to go duck hunting and stuff in a little game reserve right outside St. Joe, Missouri. He used to go there all the time, and when I heard about it, I wrote him a letter and said he'd be welcome to stay with me and I'd supply my car if he wanted to go up there and do hunting and stuff. And he wrote me back! And he said, I'll take you up on that. He never did, but I still have the letter—my son has the letter—but I guess he did remember something then.

He knew baseball, he knew how to hit, no question about it. I think he was the best ever, in my book. I told him that at that reunion. I told him, "Ted, you're going to hear this a lot, but I'm going to tell you because I played against you—I think you're the greatest hitter I ever saw." And he just beamed; of course, that's what he wanted to hear. And he was.

He wanted to take me for a ride one day. He used to fly his plane over to our field when we had a ball game. And he said, "Charlie, I'll take you up for a ride someday." And some of the other guys came over and said, don't do it, he's nuts. And I said, what do you mean he's nuts? And they said, well, you know, he comes over here and you know all those bayous we have all around the field here in Florida? He said there's one bridge under there, and someone said, "Ted, you think you can fly under that?" And he said, oh hell yes. And it would be like maybe only 6, 8 inches, maybe a foot on either side of the wingtips. And he flew under it. And I said, "Ohhh, no way! No thanks." I didn't put it that way to him. I said maybe sometime, Ted. But there's a million stories about him.

They're [the Red Sox] coming up, and they played in Birmingham. Coming north, you know, at the end of spring training [on their way up to Boston]. And he walked out on the field, and he said their pitching mound was off-center to second base, the rubber. The groundskeeper was there and he said, "Well, Ted, I'm the groundskeeper here, and I hate to tell you, but you're wrong." And Ted says, "Ehhh, it's off-center; it's not lined up properly with second base and home plate." And they remeasured it and sure enough, he was right. The grounds-keeper couldn't believe it.

There's so many stories. This guy was a phenom. One-in-a-million. And all the guys liked him.

The fans up in left field used to gamble on whether he'd swing at the next pitch, whether he'd hit it, and where he'd hit it. And if he didn't hit it or he took the pitch or took a strike, they'd get mad and boo him. They were all gamblers and they'd give him the old finger. But everyone else liked him, and he did a lot of good, too. That Jimmy Fund he founded. You didn't hear much about it, but he did a lot of good.

Don Leppert

Second base

1955: .... **Baltimore Orioles**
Career Statistics: .... **40 games, 0 home runs,**
.114 batting average

WELL, PLAYING SECOND base, of course, the first baseman played right on the right-field grass, and I played about ten steps to his right, the shortstop played normal second base, the third baseman played right over the second-base bag . . . and he never tried to hit to left field. I think if I'm not mistaken in that year, 1955, he still hit over .400.[22] You didn't have to fear him where we played him because if he hit the ball on the ground, he missed it. He just didn't hit it . . . when he hit line drives, he hit line drives and they were by you. But a ground ball for him—and he wasn't the fastest guy on the field—so you didn't have any trouble throwing him out even playing as far deep as we did.

If he hit it right to you—without a line drive being too high or a ground ball—you could throw him out. It just wasn't like him to hit a soft . . . he could hit a hard ground ball, but it wasn't so bad because we were playing so far back.

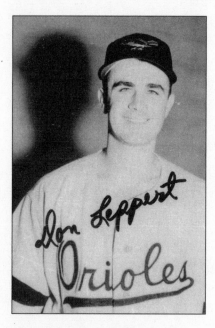

Photo courtesy of Don Leppert

Don Leppert only played 40 games in the major leagues, but he considered it an honor to play against Ted Williams.

---

[22] Williams hit .356 in 1955.

As far as the toughest—who was the most-feared hitter we had to face—I'm going to say Mickey Mantle was, because you had to play him on the very front of the infield grass, [as] he was so fast. If he hit a ground ball, you better get it as quick as you can and get it to first base, because he could beat you. I think they timed him once at 3.2 seconds going down to first base batting left-handed. You had to play him way up there on the infield grass, almost to the front of the infield grass.

I think Williams was a better hitter. Gosh, he hit more line drives . . . more home runs on a line, whereas Mantle just hit those towering home runs. Like I said, you had to play Mantle up close, and when he batted left-handed, it was almost frightening to play him up close. He hit a ball over my head, I'm going tell you what, I was playing him up close and he hit a low ball left-handed, and I jumped up and I just barely missed it going over my glove and it went out of the ballpark. When I came down, I said a little silent prayer, thanking the Lord that I didn't get my glove on it.

As far as Williams and balls and strikes, if he didn't swing at it, it wasn't a strike. He probably had the greatest feel of the strike zone of anybody that I've ever seen. That was his batting eye, really. If he didn't swing at it, it was probably a ball. He was that good.

You always watched when they were taking batting practice. Everything he hit was right on the nose. If he hit a ground ball, you knew he didn't get it good. If he hit a *hard* line drive—it might have been low—but it was by you before you had a chance to get it.

When he got on first base, he'd hardly talk to you. He wasn't that friendly a guy. He was jittery; he had all sort of little tics. And when he got on first base, I guess he was just so focused, he was thinking more about the ball game and he didn't really converse with you. But I didn't hold that against him. Hell, I'm just a rookie and this guy's a hall of famer.

[When we spoke], he didn't carry on a long conversation. You could ask him questions and he'd answer them in very short sentences. Like I said, he was always kind of jittery. But you didn't take anything personal, because that's just the way he was. But no matter what, he was a good guy. Nobody ever said anything bad against him. I mean, you had to admire him. He served two terms in the Air Force, and they said, he could identify planes—if they showed him foreign planes: Japanese planes, German planes, or whatever—that he could identify them probably five times quicker than anyone else could. His eyes were that quick.

As far as Ted Williams goes, he's got my vote. My time was short in the big leagues, but just to be on the field with that guy was an honor I'll never forget.

Al Naples

Shortstop

1949: ....St. Louis Browns
Career Statistics: .... 2 games, 0 home runs,
.143 batting average

THE ONE THING that stands out in my mind regarding Ted Williams was that he always had batting practice first. It seemed like the rest of the team just followed him. I remember the outfield (never left field) and chasing his hit balls along with a bat boy and whoever was around. The Sox would then come on the field and have their batting practice. He would then head down the dugout alleyway, and it seemed no one could enter the clubhouse. I'm not sure about sportswriters.

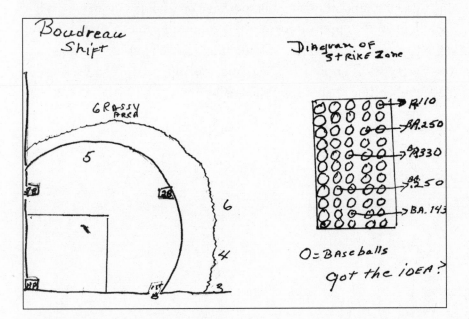

Al Naples drew his version of the Williams shift, as well as Williams' strike zone chart.

The Browns used the Boudreau shift. As you know, the first baseman played the right-field line and on the grass. The second baseman played on the grass and about 25 feet from the line of the first baseman. The shortstop was as deep as the second baseman and about 25 feet or so from second base. In other words, there were three men on the right-field side of the infield. The third baseman had the left side of the infield to himself. I imagine he could have lifted his batting average thirty points or so if he took advantage of this opportunity; I know I would have.

I know that another thing he developed was the strike zone chart. It was covered with circles representing baseballs. Each circle had batting averages in it for your chances of getting a base hit in that part of the strike zone. I thought it was very clever; show you how he approached hitting from a scientific point of view. He was an extremely disciplined hitter!

I do remember throwing him out on a one-hopper at first . . . it felt good! I had the opportunity to play a couple of games against him and the Red Sox.[23] I broke my middle finger [throwing hands], was sent to Springfield [Triple-I League], and was supposed to go back up in September, but I had not finished college.[24]

---

[23] Naples played in two major league games, and both were against the Red Sox, June 25–26, 1949.

[24] Naples never played professional baseball again.

Herb Plews

Second base / Third base

1956–59: ....**Washington Senators**
1959: ....**Boston Red Sox**
Career Statistics: ....**346 games, 4 home runs,**
.262 batting average

IWAS ALWAYS GLAD to watch him [Ted Williams] perform. Never saw him swing at a pitch and miss it completely. His hits were mainly line drives with plenty of topspin. They would sail over the infield and then sink in front of an outfielder.

At the close of the '56 season, he and Pete Runnels were almost at a dead heat for the batting championship.[25] There were three games remaining to be played in DC, and [Manager Chuck] Dressen[26] told our pitchers to pitch to Williams and not walk him. Anyway, Williams put on the greatest hitting clinic you could ever imagine. Line drives flying everywhere. Runnels was also hitting well, but all his hits were right at someone. As a result, Williams beat out Runnels for the AL batting championship by a few points.[27]

I never saw any one player hit the ball with so much authority like Williams. It's something I'll never forget. This proved to all of us why he was the greatest hitter; he really was.

---

[25] Plews is actually speaking of the 1958 season.

[26] Dressen was the manager for Washington in 1956, but Cookie Lavagetto was the manager in 1958, when Williams and Runnels entered DC, battling for the batting crown.

[27] Boston closed the season with a four-game series in Washington. Williams entered the series hitting .320, Runnels .324. Runnels played in all four games and went 5–19 to finish at .322. Williams played in three of those games, sitting out the second game of a doubleheader in the series opener, and went 7–14—with a home run in each game—to finish at .328 and lead the league, with Runnels finishing second. It was Williams' sixth and final batting title.

When in the field, we would put on some modified shift, but he seldom hit grounders to any of the infielders. Third baseman between third and second, shortstop just left of second, and second baseman in shallow right field. He could find the holes no matter what.

I wasn't with Boston long enough to ever converse with him one-on-one.[28] However, if you had a question, he would be glad to answer it. He did pretty much everything by himself. Just being around him for a short time was very special for me.

[28] Plews was traded to Boston on June 11, 1959, and played his final major league game on July 26, 1959.

J. W. Porter

Catcher / Outfield / First base / Third base

1952: ....St. Louis Browns
1955–57: ....Detroit Tigers
1958: ....Cleveland Indians
1959: ....Washington Senators
1959: .... St. Louis Cardinals
Career Statistics: .... 229 games, 8 home runs,
.228 batting average

WILLIAMS WAS SUCH a great hitter and so revered that he was almost passed over in meetings when you were going over Boston hitters. "Try to keep Dom DiMaggio and Johnny Pesky off the bases, try to keep Ted in the ballpark. We will have seven guys on the right side of the diamond, and Jackie Jensen hits into a lot of double plays." You never heard about what type of pitch to throw him or what location to try to throw the pitch; it was like it wouldn't matter. Throw and duck seemed to be our strategy.

Two games [against Ted] stand out in my mind. They [the Red Sox] came into Detroit, which was always Ted's favorite park to hit in. I would think he'd have averaged well over .400 against Detroit; he loved to hit in Briggs [Tiger] Stadium.

Future Hall-of-Famer Jim Bunning is pitching for us, and Ted hits singleton homers, but we are holding on to a 3–2 lead. Ted comes to bat with one out and nobody on. Our manager, Jack Tighe, yells out to walk him. We can't believe it, but we purposely put him on. Jackie Jensen then grounds into a double play.

The top of the ninth rolls around—same exact situation—and Tighe yells out for us to walk him again. Ted went nuts, threw his bat away, and cursed his way to first base. Jensen grounded into another double play, and we win, 3–2.[29]

The other game that stands out is one where I was playing first base and was holding a runner on. He hit a laser headed right for my nose. By the grace of God, I managed to get my glove up and slightly deflect the ball. I then heard some noises I don't ever want to hear again. The ball had hit the umpire right in the pit of his stomach and came to rest within a foot of the first-base bag. I can hear the umpire in front of me wanting to die and Williams behind me wanting to kill.

Great hitters like Williams and [Stan] Musial had such great eyes and I never saw either of them argue on a pitch. They would tell an umpire with a glance. Knowing this, I think they [the umpires] simply bore down more when those kinds of hitters came to bat. They didn't mind missing a pitch on me, but certainly didn't want to miss one on the great ones.

Williams and [Mickey] Mantle were the most feared hitters I ever played against. When they came to bat—even in batting practice—all other activities ceased. You wanted to see Ted's perfect swings and the line drives it produced and how many balls Mickey put in the seats and how far they went. In 1956, Mickey's Triple Crown year, he turned Briggs Stadium into a little league park.

I finished a season in Atlanta, and Ted was instrumental in getting me and many other players winter employment at Sears. I had lunch with

---

[29] I cannot locate the game Porter is referring to. However, Williams did hit two home runs off Bunning on July 12, 1957, in Detroit in a 5–3, Tigers win. Porter did not play in that game, however, and one of Williams' homers was a two-run shot. Also, Bunning walked Williams intentionally once, but it was with two out in the fifth, and Mickey Vernon followed with a pop out.

him a few times. He and I, Bobby Richardson and others, were asked to help open an American Legion national tournament in Memphis one September. He, along with Satchel Paige, was the most intriguing person I ever met.

Bobby Richardson

Second base

1955–66: ....New York Yankees
Career Statistics: .... 1,412 games, 34 home runs,
.266 batting average
American League All-Star: 1957, 1959, 1962–1966

I WAS A FRIEND [of Williams'] because of [our love of] the outdoors. He would slide into second [base] and say, "How are your bird dogs? Still shooting the Browning 28 gauge over and under?"

Ted Williams and Red Sox owner Tom Yawkey.

We spent an entire flight from California to New York after an All-Star Game talking about hunting and fishing and about Mr. Yawkey [the Red Sox owner], who had a big plantation in South Carolina. When he passed away, he gave it to the state of South Carolina.

Art "Dutch" Schult

First base / Outfield

1953:	New York Yankees
1956–57:	Cincinnati Reds
1957:	Washington Senators
1959–60:	Chicago Cubs
Career Statistics:	164 games, 6 home runs, .264 batting average

I **CONSIDERED HIM [TED]** a good friend of mine. The funny thing is, most people think that, because I was playing with the Yankees, we were rivals at that time. But I had just come back from overseas when I joined the Yankees, and they in turn were trying to cut my salary and send me where I could play. I had a wife and kid to support, and they called me a clubhouse lawyer because I used the G.I. Bill of Rights. I hung around until they got eleven games in front of the league and then I got part of the World Series [money, laughs], so they sold me to Cincinnati to get me out of the league because I had a real good spring training and their club was reasonably set at that time—they had won three straight World Series.

So when they sold me to Cincinnati, I went over there and played a little bit and they sold me to Washington. And it was at Washington I was playing a little first base and I had a couple of good games against Boston in Washington. I can recall that I got four hits against Boston, and every time I'd trot by Williams, he would call me a sonuvabitch [laughs]. And I got to talking to him.

[After that series], we went on a road trip to Chicago and played against Early Wynn. I think I got a double the first time up and I never got a hit against them the rest of the series. At the end of that road trip, I was having a tough time. We went back to Boston before to finish up the road trip.

I got out to the ballpark early in Boston to get some extra batting practice. I wanted to find out what the hell I was doing wrong; why I was having such a tough time. So I stuck my head out of the dugout and I hear this "Crack! Crack!" and it was Williams. He was hitting in the cage, also taking extra batting. So he looked over and saw me and said, "Hey, Dutch, come over here. You're 0–for one week, what the hell did you do?" I said, "Well, I faced that goddamn Early Wynn first." And he said, "Yeah, he can do that to you. Get in here and take a couple of swings." I said, "No, no, you finish up what you're out here working for. I got a guy who is going to pitch to me. He's in the dugout." He said, "No, no, get in here. I want to see what you're doing."

And when I stepped into the cage—before I even took the first swing, he says, "Woah! Stop!" He then went on to say, "Your hands are four-to-five inches lower then when you got those four hits against us. Move them up to where they were." I was shocked, "No kidding?" I took a couple of swings and got four hits that night,[30] and Ted called me a sonuvabitch again! He was that kind of guy. He didn't want to play against anybody that wasn't up to snuff, either. He enjoyed the competition.

But the tough part about Ted was when we had a man on first and third, and I was holding the man on first and he was the hitter [laughs], because I couldn't move! I had to play 90 feet from him.

I'd kid around with him because I really liked him. With the guys, he was always 100 percent, but he didn't particularly care for sportswriters or authorities, and he'd let them know it. But we both got [drafted]—I got drafted into the service in Korea, too, so we had some other things in common. But I really liked him.

I remember one point towards the end of the season in 1957—I think he ended up hitting .390 or something[31]—so he was spending

---

[30] Schult had four hits against the Red Sox twice in 1957: On August 9 in Boston, and on August 17 in Washington.
[31] Ted hit .388 in 1957.

part of the time on the bench. [Rather than just hanging out], he'd take a pretty close look at what everybody was doing. He was a student of anybody with a bat. If there was something that he didn't know, he'd find out.

When you picked up his bat, the distance between your forefinger and your thumb was the only part that had any black resin marks on it [laughs]. The rest of the bat was like new.

[When it came to the shift], the Senators used to play Pete Runnels on *just* to the right side of second base, and the second baseman, [Milt] Bolling, was almost where he could touch me [laughs]. So we did have a shift. And then the center fielder was over in right-center. If he got his pitch, it didn't matter where they were playing. We thought the best way to pitch him was low and behind [laughs].

If he and [Joe] DiMaggio had ever switched ballparks, they both would have broke every record there was. At one time they were talking about that trade. If DiMaggio had played with that short left-field porch, he would have left so many dents out there, it would have looked like a golf ball. And Ted in Yankee Stadium? With that short right-field fence? There's no question how many he would have hit. To me, he was the ultimate as far as left-hand hitters goes; he was the best I ever saw. He also had phenomenal eyesight. And his reactions—he was so quick with his hands. His depth perception must have just been amazing.

But right now, his daughter is frequenting the same restaurant that I go to down here all the time. The owner of the restaurant is a friend of mine and he's got my picture on the wall. She always says, jokingly, "Why do you have that picture up there of those damn Yankees . . . [laughs]." So it's a small world.

And he was living not too far from me in Ocala, where his museum was is only like 8–10 miles away. I did stop over there one time to see him, but he was not that well, I guess, or he was out fishing or doing something.

Jerry Snyder

Second base / Shortstop

1952–58: .... **Washington Senators**
Career Statistics: .... **266 games, 3 home runs,**
.230 batting average

I'M SITTING HERE right next to a picture of Ted Williams, Mickey Mantle, and Joe DiMaggio. Williams was one of my favorite players. He knew I played against him and [I also] knew Mantle pretty well. I'm from Oklahoma, like Mantle. I also have fond memories of Joe DiMaggio; he was kind of my hero, too. He was the only one that greeted me when I broke in at nineteen years old with the Yankees in spring training. The other guys kind of ignored me, but he came out and introduced himself. So I always thought of that when I think of Joe. He quit the year I was with the Yankees after that.

I played several games against Williams, mainly second base. Strangely enough, my record against Boston was the best I ever had against any other team. They never did have much pitching when I played against them. They had a good offensive club, but not much pitching. I had one of my best nights against them. I had 4 hits, 6 RBI—well, I never drove in any runs [laughs]. I even had an inside-the-park home run in that game.[32] That was by far my best game— very unusual for me.

But I did play second base and I did play, oh, I'd say 3 or 4 feet back of the infield grass . . . and Boston had a deep grass. Some of the infields were cut a little shallower than the grass angle. And he never hit me many balls. He hit the ball in the air *a lot*.

I do remember one shot he hit at Mickey Vernon. He hit it so hard— have you ever seen one that it takes off like a bullet, and it bends in

---

[32] On May 12, 1952, Snyder went 3–5, with 3 runs, 5 RBI, 1 double, 1 triple, and 1 home run, in a 12–9 win over the Red Sox in Washington.

the middle? You kind of top it, and it sinks suddenly. Mickey kind of half-jumped [laughs] and ended up catching it around his waist. It was interesting, because he was a hell of a first baseman. He did catch it, but it was one of those hard balls that . . . he just hit it with a lot of topspin on the ball. He hit a lot of balls in the air and I don't remember him hitting many my way.

But there's one play in particular that I do remember. The bases were loaded—it was towards the end of his career. I'm going from memory here, but I think it was one of his last few games. Bases were loaded and he hits this *tremendous* pop-up. I had time to think about it, you know? I probably didn't drop a pop-up but one time in my career, but I got to thinking. I thought, "God, if I drop this ball [laughs]." I did catch it, but it was funny because I still remember that play all this time. He could hit some pop-ups that were out of this world in terms of height. That's one play I do remember. It would have been horrible [if I dropped it].

[When we played the shift], the shortstop usually played, as I remember, back in second base, like an ordinary real pull-hitter. Of course, I played over toward the line, but I played real deep. It wasn't like a dead pull-hitter, a guy that will never hit to left field much. Third base would shift way over, but not tremendously. If he wanted to bunt, they'd give it to him. He could have had some [hits] easily, if he could, you know, eliminate the pitcher. Bunt it hard enough. But I never saw him try it. I did see . . . he used to, he'd run up on the ball. Did you know that? Okay, he actually would run up on a ball to try to hit it to left field. Very occasionally, but he would do it. He'd intentionally try to hit it to left field. I never saw him get a hit with that run upfield, but he would kind of fake it to try and get 'em, I guess, to keep them from doing that shift.

He'd never bunt. Never heard of him trying to bunt. He may have against somebody, but I never heard of him doing that. Mickey Mantle would bunt. He would try to pull a bunt, which is the hardest thing in the world to do and beat out. Because everybody's playing deep—now this is Mantle; Ted Williams would never do that. [Williams] would take a couple of steps and just kind of obviously try to hit it over there. I used to kind of do it too. I was a bunter. I got parts of about six years in the majors, but I was on the bench half of the time, so I wasn't a great player. But I was there long enough to get a pension and things like that.

He'd beat you a lot of times with his bat, but he'd really hurt you in the field. He wasn't a good fielder. Of course, he had that short left-field fence—he played left field—so he didn't have to do too much defense. But he and [Jackie] Jensen, when I hit that inside-the-park home run, they were playing me real short, especially Jensen. So I hit it kind of to dead center field, and that's about 450 feet in center field in Washington. Ted just loped after the ball and Jensen—I always hit to right field—they both just kind of loped after the ball. So I noticed that. I thought, "God, they're actually loafing." And they could do that, especially Ted. Anyway, I thought hell, I might get an inside-the-park home run—and I did. One of the few I've actually seen in the big leagues. You don't get those too often.

What a hitter. We had a wild left-hander, Mickey McDermott, who also played with Boston.[33] I thought to myself, this is going to be fun to watch, because Mickey was so damn wild. And he had Ted jumping around. It didn't bother him, though. He'd just take his walk. But McDermott, he got a couple of hits off of him when he got one in there. It didn't bother him one bit.[34]

He wasn't bothered by left-handers like a lot of left-handed hitters are. It's true. A lot of left-handed hitters have trouble against left-handed pitchers. I think [Williams was the best hitter I ever saw] because [he] had such a good eye. He hardly ever swung at bad balls. Another thing

---

[33] McDermott played for the Red Sox from 1948–53, and was a teammate of Snyder's on the Senators from 1954–55.

[34] Williams was just 2–14 against McDemott, with 3 walks and a hit by pitch. Both of his hits were singles.

about Williams was that if he took a strike, it was a ball to an umpire. I guess you've heard that before. Oh yeah, it was bad. Of any player I've ever seen, it was the worst, [more so than with] DiMaggio or anybody else. And he didn't get rattled by left-handers like a lot of them do nowadays. Those big sluggers. And he was a skinny guy. He was tall, but he wasn't strong looking. He had those terrific wrists and had a pretty big swing to go with such a good eye. A lot of those players that have good eyes, they don't have a big swing. But he had a big, loose swing.

He'd have 30 [home runs a season]. I don't know if he ever had 40, but 30 is good. Without the steroid[s]. I'm wondering if some of them don't—like [Albert] Pujols. He hits the ball so hard. Used to [wonder if he took steroids] when I watched [Barry] Bonds. Like, God, is it possible to hit the ball that far? And sure enough. . .

He'd talk to you about your swing. I didn't know him well, but a guy who was like a star on the club, like Vernon or [Pete] Runnels, I guess. We didn't have many stars. Anyway, he'd talk to them or even linger while we were batting at times. He was a good guy; guys liked him, but fans would boo him. In fact, I think we were there at his final three games.[35] He was being honored for something, and he finished it up off-camera, saying, "Well, you New England sonuvabitches." They were on him so much. Somebody told me he said that. They'd boo him, they'd get on him. One time—I think I read this—he was running up on that ball and hitting it in the stands in left field. I read it somewhere, but it wasn't with us.

---

[35] Snyder's last season in the majors was 1958; Williams' last season was 1960.

Chuck Stevens

First base

1941, 1946, 1948: ....St. Louis Browns
Career Statistics: .... **211 games, 3 home runs,
.251 batting average**

I **WILL OPEN IT** up by saying that I always called him, "The Thump." That goes back to high school days.

Even as a high school outfielder—he played at Hoover High in San Diego—we played in a couple of tournaments against each other, and every time he struck a ball, it sounded like you were hitting a bass drum. You knew the ball was solidly struck; that he got it right on the meat part of the bat. He did that the rest of his life; so we go back a long ways.

I'll tell you an amusing story. When we were in high school . . . there was a club at one time called the 20-30 club, and that meant between the ages of twenty and thirty, you joined this club—I don't know if you are familiar with it, or if it was a West Coast movement; I really don't know or don't remember—they taught you how to do public speaking and that kind of thing. It was kind of a constructive thing for guys that age. They [the 20-30 club of Southern California] sponsored a baseball tournament in Pomona, California, during the Easter break. Pomona High School had a massive football field and they had two diamonds at each end and had ball games going on at the same time. It was so large that the outfielders were not in conflict of any kind.

We're playing a Pasadena ballclub, their second baseman or shortstop, I don't remember what he played, was a guy named Jackie Robinson. During the ball game, I remember we were in the infield. We had the best ballclub and won the tournament, and we *knew it* going in. The umpire began screaming, "time, time, time," everybody looked around, and a ball came through our infield on the ground. We looked down

272

at the other end of the field, and Thump's galloping around the bases. He touched one off; must have hit it 400 feet, and it rolled another 200. So that's when it dawned on us that this guy had awesome power. Not just power, but awesome power.

When we were in high school, we played against Jackie Robinson, Bob Lemon, Jack Graham, [Bobby] Doerr . . . you know, there were just all kinds of guys out here that were superior ballplayers. On our ballclub in high school, Vern Stephens was the backup second baseman. I was the first baseman, and Vern played a little second. Bob Sturgeon with the Cubs played third, Bob Garbo—I think he got a shot with Brooklyn—and the best ballplayer of all was a guy named Dick Lang, who was a center fielder and he was wounded during the war, which halted his career, but he was a great ballplayer.

Anyway, getting back to Williams. Yes, we played deep . . . as deep as you could get. I used to tell him it wasn't deep enough because I was married then. He thought that was funny. I didn't, because when he hit screamers at you, they were hit hard.

[I remember] we were playing in Boston one afternoon, and he hit a screamer down the right-field line. I dove, got my glove on the ball, and it took the glove off of my hand. I picked the ball out of the glove, threw him out at first base, and he came galloping by and said to me, "Thanks a lot, asshole."

Bob Lemon and I were like brothers, as we grew up together. Lem made his first appearance as a relief pitcher against the Browns. I think the only base hit I got off him was a double to right-center. As I slide in [to second]—[Lou] Boudreau was covering—I beat the throw. But there are three of us there and I look up and Lem is bent over me, and says, "Thanks a lot, asshole." So I began to realize I must have been [an asshole], but I thought that was kind of funny coming from two of those guys who had accomplished so much in their careers.

[I remember] we had a guy [named] Ellis Kinder, who was a reliever. Williams *hated* him. Frankly, Williams couldn't hit him with a two-by-four, if you can believe that.[36] And Kinder was a free spirit. He would relieve against Williams—and you remember how Ted would scrape that right foot to kind of dig a hole? And held everybody up until he got that hole dug up, scratching around with his spikes, getting real comfortable. Kinder would patiently stand up there on the mound. The first pitch he threw at Williams would be at his right foot. And Williams, it'd just upset him. So the next thing we know, Mr. Yawkey [the Red Sox owner] had bought Kinder, and he ended up with the Red Sox. I know that he bought Kinder because Williams probably was raising so much hell about it that there was only one way to quiet him down, and that was get Kinder on his side.

I'll bet you a crisp $100 bill that Williams could tell you what the hell Kinder threw him the first time he ever saw Kinder. And he would tell you. You'd be talking about somebody, he'll start you out with a fastball then he'll throw you a breaking ball. Vern used to tell me about guys when I got out of the service. Vern knew all those guys. He'd tell me all about the sequence they'd be liable to throw. That taught me to do the same thing. But they had total recall. It was just a natural thing with him. Thirty years later he'd tell you what Kinder threw him. The only thing I could tell you thirty years later is a baseball.

But he was a good guy. He never changed, you know; I always stayed in touch with him. When I was the CEO of the players association, the benevolence association of pro baseball[37]—I did that for thirty-eight years after I quit playing. Ted was on the board with me the entire time. So we were in constant touch weekly or semi-weekly for the rest of our lives. And if the winter meetings were in Florida and Ted could make it, he'd drive into town, attend the meeting, and then go back home.

---

[36] According to retrosheet.org, Williams was 5–14 against Kinder, although the data is incomplete.

[37] Association of Professional Ball Players of America

When Ted was in Boston, we'd get out there early to watch batting practice. Everything stopped in the ballpark; not only the visiting ballclub, but the Boston ballclub, just to watch him hit. He was that impressive at the plate.

I remember him taking batting practice—it got to be a kind of a thing with me—I would look around and everybody stopped what they were doing to watch him while he was taking batting practice. Because he was Williams—normally you'd get into the batting cage and hit four or five, whatever the predetermined number was, then get out of there and the next guy would move in. It would just expedite the time you had. But Ted would get in there and take up homesteading rights. He'd swing until he got tired. The sequence was always: The first two or three swings were just singles; then the next two or three swings was him letting it out a little bit; then he'd begin to pump the ball; and the last four or five he'd swing at they might still be looking for 'em someplace. But that was always his routine. As I say, he stopped all activity, I don't care what ballclub he was playing against.

I often wondered . . . I always stayed close to [Joe] DiMaggio because of my job and we were in constant contact, and I often wondered if Joe stopped what he was doing. Did you ever stop to think of that? One of the greats looking at another great. Every time I was having dinner or something with DiMaggio, I always forgot to ask him. I would have if I had thought about it.

I'll tell you another story. We're playing in St. Louis, [and at that time] both the Browns and Cardinals used the same ballpark. By July or August, the infield was probably a little harder than Highway 40. It was *really* hard. So Williams is up at-bat, hits the ball, and pulls it into right field. It wasn't that far off the ground. I jumped and *just* made a fraction of contact with the ball and it got over my head by about 10 or 15 feet. It felt like it went off my uniform. And the ball hit and bounced way up in the air and we held him to a single, which is a victory in itself. Now, Eddie Rommel was umpiring first base. He was a really, really nice man, and everybody liked him. Williams said to me, "Damn, I hit that ball on the top half." That was why it bounded over my head and bounced so high. I turned to Rommel and I said "time." And I got right in Williams' face and said to him, "Are you telling me you can hit the damn ball on the bottom side or the top side?" And he said, "Sure." I can't repeat what I told him, but Rommel was hysterical [the entire time]. But he finally walks up to us and says, "Gentlemen, I wonder if we could get on with the ball game."

But Williams and Musial and those guys, they were endowed with a *tremendous* advantage in sight. Paul Waner told me—again, I asked him one time—how big did a baseball look to you? And he said, "Kind of like a softball." To me, the thing looked like an aspirin tablet. Those guys, they were amazing.

You know, Ted was Ted. You'd look out in left field and if he's po'd at the writers, he's liable to be giving them the middle finger or whatever. You never knew what he was going to do out there. But he was a very decent guy and was really, really interested in the well-being of the ballplayer. That was our obligation, and we quietly took care of people in our business that needed help and never divulged who they were to anybody, unless they wanted us to. And he was always concerned about the ballplayers, that he played with or against or heard of, that were in financial need.

He liked everybody on the ballclub and everybody liked him. Where Joe was always so quiet . . . because I was on an all-star ballclub in, oh boy, '50 or '51 over in Japan, and you just didn't bother Joe. You just didn't walk up and, like Williams, whack him on the back, that kind of thing, because you never knew if he was in a mood or not.

On that tour to Japan—it was during the Korean War, '51 as I remember—Joe and I are in a lobby, and a Japanese guy interrupts and wants to know if he can talk to me. So I go over, and it turns out he was a shirtmaker, and he was asking if I liked silk shirts. And they were dirt cheap [there], you know. He gave me his card, and it was on the Ginza in Tokyo. So he leaves and I tell Joe, "Man, we have to go down to this cat's place and load up, because the price is right." So Joe and I get into a cab and go down to the Ginza—that's the Broadway of Tokyo. We're walking down the sidewalk and looking at stores and one thing or another, and I hear, "DiMaggio, DiMaggio," and I look back, and there must have been a thousand Japanese people following us down the street. We get to the corner of this busy intersection, and I turn to Joe and say, "Geez, I get so tired of this. Here I am all the way in Tokyo, Japan, and they're following me [laughs]." There wasn't one guy in that thousand who knew who the hell I was. He hit me on the arm, kind of [threw me] off balance, and I went out in the street, and a cab comes within about a foot of me. So I go back and tell him, "Jesus, you almost got me killed in front of all of my fans." That was the first time I ever really saw him break up.

You must know, the entire atmosphere was so much different than it is now. Whether you were playing with or against—and I don't think there is that kind of concern now, because of the money denominator, than there was then. You made lifelong friends and you were always concerned about their well-being, whether you liked them or not, and I don't know if that exists today. I've been retired for ten, twelve years now, and I kind of lost the pulse of things, but it doesn't appear that the same kind of *that* feeling—you're a ballplayer, you're proud of the game, and you're beholden to the fans.

The thing we didn't know in school . . . Ted didn't have . . . I'm assuming because we didn't talk about it personally, but his home life must have been horrible. I suspect he had to overcome a lot. His mother was very religious, and I guess was passing out pamphlets and that kind of thing, and I don't know whether she carried that into the home, although I have since heard probably yes. But I can't say anything about the guy. And stop and think about that, we both know that he was a silver-tongued devil. You didn't turn him loose, but you never knew what some of those guys were going to say.

A funny story about Lem. I had announced my retirement after thirty-eight years, and Lem by this time was on a cane and a walker with circulatory problems, but I wanted him there. There were 500 people; big representation from the commissioner's office and one thing and another, but 500 to be exact; [Tommy] Lasorda and [Sparky] Anderson; the whole mob. Lem struggles to the microphone. I always emceed my own program, so I could keep it timely and get them in and out of there. He gets to the microphone—and I don't happen to be Catholic, but one of my dear friends is a monsignor of the local Catholic church in Long Beach where Lem and I grew up. He always did the invocation, and he was seated next to me. Lem gets the microphone and looks out at 500 people—all male—and said, "Good to see everybody, but I want to say this: Anybody that said the golden years are great is full of shit [laughs]." I looked down, and I have to prop the monsignor up in the chair because I was afraid he was going to fall out and hurt himself [laughs]. Things like that. And Ted would set that pattern. You know, if he got wound up, lordy knows what he's going to say . . . and he couldn't care less.

But he was a good guy. That's the most you can say; he was a caring guy. I think he probably would be identified with older players, probably more than anybody who stayed in touch with most of his old teammates . . . stayed in touch more than anybody I know . . . and did that until he died. The last few years John Henry pretty much kept him isolated, but before that he was a really, really gregarious guy.

Guys like Early Wynn and Lem and all of those people, they always had good things to say about him—until he walked to the plate. *Then* it got a little salty. But he was a marvelous hitter.

And then that gallop of his. When he was circling the bases, I've seen that many times; it looked like he was on a merry-go-round. That kind of lope he had.

Ted was a better hitter (than anyone else). When you're talking about the four dimensions—run, throw, hit, field—I don't think there's any contest, because the guy from New York did them all superbly. The guy from Boston, how many of the four would you give him?

It was an interesting time. And writers, again, called it the golden years. I have to go along with that. I think it was. Times were not good before the war, and then a lot of us volunteered there. Then after spending three or four years, most of us took a while to recover or readjust. But Ted, that didn't seem to bother him. It didn't look like he'd been away. I'm up there struggling to hit .250, and he's up there struggling to hit .400. And he had two interruptions like that. It was so natural with him, I reckon, that there wasn't anything that was going to get that swing or eye-hand-bat coordination ever disturb that. I think that was the reason he had all of that success. It was just a built-in thing. And he could still do it when he was nearing forty. Under normal circumstances, when a guy was forty, he was looking for the La-Z-Boy. Williams is still hitting .350. That pretty much well sums up my feelings on the guy. I respected him and loved his attitude. His ability to the ordinary ballplayer was absolutely awesome.

Once you saw him—and Musial was the same way with that unorthodox stance—you never forgot it. It was indelibly stamped. The first time I saw Musial, we had an off day, so we did something different and went to the ballpark to see the Cardinals play. And some left-hander with Cincinnati is out there—the guy could really pump—and he threw Musial a change, and I think Musial had committed a little bit for a fastball. He quickly adjusted on the change and laid one up against the left-center-field fence for a triple. And I'm thinking, uh-oh, I just saw a guy with a magic wand. And Williams could have done the same thing—and did.

Ted loved to talk hitting. Hell, he'd talk hitting to a sign post. The thing that always amused me about him . . . I sat in on a conversation with Williams, Musial, and two or three others, I think [Joe] Gordon, and they were talking about hitting. I'm thinking, here's three or four guys—[Johnny] Mize might have been in there [as well]—when they talk about hitting to me, it was always so natural for them, they had no sense of struggling at the plate. But the ordinary ballplayer, it was [always] a struggle. You're doing everything you can to maintain a presentable average, but those guys, they just walked out there and began to start whaling away—with great success. But it was interesting to listen to his conversation about hitting, because he made it sound so simple. And if you were able to apply all his theories, then everyone in the world would be hitting .400 and it wouldn't be any fun. And I think I told him that one time. He just looks at me like, "another dizzy left-hander."

Vern Stephens had the same ability—he was never a high-average hitter, but had great power for a shortstop. But once they hit against a pitcher, the sequence of the pitches they were shown that day was indelibly stamped. They never forgot it.

When he came to the plate—as you know, most hitters have a spot they can really cream the ball, low ball, high ball—Williams didn't have those weaknesses. So if you are pitching against him—and I can say this with all certainty—you would just go after him with the best you got. And obviously, most of the time it didn't work, because you're not going to throw a fastball by him. A breaking ball didn't worry him. The only pitch that would be difficult was maybe one low and in or high and away, but that was everybody's weakness.

The thing about Williams, he had great ability to keep that ball in the strike zone. If he did have a weakness, nobody knew it. You'd try everything on him, but everybody in baseball—and I never really asked him about it, what guys he had trouble with. The only guy I was aware of—because he'd was always moaning when he'd get down to first base—was Kinder.

Of course with the Browns, we didn't have too many guys you had to worry about anyway. Once in a while you'd come up with a guy that could pitch a little bit, and I guess make him work for it, but the rest of them were just struggling to get him out. He always did well against our ballclub. The only time I saw him look bad was in that World Series. He had probably just cooled off or was pressing, who knows. It happens to everybody. And I don't know if he ever went through a slump. Maybe he'd consider 1–4 a slump. Hell, 1–4, I figured I had a triumphant eye. He kept everything in the strike zone, and I'm sure the umpires knew that and were extra careful, which meant it had to be in the strike zone. There were no in-between calls against Williams. I'm sure that prevailed and rightfully so, because the umpire knew this guy had the eyes of an eagle, and he's going to raise hell if they make a mistake on him, which he did . . . quietly. I don't think he [often] showed an umpire up. It wasn't much in his nature. He didn't have to, because when you opened up the paper in the morning, he was always leading the league. That must have been utopia. When I opened up the paper in the morning, I looked to see if I was still in the league!

I was there from 1936, I guess, '35, '36, to the end. I think we graduated at the same time. I remember in '36 I guess, our ballclub, Long Beach Poly, where a lot of good players like Tony Gwynn and the like came from, knew we were going to play for the Southern California championship. They didn't have a state championship [at that time]. We had already clinched the spot for the final, and Ted's ballclub was playing Escondido, another Southern California town. I was the captain of the ballclub, and the coach took me and a couple of pitchers and drove us down to see the ball game. Ted was playing the outfield. He also pitched in school, but I never did see that . . . and his swing *never* changed. It was the same stroke as a kid that he had as a retiring adult. So that's pretty much the history of Williams.

It was a real privilege to see him at the plate. You know, it must be like the past generations when they saw people like [Ty] Cobb and

Charlie Gehringer, the second baseman, those classic hitters. It must have been the same feeling from that generation as ours, looking at Williams and DiMaggio. [That you get to watch somebody] you know is great, and will always be considered great.

Wayne Terwilliger

Second baseman

1949–51:	Chicago Cubs
1951:	Brooklyn Dodgers
1953–54:	Washington Senators
1955–56:	New York Giants
1959–60:	Kansas City Athletics
Career Statistics:	666 games, 22 home runs, .240 batting average

I "INTERACTED" WITH WILLIAMS more than once, as I coached for him when he came back in 1969 to manage the Senators.[38] My memory isn't as good as I would like, but I do remember catching a line drive off him as a player one of the few times I played third base.[39] I was totally surprised, as Williams rarely hit it to the left side, but I caught it!

[As a manager], all he demanded was that you hustled and guys on the bench paid attention to what was going on in the field. He let his coaches do their jobs—he and Sid Hudson [the pitching coach] did a great job with so-so talent. I had free reign coaching third base—as to hit-and-run, steal, etc. He never questioned me. He would talk hitting to anyone who was really interested, no matter who it was. He had a great thirst to know the finer points of photography, real estate, you name it. I learned more about hitting [when he was coaching with the Senators] that, if I had still been playing, I probably would have improved my batting average by 50 points, or at least 40! For four

---

[38] Terwilliger coached with Williams on the Senators and Texas Rangers from 1969–72.

[39] Terwilliger played third base just fourteen times in his career. On September 24, 1954, in the second game of a doubleheader, with Terwilliger playing third, Williams lined out to third in the third inning. It is the only time Williams is credited with a line out to third in a game in which Terwillger played that position.

years, Ted talked and I listened to everything [he had to say] about hitting, pitching, and more. Ted's first years as manager of the Senators was 1969, and it was the greatest year in my career—he was named manager of the year.

Was he the best hitter I ever saw? Of course!

Ray Webster

Second base

1959:...Cleveland Indians
1960:...Boston Red Sox
Career Statistics:............................... 47 games, 2 home runs,
.198 batting average

I THOUGHT HE WAS fantastic. He sort of took me under his wing, you know. Really treated me nice. I'd go into the dugout and sit down with him and we'd talk about whatever. It's been fifty-plus years ago. I think everyone looked up to him, as far as I know.

When I was with Cleveland in 1959, when he went into the batting cage everyone stopped everything and watched him hit and take batting practice.

He was an amazing guy, actually. I think he got some bad press, you know. I thought a lot of him.

What I loved about him, I'll never forget, he gave me . . . I think at that time he was a representative with Sears & Roebuck, and he gave me a fishing rod and poles to bring home. And I got some autographed balls from him. And at the time I should have had pictures taken with him, but I was only twenty-two or twenty-three, I can't recall exactly, and you don't think much about that at that time. You know, you're young and stupid.

I had scrapbooks when I was a kid growing up, and I was a Boston Red Sox fan. And I got pictures of him, and, oh God, I still got 'em. Pictures of him and I can't recall who else . . . Bobby Doerr and all those guys who played with Red Sox when I was a kid. So he was always my idol.

What got me was—you know I was playing utility mainly; wrong spot, wrong time—but anyway I got to Boston,[40] and he says, "I

---

[40] Webster was traded by the Indians to the Red Sox in January 1960.

remember when you got that double off Tommy Brewer and hit the ball off the left-field wall."[41] And here I was a nobody, you know what I mean. He had such a memory. That's just hard to believe, you know. But he was an amazing guy. I could not say anything bad about him.

He had a tremendous set of eyes. I just was honored to have the opportunity to meet the guy and play with him. Not many people can say they played with Ted Williams.

And he was a loner. Unfortunately in those days he couldn't go anywhere, a restaurant or what have you. He was the greatest at that time. That's about all I can say about him. He was a great guy.

---

[41] On September 14, 1959, Webster, then with Cleveland, singled to left field off Boston's Brewer at Fenway Park. Williams was on the bench that day.

INTERVIEWS

Bob Kline

Shortstop

1955: ....Washington Senators
Career Statistics: .... 77 games, 0 home runs,
.221 batting average

Q. Being an infielder, what was your defensive strategy against Williams, and how do you think you fared?

A. My defensive strategy against him was to pray a lot!

Q. Did your teams use the "Williams shift," and if so, did you like that and how did it fare? If not, do you wish they did?

A. My team used the shift and it helped.

Q. Recollections of any specific at-bats and/or plays vs. Williams.

A. My recollections about him: At his first at-bat on returning from Korea, I was [at] second base in the shift, and he hit a ground ball to me.

Q. What was the talk among other players on how to face Williams in pregame meetings or just in general?

A. There was no particular talk about Ted Williams between players on our team.

Q. Was he the hitter you feared the most in the field?

A. He was the hitter we feared the most on the field!

Q. Did you ever have occasion to interact with Williams? If so, what kind of guy was he like?

A. During batting practice, Ted and I had a good conversation about fishing, since he was a fisherman, and I was born and raised in Florida, where I fished all my life. We discussed different types of fishing lures and our love of fishing.

Ted Lepcio

Second base / Third base / Shortstop

1952–59:	....**Boston Red Sox**
1959:	....**Detroit Tigers**
1960:	.... **Philadelphia Phillies**
1961:	.... **Chicago White Sox**
1961:	....**Minnesota Twins**
Career Statistics:	.... **729 games, 69 home runs,**
	.245 batting average

Q. Did your teams use the "Williams shift," and if so, did you like that and how did it fare? If not, do you wish they did?

A. Fortunately, I played with him most of my career. Outside of Cleveland, I don't remember many teams applying the shift. During my career, Ted hit balls so hard it didn't do much good to employ the shift.

There is no doubt in my mind that he could have hit .400 several more times if he wanted to. But, Ted was "Teddy Ball Game." They didn't come to see the greatest hitter bunt or hit a ground ball to left field when they played the shift.

Q. What was the talk among other players on how to face Williams in pregame meetings or just in general?

A. All players respected Ted.

Q. Was he the hitter you feared the most in the field?

A. Fielding against him was a nightmare. I played third base many times against him, so I didn't feel any fuzzy feeling.

Q. You played with Williams from 1952–59. Did you ever discuss hitting with him? What kind of guy was he like?

A. He always talked hitting and tried to help not only me, but other teammates.

Gene Verble

Second base/ shortstop

1951, 1953: ....Washington Senators
Career Statistics: .... 81 games, 0 home runs,
.202 batting average

Q. Being a middle infielder—playing second base and shortstop—what was your defensive strategy against Williams, and how do you think you fared?

A. Being a pull-hitter and left-hand batter, I played almost right behind first baseman Mickey Vernon. Was very successful at [it, and] one time he hit into a double play.

Q. Did your teams use the "Williams shift," and if so, did you like that and how did it fare? If not, do you wish they did?

A. Yes, it was a challenge.

Q. What was the talk among other players on how to face Williams in pregame meetings or just in general?

A. We knew he did not swing at bad balls, so tried to throw strikes all the time.

Q. Was he the hitter you feared the most in the field?

A. Yes

Q. Did you ever have occasion to interact with Williams? If so, what kind of guy was he?

A. He was a swell guy and was very helpful when he was asked for suggestions.

Section Four: Outfielders

Chuck Diering

Outfielder

1947-51:	St. Louis Cardinals
1952:	New York Giants
1954-56:	Baltimore Orioles
Career Statistics:	752 games, 14 home runs, .249 batting average

MUSIAL OR WILLIAMS? I don't try to distinguish between [players]. I played with so many good ballplayers all around, uh, God, I guess I'd have to say . . . I'd have to pick Stan because he was a better all-around ballplayer. Ted . . . well, he was a big home run hitter. When Stan had to become a home run hitter, he did, but Ted was a better home run hitter. He could hit them probably further, but all around, Stan could do everything. Of course, Ted was in the outfield, and I guess he was probably classified as a better-than-average outfielder, a good outfielder in that respect. I don't remember much about him being an outfielder when I played against him, but as a hitter, I can remember him calling his own balls and strikes, like all those good hitters did.

I played him in center field with that shift. That was part of the shift we used on him, and I guess the rest of the clubs did as well. Because he wouldn't . . . you could give him the whole left field and shortstop, and he wouldn't try to hit it out that way. He was strictly a hard pull-hitter. And he hit the line drives, and of course hit the long ball.

I played him a little deeper than normal, because if he hit the ball high enough, it was probably gone. But what I played him more for was low line drives—to catch them balls—because they would sink. With his type of swing, you're going out there and they'd sink, because he'd put that topspin on the ball. So that's the way I played him on defense. Because I could go back and get a ball—a long fly ball, while using that fence from right-center to the right field line. It was deep in center, but the right-field fence wasn't that deep. I think there was a little hill that you had to run up to the fence. I mean, I never had no trouble going back on a ball, in that respect, so I didn't play him as deep as some of them guys did. I played him more for those line-drive hits through the infield, over the infield.

You can cut off hits. You'd rather have him hit a single or double than a home run, but you're not going to hit 500 home runs a year. I don't know what the most he hit, 40? It isn't like today where you got eight guys on your ballclub and they all hit home runs. Back in our day, you only had one or two guys on a ballclub that hit home runs. It's just a different game than when I played.

He had a good eye; he got the benefit of the doubt. Yup, I've seen that happen many a time. The good power hitters, they pretty much have their own strike zone. You respected him, like a [Albert] Pujols, no denying that. The strike zone being so narrow, it was tough without putting it into an area where he could really rack one or get a base hit.

The only incident I had with Ted was when we had our first professional alumni . . . the retirement guys. And that was in St. Petersburg, Florida. I brought a bunch of bats down there and I wanted to get these guys to autograph for me. And I went up to Ted and said how about you autographing a bat for me? And he said, "Chuck, I can't do it." And I said, "Why not?" Musial autographed a bat for me. I was getting different signatures on one bat. I wasn't just asking for *his* autograph, but I wanted his signature on a bat with the other big stars. And he said, "I can't do it." And I said, "Why not, Ted?" And he said, "Because I got a contract." I was like, my God, I'm not going to sell the damn bat, I just want it with your name on it. He said, "I won't do it Chuck. I'll sign anything else, but I won't sign the bat." No thank you. And that was the last time . . . that was really probably the only time I recall having a conversation with the guy. Those big guys don't talk with rinky-dinks. That's what I called myself, a rinky-dink.

Joe Hicks

Outfielder

1959–60:	**Chicago White Sox**
1961–62:	**Washington Senators**
1963:	**New York Mets**
Career Statistics:	**212 games, 12 home runs, .278 batting average**

FEEL LIKE I didn't play against the "real" Ted Williams. It was 1960, his last year. Still he hit over .300 with almost 30 home runs and forty-one years old. Most all players would be pleased with stats like that, but it seemed like he was such a perfectionist that he was embarrassed by them. I'm sure the last player to hit .400 didn't want to play any longer when pitchers who he used to feast on were getting him out—he was just too proud to play the game any longer.[1]

---

[1] Williams batted .316 and hit 29 home runs in 1960, his last full year.

Jim Landis

Outfielder

1957–64:	Chicago White Sox
1965:	Kansas City Athletics
1966:	Cleveland Indians
1967:	Houston Astros
1967:	Detroit Tigers
1968:	Boston Red Sox
Career Statistics:	1,346 games, 93 home runs, .247 batting average
American League All-Star:	1962

Jim Landis said, in his era, no one compared to Ted Williams.

YES, HE IS definitely the best I ever saw. Oh my God, yeah.

One of the greatest things I think he did was study the pitchers. I mean, he had great ideas on all of them, and if you look at his record—records, I should say—he had some of his best luck against the greatest left-handers. He was just a knowledgeable man and he watched [everything].

And I'll tell you something—I was in a rut, so we were in the runway that both teams came down in the old ballpark of the White Sox, and Nellie Fox said, "I was going to ask him something." And Ted came down and Ted says—from left field now, remember this—it [my slump] had something to do with my hands. And he watched that from left field! That's how recognizable [he was] with things. I was totally amazed. But it helped, believe me!

I can tell you, I always went by Nellie Fox. He got along with Ted real well and liked him. I always figured if Nellie was that way toward him, then Ted had to be a pretty good guy.

I didn't talk to Ted, really. I was much younger,[2] and these guys were great vets like that. You just sort of looked at them and that was about it.

I definitely played him to pull and plenty deep. I don't care where you played him. He proved it by his averages it didn't matter where you played him.[3] You had three infielders to one side, play him to pull, whatever it was, it didn't matter.

I can remember one game and two balls in the same game, I took off towards right-center and thought *I got a shot at that ball,* and all of a sudden that backspin on that ball . . . and both of them went into the stands at the White Sox ballpark. What can you say about that? That's how good he was, and those fences were something like 350, 360, somewhere in that range.

I don't know what else to say about him as a hitter, my God. I think everything that he has in his averages, they speak for themselves. And like I said, he hit the best pitchers just as well. It didn't matter. And he studied them; he was very knowledgeable on all those pitchers.

I think the funniest thing I ever saw was Billy Pierce threw him a fastball—it looked like a strike, you know I'm out in center—and the umpire called ball four, and Billy Pierce jumped up about a foot in the air and straight back down. You know, you get a strikeout on that guy. . . . He probably did get a break, but give him credit.

---

[2] Landis was twenty-three when he broke into the majors in 1957; Williams would turn thirty-nine in August of that year.

[3] Landis was a five-time Gold Glove winner, from 1960–64.

He had such a goddarn good eye, too, they had to go along with that somewhat. What can you say but [he was] one of the greatest I'll ever see.

In my era, nobody compared to him. Nobody. I mean, I don't even know his stats to be honest with you, but I bet everything is outstanding. And if he didn't go into the service, my God, the home runs he would have hit. I'll always remember him as far as hitting the ball. You know, you always will remember some things, and Ted Williams will always come to my mind. I'm so glad that I got to see him. He was the greatest pure hitter ever. I just keep saying it, but that's what I feel. I haven't seen any better than him in all these days still, you know. Don't make me say it again!

Wally Westlake

Outfielder

1947–51: ....Pittsburgh Pirates
1951–52: .... St. Louis Cardinals
1952: .... Cincinnati Reds
1953–55: .... Cleveland Indians
1955: .... Baltimore Orioles
1956: .... Philadelphia Phillies
Career Statistics: .... 958 games, 127 home runs,
.272 batting average
National League All-Star: 1951

IHAD LITTLE ASSOCIATION with the "Big Guy." When I played
with Cleveland, I was just a part-time player. My association with
Ted, little as it was, was about the fly rod, not the bat. I do remember
that when he walked into the batting cage, we all stopped to watch.

INTERVIEWS

Joe Durham

Outfielder

1954, 1957: .... **Baltimore Orioles**
1959: .... **St. Louis Cardinals**
Career Statistics: .... **93 games, 5 home runs,**
.188 batting average

Q. When you played right field, what was your defensive strategy against Williams, and how do you think you fared?

A. Williams = play him extremely to pull.

Q. Did your teams use the "Williams shift," and if so, did you like that and how did it fare? If not, do you wish they did?

A. Yes, we did use the Williams shift.

Q. Recollections of any specific at-bats and/or plays vs. Williams.

A. No

Q. What was the talk among other players on how to face Williams in pregame meetings or just in general?

A. What can you say about a legend like Williams?

Q. Was he the hitter you feared the most in the field?

A. Yes

Q. Did you ever have occasion to interact with Williams?

A. No

Jim McAnany

Outfielder

1958–60: .... Chicago White Sox
1961–62: .... Chicago Cubs
Career Statistics: .... 93 games, 0 home runs,
.253 batting average

THANKS FOR THE opportunity to recall some very special memories. Ted Williams was my hero!

Q. When you played right field, what was your defensive strategy against Williams, and how do you think you fared?

A. I always played deep and ready to cut across on him.

Q. Did your teams use the "Williams shift," and if so, did you like that and how did it fare? If not, do you wish they did?

A. Yes, "the shift" fared well for us. One time Nellie Fox came almost all the way out to my position in right field to catch a ball off his bat— we were ready for him.

Q. Recollections of any specific at-bats and/or plays vs. Williams.

A. I recall one time catching a line drive off his bat that was the hardest ball I had ever caught. It stung for awhile!

Q. What was the talk among other players on how to face Williams in pregame meetings or just in general?

A. Pregame reminders: Keep the ball away and no good pitches.

Q. Was he the hitter you feared the most in the field?

A. He was the most feared hitter, and Mickey Mantle was next.

Photo courtesy of Jim McAnany

The minor-league and major-league batting average leaders from 1958—Jim McAnany and Ted Williams—pose before a game in 1959.

Q. Did you ever have occasion to interact with Williams?

A. I was a twenty-four-year-old rookie and still getting used to being a major leaguer.[4] I had won the Silver Bat for hitting .401 in Triple-A the previous year. Ted Williams won the Gold Bat that same year.[5] When the Red Sox came to play us, I was called out of the dugout before the game. I was asked to stand next to Ted Williams for a photo shoot. Each of us is smiling and holding a bat. A very memorable moment for me!

---

[4] Actually, McAnany was twenty-two as a rookie in 1959.

[5] In 1958, Williams led the American League in hitting at .328, while McAnany led all of the minor leagues with a .400 batting average for Colorado Springs.

Roy Sievers

Outfield / First base

1949–53: ....St. Louis Browns
1954–59: ....Washington Senators
1960–61: .... Chicago White Sox
1962–64: .... Philadelphia Phillies
1964–65: ....Washington Senators
Career Statistics: .... 1,887 games, 318 home runs,
.267 batting average
American League Rookie of the Year: 1949
American League All-Star: 1956, 1957, 1959, 1961

Q. What was your defensive strategy against Williams, and how do you think you fared? When you played first base, did you play especially deep?

A. I played Williams deep at first base.

Q. Did your teams use the "Williams shift," and if so, did you like that and how did it fare? If not, do you wish they did?

A. Yes, our team used the Williams shift. It worked fairly well at times.

Q. Recollections of any specific at-bats and/or plays vs. Williams.

A. Williams and I were going for the home run title. Playing in Washington, Williams' first at-bat—hit a line drive that missed going for a home run. If it happened, he would have been one ahead. My second time at-bat, I hit a home run to go ahead.[6]

---

[6] Sievers led the league in home runs in 1957 with 42. Williams finished in second with 38.

Q. What was the talk among other players on how to face Williams in pregame meetings or just in general?

A. We all talked about Ted Williams and what a great hitter he was.

Q. Was he the hitter you feared the most in the field?

A. Yes, he and Mantle. I didn't fear Williams—played him like most every player.

Q. Did you ever have occasion to interact with Williams, perhaps at first base? If so, what kind of guy was he like?

A. Williams was a great guy on and off the field. Back when I played, you didn't talk to the other players—especially during the game. Williams and I became good friends 'til he died.

Photo courtesy of Bob Wolff

Me interviewing Ted Williams and a young fan.

AFTERWORD

I **STILL MARVEL AT** the most unusual schedule of events that led me to the major leagues as a broadcaster. In my school days, playing sports was everything to me. My ambition was to make it as a major league baseball player, and didn't pay too much attention to the sports broadcasters. I knew that most were hired because of their voice, not their athletic ability. I was a fan of the big band era though—my family had a musical background—and my younger sister Margy and I harmonized on many of the New York City amateur shows where I also played my ukulele. Little did I realize that in my college days, I would sing with the college dance band and, when I became a sportscaster, would use my singing technique on the most exciting calls in sports.

I always felt, though, that the skill more important to broadcasting than a good voice was the content. That was particularly so in television, where one picture is greater than a thousand words. Content is the key to holding an audience, and still is. Content has to have appeal, though. One has to grip the audience through stories, revelations, humor, explanations, and personality—or being different in some fashion. Ted Williams had that mystique. He had his idiosyncrasies, and he was stubborn too. Ted believed in his baseball views and disdained many societal customs. Being different is an asset in attaining a TV audience, but what matters most is true talent. Ted had that.

Ted would never wear a tie and didn't believe in tipping his cap to thank those who were applauding him. A great hitter in olden days,

Lefty O'Doul, had told Ted never to change his classic swing. Ted never did, even when opposing teams used a defensive shift against him. With all the fielders on the right side, giving Ted the option of slapping the ball to left for an easy single or possible double, he decided to compete against this defensive strategy by lining hits to right field out of reach of the fielders or hitting long drives over their heads. One cannot quarrel with a player who, in 1941, had an astounding season, finishing with a .406 batting average. Baseball players are often superstitious. If the quirks helped Ted psychologically, who can complain?

I first met Ted Williams in Washington, D.C. I was the first television sportscaster in the city—the TV voice of the Washington Senators—and Ted was the most in-demand ballplayer of his era. It was vital for me to get him on the air. Ted seemed rather aloof in his relationship with the media, so I checked on his mood with a few of his teammates before approaching him for his first appearance with me. Ted agreed, and we had a most enjoyable session together. He seemed completely at ease answering my baseball questions, in fact appeared grateful at the opportunity to express his views. I always wanted my guests to leave our time together feeling as though they had an enjoyable experience. This certainly set the stage for future ones.

Whenever possible, I tried to spend some time with my guests in a social way without discussing an on-camera session. I learned what topics the potential guest enjoyed discussing and what made them smile, and Ted was no exception. I learned that he seethed with anger at himself if he didn't fulfill his own expectations on the ball field. When Ted stepped into the batter's box for practice swings, there was silence in the ball park. All players—both sides—as well as the media stopped what they were doing to watch the master in action. Fans always arrived early to enjoy this extra bonus.

Ted exhibited artistry at its finest with exploding line drives and a few towering homers; but occasionally, there were a few innocuous dribblers or routine pop-ups. Reporters learned on these occasions to move quickly out of the way when Williams started back to the dugout. Ted would get so mad at himself that he would not tolerate any questions or baseball banter before the game. I learned quickly to give him ten or fifteen minutes to cool off before resuming a lighthearted conversation; and luckily, it never interfered with our friendship. I was always surprised that practice could cause him such consternation. Maybe such intensity contributed to making him such a terrific player.

When it came to interviewing, whether the Virginia Slims Tennis matches, handlers at the Westminster Kennel Club Dog Show, or just athletes from the major sports, I always used my three-act system:

> **Act One** was an unusual question which brought a laugh or a smile to make them relax.
>
> **Act Two** was about something newsworthy they had performed in competition.
>
> **Act Three** was something of a personal nature about them so we could conclude with a story ending on a happy note.

One day before a Red Sox game in Washington, I noted that Ted was in a good mood and asked him if I could spend a few minutes with a TV camera on him to just discus his baseball techniques. I said this would benefit young players who wanted to follow his beliefs, his examples. "Ok," said Ted, "let's do it right now." I motioned to my cameraman and we stood near the dugout on the first base side. I had the microphone in one hand and my stopwatch in the other. I never use notes in an interview; all I needed was my curiosity, as I had enough questions for a two-hour documentary. My technique is similar to having lunch with a friend. No one brings notes to start the conversation.

> "Ted, I always notice that you keep flexing your fingers while you grip the bat. What's the purpose of that?"

"Bob, I use a lot of pine tar on my bat, and don't want the bat to slip out of my hands. But I don't want to hurt my swing because my hands are sticking to the bat, so I test my fingers all the time to make sure they're not going to stick there when I need them."

"Ted, you take a lot of pitches at the plate—including some good ones. Some other hitters usually go for the first pitch, believing it will be a fast ball over the plate and that the pitcher wants to get ahead in the count. What's your theory on this?"

"Bob, if it's early in the game and I'm not that acquainted with the pitcher's style or his stuff, this is my chance to look at what he's got. I don't want to swing at a slow curve and get angry at myself for swinging at his pitch, rather than one I can hit well. It's sort of a guessing game, but I'm always looking for a pitch I can drive well. Now the other night I took one pitch too many, but was ready for the next at bat and had learned what to look for. Figuring out what the pitcher is going to throw is important to hitting well."

"Ted, you seem to take batting practice very seriously. How important is that to how you'll do in a game?"

"Bob, it's an important dress-rehearsal. It's a final practice before the game. I'm saying to myself—need a fly ball to right—sacrifice fly to bring home a run—a line drive to center—or whatever. This time for me isn't to exercise my muscles; it's to do something specific to win games. The best hitters take it seriously."

This is just a sampling of my TV conversation—but with Ted, a perfectionist, batting practice was serious business—done with a purpose.

I remember another time when the Red Sox were warming up for a game; I was walking towards the Sox dugout with a mic in my hand. Ted was playing catch and I had no intention of interrupting him, as I already had my guests lined up. Ted scowled when he spotted the mic. . . . Guess he figured I wanted him for a show. I was taken aback when I saw the look on his face. The mic must have looked like a bayonet. There was not time for pleasantries, though, so I just kept walking.

After the game, I visited him in the clubhouse. "Ted, I came close enough to wave hello, but was concerned with your look of disgust.

I've always considered you a friend and I couldn't understand your facial reaction. What offended you?"

"Bob, it certainly wasn't you. I just didn't want to do another interview—I've had my fill this past week and I guess I overreacted."

"Understandable, Ted, so here's what I suggest. As a TV and radio guy, part of my job is interviewing players on the pre- and post-game shows, but you're doing me a favor by going on. So tell me when you'd like to do so and the rest of the time when I come by it'll just be to say hello, offer you a ride back to the hotel, or just to talk baseball."

Ted seemed to like the idea, so he said, "Tell you what, kid. If my average is around .330 or I've hit 20 home runs when I come in next time, you can count on me. The rest of the time, grab somebody else."

"That's great with me, Ted. I'll be pulling for you to hit those numbers whether you do the interview or not," and we shook hands.

The last series before Ted came to Washington; he was home at Fenway Park and made headlines there. Ted had become upset when he was booed after misplaying a windblown fly ball. When he came up to bat the following inning, Ted spit on home plate, thumbed his nose at the press box, was fined $5,000, and vowed after the game never to speak to the press, TV or radio, again. Ted's next stop was Griffith Stadium in Washington.

I got to the park early and saw Ted dressing for the game. After a warm greeting, I said, "Ted, I've got a problem. According to our agreement, you said you'd go on TV with me if you hit a certain batting average and the number of home runs you specified, and you've easily passed that amount. Here's my issue. I read that you were through doing interviews. To add to that, you're a good friend; so if you go on as promised, I'll have to ask you about your recent actions in Boston. I don't like asking those questions, but if I don't, the public will think I'm a bad reporter and my station will feel the same. So you can just refuse to go on with me despite our contract, and our friendship will still remain. But if you do go on, I'll have to ask you how you feel about it now—I can't avoid that. So it's your choice."

Ted then said, "Where do you want to do the interview and what time?" After telling him where and when, I said, "How about my questions?" Ted said, "Anything you want to ask."

The interview was done. Ted expressed his being contrite about his behavior. He also said that he could take criticism, but not when things were written about him that weren't true, and he hoped the fans would understand. I took that interview, added one with switch-hitter Mickey Mantle, in which the slugger confided that he was strictly a right-handed hitter and the only thing he could do lefty was wallop homeruns. No home run hitter was ever faster at beating out drag bunts. Like Ted, Mickey is an all-time great. With these two interviews as a pilot film, I went to New York and met with General Manager Lev Pope of Channel 11, where I telecasted Madison Square Garden events. They also carried the Yankee games at that time. We ended up selling Colgate-Palmolive my interview series with ballplayers from all clubs. This became the Yankees pre-game TV series, the Red Sox pre-game series, as well as Washington's and Kansas City's. The next year I formed my own production company and increased our coverage to the national scene.

The interesting thing about that interview was that it had been interrupted by an unusual happening; a hazard of live television. I did my best to make light of it, but hoped it would not changed the mood of the show. Let me explain that, in all my years of interviewing, I always did first-take shows. I have three important reasons for this:

1. All the players were on a busy schedule getting ready for the game. They couldn't wait for another try.
2. My schedule included doing a minimum of four interviews before each game, then pre- and post-game TV and radio shows, post-game taped, and then the play-by-play. No time to start re-scheduling.
3. First-takes are always more spontaneous. On second takes, laugh and smiles seem more rehearsed and not as genuine.

So about halfway through my filmed questioning of Ted, a fan climbed over the low ballpark barrier, came onto the field, walked right up behind me, and asked for my autograph. I didn't want to reveal my being upset on camera, believing that this important interview was being spoiled, so I smiled, explained I'd take care of the autograph a bit later, and continued speaking to Ted. The fan started to leave, and then returned to ask, "Is that Ted Williams with you?" Again a big smile, a "yes," and again, "please come back a bit later." This time the fan left.

I was afraid to look at the filmed result, so I stayed outside the viewing room, disheartened that this sought-after prized interview might no longer be good enough to use.

As the TV staff viewed it, I kept waiting for their verdict. Through the wall, however, I heard chuckles of mirth and then unrestrained uproarious laughter as they viewed my forced smile next to Williams' facial agony. The close-up of Ted showed him scowling, then enraged, and then his lips muttering a few swear words illustrating his wrath. This was visual proof of Ted's emotion, which was what the interview was about.

The true greats—in sports or otherwise—enjoy winning as we all do, but some become so used to praise that losing moments may have an even greater effect on them. Ted's reactions were genuine and honest, but sometimes resulted in far more coverage than his many good deeds.

The Williams interview remains one of my most cherished memories, particularly his last line in the interview. Ted said, "Bob, the reason I'm doing this with you is because you've always been so fair with me." I was flattered by his comment. Ted was certainly fair with me, and still I remain appreciative.

When Ted ended his career as a player and became manager of the Washington Senators, he had mellowed, realizing he could impart knowledge to his players—but not his talent. His players respected his advice and his patience with them.

Now at the age of ninety-two, I'm still talking on News 12 Long Island TV and am cited by the *Guinness Book of World Records* as the longest-running sports broadcaster in the world. I currently have no retirement plans—I enjoy working—but I do admire those who leave on a high note.

When Ted Williams announced his retirement as a player, he knew that his farewell game deserved a terrific ending. He provided that himself. On his final at bat, Ted put everything within him into stroking a pitch of his liking, smashing the ball into home run land at Fenway Park. That personified Ted the legend—a hall of famer who did it his way.

After serving in the Navy during World War II, I signed on as the Sports Director of the *Washington Post*. In 1947, I achieved my major league dream by becoming the Washington Senators' first TV play-by-play announcer. Sports Director Paul Jonas of the Mutual Broadcasting System signed me on to do national radio play-by-play, including bowl games and the Game of the Day. In 1954, I began a fifty-year run televising Madison Square Garden events, and in 1956, I broadcast my first of three World Series, which included Don Larsen's perfect game. I was also lucky enough to cover Jackie Robinson's last major league hit. In 1962, I became NBC-TV lead play-by-play announcer. My family and I have been thrilled by my inductions into the baseball and basketball Halls of Fame, the Madison Square Garden Walk of Fame, and the Sportscaster-Sportswriters Hall of Fame. Everything seemed to happen for the best. One can't ask for more. I've been more than fortunate and I'm truly grateful.

—Bob Wolff, December 2012

ACKNOWLEDGMENTS

AS WITH ANY project, there are a number of people to thank and recognize. First off, I'm not sure any of this would be possible without all the data compiled by the folks from retrosheet.org and baseball-reference.com. They certainly make the life of any baseball researcher—and fan—easier and a lot more fun. Also, Jack Smalling's *Baseball Address List* was an invaluable resource in contacting all these former major leaguers.

Even with all of this information at my fingertips, I still wasn't sure if this was a viable project or not. My gut said yes, but I guess I also needed some positive reinforcement. Enter two co-workers: Enrique Rodriguez and Sam Manchester. I innocently floated them my idea to get some feedback and both gave honest, enthusiastic, and positive responses that spurred me on to get started. In fact, Enrique was so enthusiastic that he not only kept asking me about updates on the project, but he also designed the graphics you see on these pages. I cannot thank him enough for his encouragement and enthusiasm, even though I try.

Jason Katzman with Skyhorse Publishing was aggressive and gung-ho about this project from the moment he called me. This book is in part a testament to his ideas, guidance, and pursuit of the best possible product.

And, of course, I have to thank each of the former major leaguers who corresponded back with me, whether they could help out or not.

FACING TED WILLIAMS

Although it's funny how many times a former player would tell or write to me that they couldn't offer much, whether due to memory or not having faced Williams often, and then go off and tell a great story. I thought I was really onto something early in the process when a few of them told me that this book is something that they'd really like to read. Boy, talk about feeling like hitting a game-winning home run when you hear something like that! Not to mention a lot of them just liked talking about Williams—he was a hero to many of them as well—and they would tell me that in those exact words. I had a couple of people thank me for allowing them to just discuss Williams for a few minutes. There was a definite reverence and respect for the man, not only as a ballplayer, but as a person.

Finally, and in cliché-speak, last and definitely not least, a giant thank you to my wonderful family. My boys, Laben and Kieran, keep alive my fire for the game of baseball with their enthusiasm and questions. My wife, Shelly, is always there encouraging me to forge ahead—even if she has no idea what the heck I'm talking about half the time... okay, three-quarters of the time. Without them, I don't know if I'd have the desire, passion, or energy to undertake a project like this. I love them, feed off their love, and in turn, love doing something like this.

By the way, I know Ted Williams didn't have much use for the media—and maybe even pitchers—but I can only hope he'd take some appreciation in reading this and learning what his colleagues thought of him. Heck, he might have even gotten a big laugh out of it.

Dave Heller

INDEX